A TRILOGY IN

MAYA

BOOK ONE

VIEWPOINTS: INTEGRATING PARALLEL UNIVERSES

LLOYD LEIDERMAN

BALBOA.
PRESS

A DIVISION OF HAY HOUSE

Scripture quotations marked KJV are from the Holy Bible, King James Version (Authorized Version). First published in 1611. Quoted from the KJV Classic Reference Bible, Copyright © 1983 by The Zondervan Corporation.

Balboa Press books may be ordered through booksellers or by contacting:

Balboa Press
A Division of Hay House
1663 Liberty Drive
Bloomington, IN 47403
www.balboapress.com
1 (877) 407-4847

Because of the dynamic nature of the Internet, any web addresses or links contained in this book may have changed since publication and may no longer be valid. The views expressed in this work are solely those of the author and do not necessarily reflect the views of the publisher, and the publisher hereby disclaims any responsibility for them.

The author of this book does not dispense medical advice or prescribe the use of any technique as a form of treatment for physical, emotional, or medical problems without the advice of a physician, either directly or indirectly. The intent of the author is only to offer information of a general nature to help you in your quest for emotional and spiritual well-being. In the event you use any of the information in this book for yourself, which is your constitutional right, the author and the publisher assume no responsibility for your actions.

Any people depicted in stock imagery provided by Getty Images are models, and such images are being used for illustrative purposes only. Certain stock imagery © Getty Images.

Print information available on the last page.

ISBN: 978-1-9822-1946-8 (sc)
ISBN: 978-1-9822-1947-5 (e)

Balboa Press rev. date: 01/24/2019

To the lightbearers of Earth
weaving their deathless solar body
in and as the One

ABOUT THE AUTHOR

Lloyd Leiderman attended the Rochester Institute of Technology, attaining a BS in photographic science and instrumentation. He worked as an optical physicist at Technical Operations, Inc., a premier optical R&D lab; an optical engineer at Stocker and Yale Corporation, and a statistical analyst at Avco Everett Research Laboratory. He then worked as a computer programmer and copy editor for The Summit Lighthouse, Inc. After that he served as a CNA: Certified Nursing Assistant, helping people with their activities of daily living. Now he is a writer and practitioner of spiritual techniques designed to anchor divine light and virtue individually and in world service.

Lloyd can be contacted at the email address:
lloydsupport@mcn.net

Be sure to visit his website at:
https://lloydleiderman.com

ACKNOWLEDGEMENTS

I am most grateful to Keith Dowman for the use of his insight in his Books *Maya Yoga: Longchenpa's Finding Comfort and Ease in Enchantment* and *Spaciousness: The Radical Dzogchen of the Vajra-Heart.*

Thank you to Daniel Ladinsky and his magnanimous agent Melissa LaScaleia for the use of his translation of the poem "Laughing at the Word Two," from The Gift by Daniel Ladinsky, copyright 1999, and used with permission.

A huge thank you, also, to Gvido Trepsa, Agni Yoga Society, Vice President for the use of El Morya's wisdom from His Agni Yoga books, as well as for the Nicholas Roerich painting "Mother of the World."

Thank you to The Summit Lighthouse for use of the Chart of the Divine Self. I am not sponsored by, nor do I represent any organization, but I wish to point out a great gift of loving wisdom as the teachings of the ascended masters which can be found at https://www.summitlighthouse.org/.

CONTENTS

PREFACE

This Trilogy is intended for people who have already established in their mind and everyday experience that they are not just the body they are wearing, and that the material world seemingly out there is a product of consciousness, not the reverse. These understand that their apparently separated human being is one of many they have entertained over the centuries, and like those, it will fall away like an autumn leaf when their current season expires. This understanding, far from frightening them, is embraced as joyous opportunity to realize immortal union in and as the One.

But most importantly, they know that they now possess a highway system within their everyday experience, which remains after the accoutrements of embodiment are no longer accessible. Therein—in the NOW—they experience the gratifying and inspirational fulfillment of their infinitely mysterious Selfhood.

Why I Invited My Higher Self To Inspire Me to Bring This Book to You

Yogi Vasiṣṭha imparts to Rama, a Hindu God of the Logos:

"O Rama, if you thus overcome this sorrow of repetitive history (*samsara*), you will live here on earth itself like a god, like Brahmā or Viṣṇu! For when delusions are gone and the truth is realized by means of enquiry into self-nature, when the mind is at peace and the heart leaps to the supreme truth, when all the disturbing thought-waves in the mind-stuff have subsided and there is unbroken flow of peace and

the heart is filled with the bliss of the absolute, when thus the truth has been seen in the heart, then this very world becomes an abode of bliss...Such bliss is possible only by self-knowledge, not by any other means. Hence, one should apply oneself constantly to self-knowledge—this alone is one's duty"[1]

To fulfill that duty, my friends, is my wish for you, for me, for everyone else. I, from birth, have been, shall we say, afflicted, with a flood-tide-like need to attend to "enquiry into self-nature." I am unable to live a happy-go-lucky life. Yet, far from being habitually solemn, I do sometimes need to "cool my jets" on occasion, as a good friend used to implore. But I also can't just flop around like a caught fish on life's surface decks. Such meaningless existence, to me, is to live as a renegade to my core.

Oh, I see you have not put this book down yet. So I am safe to assume that you share my need in this regard. So keep reading. Then we can ooh and ah together at the infinite vistas all around here.

The spiritual endeavor of the Lloyd who began writing this book was copacetic. He was cruising along like a gardener implanting infinity in the folds of his soil and submitting his soiled garments to a Violet Flame wash regularly. Little did he know the joyous integrating baby step that lay in wait for him, which you're now perusing.

Pen in hand, he poked and prodded his Higher Self into capitulation time and again to satisfy his questing soul. That, often as not, would plaster a brightening smile upon his gumshoe countenance. For answers came about, including to some questions his ignorance disallowed even asking. Now Lloyd in a new edition is pleased to share these insights with other spiritual gumshoes eager to bless their own endeavors with smiley, radiant immanence.

Your Spiritual Unfoldment Is an Inside Job

You are in charge of your spiritual unfoldment. No one else can do that for you. No writer or guru—not even a great cosmic master—can weld a liberated "You" into your Being. Reading a spiritually oriented book can open doors of your mind and your heart; but you must walk through them and assimilate the divine virtue you find.

Masters of great spiritual attainment can bless you immensely to eliminate blockages upon your Path. Books can serve up explanations of complex subjects and usher them into your understanding so clearly that they become common sense to you. You can serve in a community with spiritual comrades and adopt the OM-singing aura of the Buddha's sangha. But ultimately, the spiritual Path remains yours to walk alone—all One.

You are unique, and no master or teacher can fiddle with that, for your free will is sacrosanct. Nevertheless, we are certainly not bereft of spiritual help here on Earth. Indeed, your normal, everyday awareness is intended as a sacrament that awakens you to the same spiritual depths from which every master and Cosmic Being draw their sustenance. You can find them there, present in your heart, eager to impute their awakened joy to all who will avail themselves of that open door to unity.

Awaken—Activate—Surrender
Infinite Selfhood's at the Ready

In the face of all that help, you'd think that walking the spiritual path would be a breeze. And it is, when the breeze comes styled as Holy Spirit winds. But, so often, souls misplace their attention and entertain joker man phantoms who convince consciousness that the stuff that outer perception reports is a gaggle of separated entities.

Failure to sunder that sense of separation will only repay you with the low self-esteem of racing through life for nothing more than a participation medal. Then, when you turn the page on this embodiment, you'll see that you often didn't even earn that.

Life doesn't owe anyone a living.
You're here to work hard at not working at all.

Yeah, yeah; ya gotta do what ya gotta do to survive. But your Real work is living your unique answer to "Who are you?" Living in and as that infinite answer will spoil you with light's effulgence. On the other hand, you've also made some mistakes, and that karmic energy awaits reintegration with your Real Self. Immortals working with you upon your spiritual Path must be careful about how accessible they make that to you. They don't want to throw you for a loop; so only little bits of karma are released for you to balance daily.

We Attend the University of the Spirit

I, along with probably millions of others now on earth, am a student of the ascended masters: the Beings who have graduated from their human mortality into their immortality. That, in no way, says or is meant to imply that I am special in any way. I am still a regular old inquisitive, speculative human. So you should read this book, not because you might think I have some kind of inside track, but because you are willing to consider viewpoints about spiritual life that may prove useful to you.

I am so grateful for the teachings and magnificent blessings the ascended masters have released to their students, especially over the past hundred and fifty years through such organizations as the Theosophical Society, the I AM Activity, the Agni Yoga Society, the Self Realization Fellowship and The Summit Lighthouse. I am also grateful for the outpourings of heart from holy ones and teachers like Sri Ramana Maharshi, Nisargadatta Maharaj and Sadhguru Jaggi Vasudev. Spiritual instruction has also arisen through masters of light who have delivered their teachings in more ancient settings, such as Lao Tsu, Bodhi Dharma, and many Zen masters, who found it necessary to bop certain disciples in the bean with their staff when those seekers would insist upon figuring out how to become one with God by a mere twiddling of consciousness or hitting it with so gross a monkey wrench as their human brain.

All of the above teachers would be the first to inform you that spiritual teachings and any inspirational worded expressions are but catalysts intended to bring those imbibing them into consonance with their inner salon where they commune in and as the One's immanence. I surely don't place myself on the dais with such spiritual lights as those mentioned above. But my own inner need to share insight with others runs in tandem with them.

Although I sometimes share direct quotes from the ascended masters, I have no conscious face-to-face contact with them. Quoted ascended master teachings come from the published work of their Messengers Mark and Elizabeth Clare Prophet.

This Book Is a Resource

You're not meant to read this book like a novel. Dip into it as your ongoing assimilation of its spirit allows. Parts Two and Three of *Viewpoints* carry the core of its insight into the structure of consciousness and the nature of *maya*.

Divine Alchemy

Divine alchemy is the means by which divine Agents gain greater humility. That is, it's how they seal themselves in ever more inclusive fields of the One I AM Presence.

I aspire to be a divine alchemist: one who is skilled at God's transcendence. That is, I devote myself to honing my ability to enable higher frequency findings as receptor cells that can host and assimilate expanding courses of infinite mystery. Thus I invite you to engage my sharing here as entry points to greater Self determination and spiritually enfranchised attunement. For, as Neill deGrasse Tyson said to James Altucher in an interview, "Curiosity is freedom."[2] Curiosity may kill cats, but it lubes human minds and hearts out of seized up preconceptions.

As my curiously disposed eighth-grade math teacher Mr. Amtower told me one day after school, "The more I learn, the more I find out I don't know." So let your creative musings introduce you to unsung worlds that await no more than your attention to get them singing like meadowlarks at dawn.

The musical prodigy August Rush exults and relates in the film of that name, "The music is all around us. All you have to do is listen." And I would add, once you imbibe the music of Your spheres, let your super additive dominion share out its harmonies to near and far off worlds. Yes, yes, yes. This is definitely doable, for the abundant life IS. But its graces come about in proportion to the degree that you provide life its living by greasing its wringer with infinite mystery. Don't try to understand that; just kinda let it settle in.

Realizing Oneness Is Step One
Of the Spiritual Path

Many souls are quite content for their spiritual Path to simply encompass realizing their oneness with infinite divinity. And since only the One IS, and since ALWAYS "of myself I can do nothing," it is ALWAYS by infinite mystery's grace that a divine Agent can "do" anything at all. Thus it just might be true that the simple Path of realizing the One may forever and always be THE Path.

But...

Then why did the master Morya write so very many Agni Yoga books, in which so much of what He has to say involves a great deal more than judo chopping human dullards into a greater realization that only the One IS?

I believe it's because alchemical science is Real. Aspects of the structure of the divine One must be learned and mastered for Beings to graduate to levels of humility at which they can skillfully nourish entire life waves, planets, solar systems, galaxies....

That is why I, as a regular old human, am inspired to fervently adapt my consciousness to gaining the preliminaries of cosmic alchemy. That's why a book such as this is not mere mental masturbation. It's an invitation to gaining a skill set that will do your Mom proud. Deep meditation on the concepts I discuss herein can matriculate you into more advanced programs of the prep school that fits you for your career in and as your immortally fruitful ever new day. We have greater worlds to sing.

Since I'm Not an Ascended Master
Anything I Write Is Laid Over
With My Own Flibbertigibbets

Unless I'm quoting a master, I must insist that you take what I say simply as my own viewpoint. Receive it as an invitation to draw it through your own take on life to seek some level of resonance we can profitably share. Moreover, my viewpoints may amuse, but to render them useful, you'll need to read between the lines. Entwine them with your own warp speed visions, and weave them into your own living bouquet.

The Bottom Line

If you intend to read this book for intellectual content, you can put it down after reading only the next sentences:

> **Only the One IS, evolving in and as the ever expanding consciousness of joy. Anything that seems to be separate is but metadata, which is only useful as a catalyst to realizing the One.**

Incidentally, the metadata, the outer material universe that consciousness captures with perception and mechanical instruments is also Real. Its phantom insubstantiality—eternally speaking—is irrelevant. "In the moment" an entire experience is Real. Its eternality for you only depends upon the posture consciousness makes of it. Slouching into separative lies earns you a chance to karmically revisit them sometime later. Whereas, upstanding, unitive Truth renders infinite mystery into perception's mix. That imputes to consciousness eternal Beauty.

That's it. You got it all.

Here's Swami Muktananda imparting a similar message:

> **"[Vasiṣṭha's Yoga's] main teaching is that everything is Consciousness, including the material world, and that the world is as you see it. This is absolutely true. The world is nothing but the play of Consciousness... Abhinavagupta, the great tenth century scholar of Kashmir Shaivism, once said, 'Shiva, the independent and pure Self that always vibrates in the mind, is the Parashakti that rises as joy in various sense experiences. Then the experience of this outer world appears as its Self. I do not know where this word "samsara" has come from.'"[3]**

See...I didn't make my motto up: only the One IS.

This Is a Speed Trap
The Cop's Hiding Out Behind Each Word

The intention of my spiritual writing is to share inspirational viewpoints I have experienced. All of this book's detail is intended to caress you into a greater realization of the One. This a meditative adventure I am inviting you to share with me. So speed readers will miss most of the joy I have encountered in its writing.

You may, at times, feel that I am going around the mulberry bush or jumping about layer upon similar layer in an onion when I ought to just come right out with what I have to say. But I'm usually referring to the living mystery of consciousness beyond intellect, and words alone cannot encompass that. So please let me forthwith apologize for not accomplishing the impossible.

Expect to Change

I have a normal, everyday human brain that has been programmed to perceive the outer world in which we live in a peculiar way. Assuming you are similar, masticating this book may bend your everyday awareness out of its accustomed shape like it did mine. Such disturbance may hurt a bit, but that's okay. Just ask our Divine Mother to kiss it and make it better.

There's Some New Stuff in Here...Really

Many people who have studied the teachings of the ascended masters for decades may think some of this book will be just more of the "same old same old" because it reiterates a knowledge of consciousness long ago assimilated.

But there is much new context here that is well worth consideration. Indeed, introducing more inclusive context is the crux of all spiritual evolution. So you'll find what I hope to be a great deal of useful insight in the worded expressions. But their non pareil Allness will come only by following the worded vectors into the wild blue here-now yonder.

This is doubtlessly the most mind blowing book I have attempted. I know...because I've been picking up brain parts off the floor for quite a while now, trying to force them to fit back together again. But there's always an extra piece of something—who knows what—missing after I think it's worthy of a try to be sorta normal again. It's like what usually happens when I take apart a car or clock or some such. Invariably a spring or an odd shaped thingamajig pops out onto the floor. If I'm lucky enough to find it, I'm mighty hard pressed to figure out, first where it goes, and then how to get it back in there where it belongs so it's possible to get the consarned thing working again.

Since that's pretty much impossible for humans to do with consciousness, people have come up with phrases like: let it be; live and let God; God is my co-pilot; don't sweat the small stuff; OM. So if any things I say seem a bit too weird for you, like my above ill-fitting brain parts, just pop them into your inner fiery hearth. Maybe they will bloom something useful from there.

The way I see it, normal, everyday mentality and perception can ever so easily get stuck like glue on hunks of *maya* zipping by, or even laid out flat, nice and purdy for you to ponder. For many of us normal everyday-life critters, it takes the likes of a 2x4 upside the head to shake such somnambulistic lull up to the extent that light and only light has a chance to envelope and enrobe us in a Holy Spirit unifying whirlwind. I offer this book as just such a 2x4.

Spirituality Is a Vector, Not a Destination

True, a book is but a bucket of words. But treat those you'll find here as pointers beyond, and you'll coax infinite mystery to enjoy romping through your own self-styled maze. Your Real Identity is far more than what your awareness focuses: the outer appearance of yourself and all you perceive. Instead, the Real You persists as THAT which gives rise to birth and death. And it accomplishes its alchemy many times per second.

Don't Walk Through Life Flat
Like a Worn Out Shoe

Of course, the sense of separation that most people impute to the *maya* of false conception can inflict pain, suffering and a host of other downers. But the real You never met anyone but sincerity, fulfillment and victory. So enjoy yourself, because:

Only the One IS.

Let's Get Real

Note well, that this book is not intended to hypnotize anyone into thinking that life is an amazing, delicately fragrant rose garden, even when you encounter difficulties and the grime of outer circumstance. I do not desire to lead you or myself about by the nose through a la-di-da existence when you and I actually need to get down to cases and balance enough karma to realign viewpoints and vistas to accommodate a preponderance of light, the radiance of divine virtue. Such spiritual work will bring consciousness into direct consonance with the One's ultimate, omnipresent Beauty.

Yes; I suppose it can be truthfully said that instantaneous enlightenment—accelerated satori, the sort of total Self realization that can fit you for immortality—is possible. Tibetan Radical Dzogchen bets its boots on that.

But my experience with normal, everyday humans like myself belies such optimism. Even though snatches of beatific vision come, sometimes quite often, the work of the ages remains an ongoing slog for pretty much all of us.

I use that word "slog" not to belittle the effervescent, amazing, fantabulous, miraculous, serendipitous, consumption of light-light-light that every moment of the Homeward Path offers. I use that word to get real.

A magic, instant enlightenment switch does exist.

But ordinary humans rarely find it in hand. First they need to realign a considerable percentage of their conscious awareness to light and only light. Thus, I would point you to liberation as a process punctuated with a series of instantaneous realizations which enables soul to deconstruct *maya's* apparent separatist lies and to transform consciousness into THAT of divine Truth's Real, living, flaming imagery.

Even as the sense of separation lies in wait to hoodwink you into settling for its netherworlds, you can turn the tables on it. You can encourage your consciousness to implode provinces of deceit and subversion.

In this book, I give you conceptual tools that will enable your soul to demand your inner Gorbachev to tear down phantom fortified Berlin walls.[4] I encourage you to use those inner implements of deconstruction to transmute false conception into treasures. Don't let divine artifacts sit around gathering dust. Get the rat-a-tat-tats going. The Great, Great Silence won't mind.

You're Missing in Action

Buddhism and the Vedanta style called Advaita would have you clean house so thoroughly that only nothing is left to do itself. Nisargadatta's chief disciple Ramesh Balsekar put it this way:

> **"The Individual's Problem: The conditioning of the *'sea of samsara'* is so strong that you are compelled to seek the state of *nirvana* from an outside source. You pray: 'I am drowning in this ocean of misery, O Lord, please save me.' Then you are told that liberation is not all that easy or simple, that you must make long and arduous efforts before you can attain liberation. Various paths with names and rites and regulations are prescribed. Then you are told that you are not bound at all, and that, therefore, the question of freedom does not arise. However, all this is happening to a 'you'; this is being told to 'you.'**
>
> **"Is it not simpler, and more direct, to understand at once that there is no 'you' at all, that the 'you' is a concept created by the mind. 'You' are an illusion. In such understanding there is no conceptualizing, no mind acting as the comprehender ego— 'you.' Such understanding, without any 'you' as the comprehender, is pure understanding or apperception. Such apperception—or, rather, such apperceiving—is all there Is: Consciousness, or Awareness, or God, or whatever you may call it, whose only 'doing' is witnessing (without any judgement) the entire functioning of the total manifestation.**

"The earlier stages are part of the circle which gets completed only with the final annihilation of the 'you' or 'me.'"[5]

[Here, here!!! Says my parliamentarian. Also, I'm gratified that Balsekar illustrates how important it is to choose the right words. He says, "Such apperception—or, rather, such apperceiving—is all there is." Surely that change of wording from "apperception" to "apperceiving" is subtle splitting of hairs. But it functions as a great big change. "Apperception" implies some kind of finished state and that there is someone doing the apperceiving to achieve that state. The word "apperceiving" alone leaves the notion of an endlessly ongoing mode of Being and of a doer being unspecified and completely unnecessary. Book Two of this Trilogy— Only the One IS—deals entirely with this need to free the subconscious from word traps that imprison consciousness in the sense of separation.]

While it is reasonably easy for us to understand Balsekar's point— that there is no "you" to be doing anything, it's quite another to BECOME that mode of Life, to gad about of yourself, doing nothing. That jocular image is mine. Master Morya elevates its notion to your realizing it as solemnity. In any case, I hope that my Trilogy will contribute to that spiritual skill in you.

Catch Your Busybody's Self
In Its Acts

After so many lives ensconced in *maya's* funhouse, doing stuff, the "doing nothing" which produces spiritual liberation involves catching your busybody self in its acts. That can take lifetimes of meditative practice.

But such spiritual practice is not necessarily sitting in meditation or participating in rituals; though, I don't encourage you to avoid them. Ultimately, spiritual practice is adopting the be-here-now approach to life, whether you are sitting quietly or moving about, engaging an art form or tabulating figures. The good news is that you have already completed a lot of that. It's unlikely that you would be reading this book if you haven't.

This book intends to incite you to actively bless THAT which you already are and to continuously complement those fire blossoms with the fertilizer of divine Love, I AM THAT I AM. Thence, God's gracious gratitude will pour more fully all over and in you. You've got a money-back guarantee on that; shipping label provided.

"In and As"

I want to quickly point out my intentions to you English teachers out there who might get on my case for overly using the phrase "in and as." I might say, for instance, that your soul shines in matter *in and as* the One. Or I could write that God impresses victory *in and as* his creative engrams. For many years, I have felt the need to use this phrase because either word alone is misleading.

After Writing Volume Three, *The Magic in Maya*, I have seen that my feeling emanates from an inner knowing that the unifying Holy Spirit (the Zoroastrian *Spenta Mainyu*) and his diversifying "evil" spirit brother (the Zoroastrian *Angra Mainyu*) are twins. They both partake of the One; both derive life from God's white fire core. It is the sense of separation attached to the energy veil (evil) that leads to denigration and moral depravity. Devoid of the sense of separation, the energy veil becomes liberating, juicy living Art.

Speaking of identity, for instance, you become aware *in* the One (as one piece of the whole pie looking at others in the energy veil), but you are also acting *as* the wholeness of the One. (Each piece has all of the qualities of the whole pie.) So whenever you read that phrase—in and as—understand that I am saying that you will miss my point if you are not meditatively practicing the Presence as you read. "In and as" is a tipoff that I am especially harkening to inner depths.

Repetition Beyond Mantra

Also, I beg: Stand back, ye strict editorial police. As usual, this book uses a lot of repetition owing to its holographic nature. Each point I make partakes of all of the others, and sometimes it is necessary to impart that unity and the fullness of what I wish to convey by couching a new point in already related concepts.

Is Your Fancy Tickled?

I hope that this preface has tickled your fancy and that you're fascinated, gladdened, captivated or even just curious. Some ah-ha moments await your company to breathe in you.

FOREWORD

My purpose in this foreword is to ensure that you understand the terms I repeatedly use as I intend them. The meanings of some of these may be self-evident, but to get the most from this book, you need to know specifically what I am alluding to when I use these words. So please allow me here to lay out the turf we will be traveling upon together.

The Chart of Your Divine Self

Several organizations present charts of your divine Self similar to the one shown below, so it is important for me to explain what I mean when I refer to the aspects of consciousness it depicts.

I have chosen to use this particular chart because it emphasizes the arena where most readers of this book stand upon their spiritual Path: working out their karma in the human incubator realm of evolution leading to their immortality.

The chart pictures a single I AM Presence, surrounded by the Causal Body, as one of Your "twin flames" (explained in Part Two) evolving the infinite One into ever greater coefficients of joy. Emanating from the Presence is the "tube of light," which seals its interactive Selfhood in divinity. It further shows soul gaining mastery "below" in the outer realm of form, invoking and surrounded by the Violet Flame as she deals with her karmic interactions.

Between those stands the Holy Christ Self, your Higher Self, mediating the infinite One on behalf of the soul's schooling and mastery.

Used by permission of The Summit Lighthouse, Inc.

- **Top Figure: The I AM Presence.** Your eternal God Self—a state of Being at One with all Life worlds without end. The color spheres of light surrounding the I AM Presence are called the **Causal Body**. These spheres of light/consciousness contain the primordial, immaculate patterns of your divine personality. These patterns become your "treasures in heaven" after soul, the lower figure in the chart, assumes them in consciousness and transforms them as divinely realized Art. (Since the Chart above is shown in black and White, I need to tell you that the Causal Body sphere colors are, from center to periphery: white, yellow, pink, violet, purple and gold, green and blue.)

- **Middle Figure: The Holy Christ Self**, also known as your Real Self, the inner Buddha, the higher mental body, the Word, the Logos, the Son of God, the Daughter of God. This aspect of your Being is the masculine polarity of your I AM Presence in evolutionary mode. He mediates between your soul and your I AM Presence while your unascended (mortal) soul learns to love as God loves. (I explain how the cap "D" Daughter of God can be seen to reside at this masculine level later in Part Two.)

Ervin Laszlo quotes cardiologist Pim van Lommel, who describes this, your Higher Self:

> **"Our waking consciousness is only a part of our whole undivided consciousness. There is also an extended or enhanced consciousness based on indestructible and constant evolving fields of information, where all knowledge, wisdom and unconditional love are present and available."**[6]

- **Lower Figure: Soul.** This is your opportunity to engage consciousness as the feminine polarity of the I AM Presence in evolutionary mode. Pure soul is now and always has been One with her Holy Christ Self.

But there's a fly in the ointment. Soul attends "school" in the space-time realm where she learns to master energy flow as divine Love and to realize her unity with her masculine consort (her Holy Christ Self) and her I AM Presence. After soul undergoes her final earthly initiation, the ascension in the light, she fully, permanently realizes her immortality. Hence forth She eternally acts, one with Her Holy Christ Self, as the joyous expression of the I AM Presence in evolutionary mode. As such, the I AM Presence evolving through Christ/Soul progresses into greater and greater realms of activated humility to assume spiritual offices as a planet, star, solar system, galaxy, universe, multiverse and beyond. If you really "get" that, my guess is that you will never have self-esteem issues.

Note also the lower figure, soul, is shown enveloped in the Violet Flame. This flame is perhaps the greatest gift the ascended masters have ever delivered to unascended souls. It transmutes bad karma on contact, returning the spectra of its mangled patterns to innate, immaculate purity.

As positive as the above may seem, there's yet another big fly in the ointment. All that talk about soul being the always an eternal consort of her Holy Christ Self refers to the **pure** soul before she has created any bad karma. It also refers to the pure centrosome of her being even after bad karma has accrued to her.

The big exception, however, is that the soul can be lost. It is possible for her to create so very much bad karma that the Lords of Karma (the Cosmic Being adjudicators of divine justice) deem it impossible for her to ever balance it. At that point, the soul experiences the "second death" wherein all of the energy she has ever qualified is transformed: repolarized and returned to its universal divinity as the One.

I am not aware precisely of what happens to that bad karma during the second death, but I suppose that the malformed patterns that the soul imposed upon her Causal Body's basic immaculate *maya* are alchemically transformed back to their original engrams/patterns. In other words, the akashic records of the soul's bad karma are removed, much like light removes darkness. It seems to me that the patterns of all of the good "extra" Beauty that the soul may have brought about would also be transformed back to its innate Causal Body engrams, but me not know nuttin' 'bout dat.

The Nature of Consciousness and *Maya*

In college, I had a physics professor who often demanded that we define our terms. He was good at telling when we were tossing jargon around without really knowing what the heck we were talking about. So, since this book concerns the nature of consciousness and *maya*, I see Prof. Hollis Todd standing before me now demanding that I clearly define the words consciousness and *maya*.

This is not going to be easy. I could say consciousness is the stuff out of which all experience is woven. Okay, then, so what's that stuff? Of course, the ultimate stuff is infinite mystery. But that probably gets you within a millimeter of calling me names and trying your best to keep from slugging me. All a statement like that can lead you to is a shrug of your shoulders. It's way too general to be useful. It says nothing at all about all those tables and chairs seemingly out there, and love and anger and the urge to help little old ladies across the street.

So a useful definition must involve the stuff we commonly interact with as well as the infinite realms beyond our senses. A good definition should imply how consciousness differs from the One about Whom Naught Can Be Said and also relate something about why it exists at all.

One thing's for sure. I can't just come out and say what consciousness in humans and immortals is because it's individually infinite, and it's ever so obviously not just a gaggle of matter. So you're definitely going to have to settle for some poetics.

Also, consciousness inheres in life forms below the human. Lower life forms can be said to be conscious in that they can repeatedly identify categories of life that differ from their own self-identity. At the mineral level, chemical equations are possible because elements "consciously" combine in certain ways. That is, an element responds differently to each of the other elements. Plants act similarly, but they can also seek nourishment. Animals add likes and dislikes, procedural abilities and the ability to actively move about. They enjoy some freedom of choice, yet they are largely governed by instinct.

Currently, only humans can actively engage divine transcendence (through the living flame of God in the heart). Only humans can consciously expand their identity unto their infinite Individuality, their Individual immortality. In this book, I will only address consciousness as it appears in humans and immortals.

We Must Settle for Similes

Since anyone using words can't just come out and say the infinite, the Fourteenth-Century Tibetan Buddhist mystical poet and sage Longchenpa found it necessary to describe attuned consciousness with eight similes: dream; magic show; optical illusion; mirage; reflection of the moon in water; echo; the city of the Gandharvas; and apparition.[7] By accepting Longchenpa's invitation to his poetic dances (see the above endnote), you can find inner resonances that will produce in you a deeply rewarding appreciation of the One I AM.

I hope that my attempt to bring the nature of consciousness to light here will help you similarly. I'm going to dive below the realms of effects into a more archetypal approach that should help understanding what consciousness is, not just how it affects the outer, everyday realm.

Start by noting that all the One can "do" is to realize I AM: the One and only Individual. Given that the One is infinite, that in itself, is quite a magic trick. But, that alone, is not yet consciousness. Consciousness involves realizing I AM the One from myriad viewpoints.

Ultimately, in Truth, only the One can be cognized. But more important, only the One can Really be re-cognized. The One re-cognizing Self is also known as divine Love. And you know what the song says: Love and marriage leads to a baby carriage.

Thus, consciousness is actually a synonym for the alchemical process of multiplication. Consciousness is I AM Selfhood acting as an exponent—a multiplier—of the One.

This processing is the transcendence that paradoxically enables infinity to become more infinite. Moreover, each instance of "greater" infinity signals a deeper humility in the conscious One's agent. That agent's consciousness can then be said to be more inclusive. That is, such a One is then able to nourish more of Life. For example, a conscious agent of the One, whose body expresses Selfhood as a solar system will "eventually" graduate to a "level"[8] of the spiritual Hierarchy at which they will express Selfhood as a galaxy, and endlessly beyond.

On the other hand, energy flowing through mechanisms of perception as memories, thoughts, feelings and physical sensation in ignorance of the One sustains an imbalance in lieu of divine Love. That is, consciousness is misused when it entertains the sense of separation. These vibrations produce spectra known as bad karma.

But that darksome activity must also be called consciousness because, like divine Love, it is awareness "driven by" the magical urging of infinite mystery. (But I choose to view such activity as unconscious ignorance. I prefer to use the term "consciousness" only to refer to awakened Self awareness in and as the One.)

What Is Consciousness?

So now I can take a poke at saying what Real, Infinite Consciousness is:

Consciousness is infinite mystery empowering the One as active Self awareness from a plenum of viewpoints. This divine Love enables to the One

and all focused agents of the One transcendent joy. Corollary to such joy comes humility and the requisite nourishment of ever-expanding Self expression, colorfully blooming as divine virtue.

Here's another try:

Infinite mystery drives consciousness as an awareness of I AM Selfhood. That drive imputes Life to its agents as flavors of the One. Cap "L" Life radiates light as infinite mystery's joy. Small "l" life insinuates sleepy eyed, more or less sordid separation.

Consciousness as a Question

Quantum physicists put it this way: Reality—consciousness—only exists as an answer to a question. Without a question, nothing can really exist. That's their endorsement of infinite mystery as the ultimate provenance of consciousness. So we can say that infinite mystery imbalances the One by suffusing it with questioning as potential. Consciousness restores balance to the One by completing the circuit of an enlightening question as divine Love. Consciousness alchemically enables the One to act, to experience joyous Selfhood and remain One.

Consciousness as a Transform

We can also relate to consciousness as a mathematical transform, such as the Fourier transform. That changes a functional representation of an image that can be seen into a functional representation of the wave frequencies and phases composing that image. The content of the image remains the same. Only the way it is described changes.

Consciousness works the same way. It is an operator that transforms subsets of infinite possibility (derived from the basic immaculate *maya* in our Causal Body) into expression that's accessible to our sense perception. Inversely, it transforms the sense perception we experience in our everyday life into the inner radiant Art of our treasures in the heaven world of our Causal Body. The infinite archetypal meaning/content THAT I AM of both representations never changes.

Consciousness as Presents to Presence

A long time ago I realized that the reason for the whole shebang (feminine energy activating man/manifestation) is like a little child sitting at a Christmas tree eager to find out what is hiding in all those beautifully wrapped presents. This harkens, again, to quantum physicists saying that everything out there answers a question. "What's there? Who/what AM I NOW.

Nowadays I refer to the only thing that's really Real as infinite mystery. So now let me give you my downright simplest definition of consciousness:

Consciousness is divine wonderment.

What Is *Maya?*

Keith Dowman describes four types of *Maya* in his book *Maya Yoga.*[9] These are:

1. **Basic Immaculate *Maya***
    I refer to this as the patterns of divine individuality (God's personality) inherent in the Causal Body. Dowman calls these "the fundament of the clear light of the nature of mind."

2. **The *maya* of false conception**
    This is the outer, phantom world we impute to consciousness with our sense of separation.

3. **The *maya* of the method used (the spiritual practice) to decontaminate the *maya* of false conception and recognize the nature of mind.**
    Dowman refers to this *maya* as "an agenda that turns back the ever-proliferating elaborations of the intellect upon themselves."

4. **The *maya* of primordially pure pristine awareness.**
   This is what is often called the "treasures in heaven." It is the radiant soul Art that results when her Identity is recognized in and as the One.

More About Basic Immaculate *Maya*

This is Keith Dowman's English translation of a Tibetan term. I will be using it often in this book, so I want to be sure you understand it and can relate to its implications.

Basic immaculate *maya* refers to the patterns of a Causal Body that render its I AM Presence a unique, divine Individual. These patterns are the soil, so to speak, of consciousness. They are the raw material out of which divine Art blooms as treasures in heaven. Soul kneads and caresses these patterns with the divine Mother's masterful magic. All of this activity invests the One, the I AM Presence, in divine consciousness: the awakening of possibility into patterned, Self realized conduction.

Of course, to err is human, so people often engage their souls with illusory patterns of bad karma which must eventually be healed. But that's just the "rest of the story." In this book, I will be concentrating upon viewpoints through which soul completes her lessons victoriously as the *maya* of primordially pure pristine awareness.

The Spiritual Hierarchy

Throughout this book, I often refer to the spiritual Hierarchy. I have found over the years that humans have a very strong penchant to misconstrue this concept. So now I equally strongly wish to obviate that.

The spiritual Hierarchy is a synonym for "Only the One IS." You ARE the beginningless, endless spiritual Hierarchy extending before and beyond quarks and multiverses. Unlike what is usually thought of as management levels where bigger bosses boss around lesser bosses and peons, this spiritual Hierarchy bosses nothing and no one in that manner. Agents of this Hierarchy NEVER circumvent God's will. They KNOW that any element of consciousness worth a dispensation of their attention—and that may appear to be bossable—IS God. So any direction imparted is delivered in a cooperative spirit.

In fact, the purpose of spiritual initiation, which raises one to a "higher" (more inclusive) position in the spiritual Hierarchy, enables consciousness to nourish more and more of Life by certifying one's humility.

As I'll be explaining later, your outer, everyday space-time life is a universe of consciousness expressing an inner, time-space parallel universe that offers your soul direct access to all the possibilities inherent in infinite mystery. Should you possess the consciousness or living technology to plumb infinitely, you would find that the outer, ever-changing world you traverse is identically equal to God's panoply of inner multiverses. Your consciousness appears limited only by the breadth of its focus, its awareness.

That is, the momentary circumscribed focus of your consciousness does not alter its Allness. The apparent limitations you may experience speak to the packaging that your ego habitually boxes you in with, not your Selfhood's inherence.

The infinite flaming One is omnipresent and open for you to realize union as your spiritual aptitude admits. As Charles Wyzanski said, "You are implicated in an enveloping mystery."[10] So sing your Truth like a canary from the witness stand.

The final word on this is that you ARE the spiritual Hierarchy. You are the One. Aspects of your Self have already gone before you to realize a greater unfoldment of the One than does the focused element of the One you currently identify with. Your ever ongoing spiritual initiations fit you to realize and recognize the endlessly transcending versions of your very own Selfhood.

Again, and again, and again: These viewpoints of the unlimited spiritual Hierarchy ARE You. You can consider your currently limited views of the great Cosmic Beings, the Gods and Goddesses, all immortals (and, for that matter, mortals, too) as previews of your coming attractions. They are elements of your own body, consciousness, being and world. Only the One IS.

Please grok that and then write to me to complain that I have wasted your time pushing pages of ever-so-obvious stuff upon you.

OVERVIEW

The three books of *A Trilogy In Maya* are:

1. ***Viewpoints: Integrating Parallel Universes***

   Consciousness creates and experiences your streaming identity. Moment by moment you assume viewpoints that cast your life upon infinite mystery's arenas. These parallel universes can be integrated to empower you as an agent of joy. By adopting viewpoints of divine awareness, you can recognize your Self as an immanence of light richly endowed with divine virtue. This book is a road map leading you along light's endless highway.

2. ***Only the One IS: Assuming Truth's Posture***

   Most spiritual teachers necessarily guide aspirants with words. That's tricky because all words are based upon conceptual duality. Thus, to usefully encourage resonance with the One, spiritual teachings and Self conception must avoid subconscious programming away from Oneness. This book empowers you to avoid carelessly using words, even as prayer, which can unwittingly imprison soul in false conception.

3. ***The Magic in Maya: Being an Inquiry into God's Destiny.***

   The Magic in Maya discloses how the divine One uses the energy veil to enable infinity to "grow" and realize joy. The Zoroastrian Twins *Spenta Mainyu* and *Angra Mainyu* are shown to bring alchemical verve to everyday life. Their interaction gift wraps the imaginative presents you momentarily accord in and as your I AM Presence.

THIS—BOOK ONE—COMPRISES:

PART ONE

Bare wire Love. Living fully energized...found AWAKE and ALIVE in spontaneity's swoon.

PART TWO

Sets the stage upon which our solar evolution plays out.

PART THREE

Describes the parallel universes of time-space and space-time. In these realms, our mortal, incubating soul prepares for her Life of ever ongoing Artistry, which portrays her eternal service in and as the spiritual Hierarchy.

PART FOUR

Considers consequences of developing a conscious awareness of parallel-universes, which invites evolving souls to ride infinite mystery's night train in broad daylight.

PART ONE

Bare Wire Love

At first, I intended to put this part at the end of this Book One, but I decided to include it here at the beginning to forthrightly convey the One's fervor for divine immanence.

Of Myself I Can Do Nothing
And No Object or Any Kind of Perception
Is Doing Anything Either

Everyday life is goes on and on in its petty pace, its imagery not much different from the displays "inside the museums, [where] infinity goes up on trial."[11] The One's unbounded Rascal—ever cross-examined on space-time courtship's stand—offends both the compartmental logic and statically exuberant charades that our ego centered busybodies so take for granted. But ego's objections to spontaneous joy take eternal Life to task in vain.

Eternity's Real Actor always gets off scot free. Grasping notions and human predilection can't touch THAT One. For its bare wire Love recognizes and embraces only the Self that Mystery esteems, unheedful of beginnings and endings. Eschewing categories, unclad, such Love spontaneously reveals imagery as harmony: harmony that dances free of sleepy-time life's jingle-jangle, masquerading convictions.

Bare wire love's harmony is a standalone field recognizing no separated parts. It's not something produced from components. Divine harmony expresses divine Love as joy caressing mystery. Moreover, inharmony doesn't even exist, for it doesn't eternally persist. It's like a passing thunder clap.

Only the One IS. Every element of conscious Reality instantaneously lives as an *objet d'Art* pronouncing eternity. Hence, apparently cascading transcendent states of consciousness change no thing. In this timeless state, bare wire Love's Real imagery is incomparably beautiful. Can't get more incomparable than instantaneous. So the Real song goes: "Everything is beautiful; in its own Way, Truth and Life."

In both Spirit and matter, "things" are said to exist because agents of the One form a consensus ratifying elements of infinite possibility shared out and mutually configured I AM THAT I AM. Moreover, a so-called "object," is radiantly enhanced whenever more viewpoints join its antahkaranic mix.

Life consists entirely of consciousness enabling viewpoints as births of a new, unique Being each New Day—each cycle of awareness. For, as quantum physicists have discovered, an "object" only "exists" by virtue of its observers. Thus, creators...observers...no dif, really.

"Each" divine Individual takes for their Identity at any stage of spiritual evolution some compendium of such Beings. Sustained awareness of personal divine Identity is possible because the organizing principal I AM has conducted those Beings into an opus in the music of the spheres. Yet, divine identity forever includes ever more BEING as in its Identity. So, given that the notion of persistence is a fool's errand, who am I this instant?

Now you know why I'm fond of declaring that only the One IS.

But getting down to cases, it's more fulfilling to say only Love IS. For, without divine Love's I-Thou Self-identification I AM THAT I AM—wholly resolved in the final Truth—even the One would amount to no more than some ghostly silly prank. But, not to worry. Bare wire Love's no prankster. Aye, any attempt to clad its zingy Beings walks the plank straight down the deep to Davey Jones' locker.

Everything you perceive as bare wire love is a moment's consensual celebration. It's a party of One partaking of favors, the favors of infinite mystery's unfathomable grace. And the Life of the party recognizes You as the One and only celebrant in the room providing that party's endearing ambiance. What could there BE without You?

Bare Wire Love Induces Beauty

I'm reminded of the exquisite, living threefold flame chalice that the ascended master Paul the Venetian fashioned as a gift for the Being known as the Maha Chohan. Nothing really changed upon Paul's fashioning that chalice. Its possibility was always there. Any ascended master had the same opportunity as Paul to bring together the elements of that piece of Art. But they didn't. It took Paul's special knack, the flair he has developed to ride the One, magnetizing components of consciousness that He massages to flourish as Beauty.

Paul's Art Lives. That's because he fashions it of bare wire Love, which favors all who enjoin His consensus as bosom buddies partaking of its grace. Like that other Paul, His works are all things to all people. His consciousness, enlivening His works, imposes nary a preconceived notion. Thus, each viewer is unhampered as they resurrect such a divine artist's confluences of the One as jewels, faceted, quickened awake, and rendered unique as their very own consciousness.

Growing Beauty is not a manufacturing process. It's awareness inviting divine virtue's possibilities to settle into patterned, focused Self reflection. It's bare wire Love's own brilliance inducing consciousness. It's a vote for a consensus. The only "change" is an observer's welcome of Paul's artistry into their own consensus. "Change" consists of the erection of receptor cells in consciousness, not in the fabrication of "things" to perceive.

The Alchemy of Your Love
Plays a Singular Part in Life's Growth
Bare Wire Love's Fiery Blossoming Deepens
The One's Own Provenance

I'm also reminded of the Black[12] Virgin of Montserrat, Spain focusing the night, Spirit, side if Life. She is not just some stand alone, standoffish statuesque image of feminine deity. She lives. Not as a walking, talking human, but Alive, nonetheless, as an overshadowed focus of Mary's Real Being.

For sure, the statue's consensus alone magnanimously amplifies Mary's purview. The statue's forehead is polished smooth and shiny by the innumerable kisses of the devotees who have passed her by and reconfigured her, each one, with their own heartfelt love and devotion.

The first day she was installed in her resting place, aloft in that cathedral, her consensus was but a shadow of what she has become. It's like the buildup of sandstone. Over and over and over again, Love's consensus builds upon itself owing to the virtual parade of devotees bequeathing their passion upon her. Her virgin enchantment deepens and expands as she partakes over the years of bare wire Love's blossoming exultation. In turn, each devotee receives the impress of all the Loving interchanges that preceded theirs.

Physically, the Black Virgin's statue is but colored wood. Anyone viewing her outside of bare wire Love's precinct would likely consider her but one more Spanish tourist attraction. Even so, her accrued effulgence of Love might, just might, put a bit of a chink in such human armor.

And such a tourist may find themselves lifting their eyes heavenward while emitting a vaguely confused "Hhhhmmmmmm. I wonder what's happening here." Since you are reading this, such a reaction would not likely be yours, but its contrary, an appreciative, hushed awe would likely linger with you, modifying all other aspects of your life.

It's commonly accepted that intense foci, such as the Black Virgin, effectively modify observant consciousness. But what about all that other stuff, the "things" you perceive everywhere? Do you just pass them by with nary a shrug like I often do? Or do you share my conclusion that nothing can exist at all without at least a modicum of bare wire Love's foundation (the white fire core of each and every element of being), be it from humans or other forms of Life.

Every rock, bush and flower—every "thing"—invites you to share its awe inspiring favors, its inner radiance. And, when your practice of the Presence is successfully online, you will drink in your very own Self radiance, which such Real imagery focuses. Sanat Kumara declares God's invitational play when he divulges bare wire Love's omnipresent Ruby Ray entreaty, "Drink Me, while I AM drinking thee."

Mother Mary's Fatima Statue

A third noteworthy instance of overwhelming consensus is the statue of Mother Mary at Fatima, Portugal. It is located where Mary appeared to the three children. Now a small chapel surrounds it. The Rosary is given there 24-7. Visiting priests come from all over the world to offer their personal devotions and for the honor of leading the Rosary. And when a live leader is absent, a tape is used.

The devotion to Mary at Fatima is remarkable. That Fatima statue is hoisted upon a small platform every evening and carried aloft around the grand plaza in a procession. Most in that throng carry lit candles and sing devotional songs to their divine Mother.

I needn't tell you the humongous consensus which that statue bears as Mary's amazingly tangible Presence throughout Fatima. It holds a comprehensive balance of spiritual light for all the world. Yes, the world is quite a mess now. But what it would be without such foci and devotion thereto as this little Fatima statue of Mary and the one at Montserrat would produce some pretty fearful imagery.

The Phantom "Objects" We So Take for Granted
Opportunity for Great Service

We can appreciate, then, that every perceptive act enjoining bare wire Love magnifies the One. And as consciousness bandies itself about attuning thereto, it bestows its unique give and take upon all Life as its Great Service. Consciousness mixing and matching every creation from the infinite pool of possibility beatifies Indra's jewels accentuating divine Love's holographic antahkarana.[13]

Antahkarana

The God Indra's jewels are said to focus God supposedly as objects, but such "objects" do not exist in the way our physically grounded mind supposes. Each object is more like a proposal, an invitation *from* the One and *to* the One for a dance. The more elements of consciousness agree to that dance—the greater its consensus—the more pronounced it becomes, the louder blares its Word. Yet no object ever really takes any precedence. For absolutely, with no exception whatsoever, ONLY the One IS.

It's useful, here, to review the antahkarana to assimilate Reality's insubstantial, yet boundlessly foundational nature:

> **"Indra's net" is the net of the Vedic god Indra, whose net hangs over his palace on Mount Meru, the axis mundi of Hindu cosmology and Hindu mythology. Indra's net has a multifaceted jewel at each vertex, and each jewel is reflected in all of the other jewels. In the Avatamsaka Sutra, the image of "Indra's net" is used to describe the interconnectedness of the universe:**
>
> **"Far away in the heavenly abode of the great god Indra, there is a wonderful net which has been hung by some cunning artificer in such a manner that it stretches out infinitely in all directions. In accordance with the extravagant tastes of deities, the artificer has**

hung a single glittering jewel in each "eye" of the net, and since the net itself is infinite in dimension, the jewels are infinite in number. There hang the jewels, glittering 'like' stars in the first magnitude, a wonderful sight to behold. If we now arbitrarily select one of these jewels for inspection and look closely at it, we will discover that in its polished surface there are reflected all the other jewels in the net, infinite in number. Not only that, but each of the jewels reflected in this one jewel is also reflecting all the other jewels, so that there is an infinite reflecting process occurring."[14]

Your consciousness focusing upon any one of Indra's jewels—any object, be it physical, a thought or a feeling—is like setting up a mirror at every other of Indra's jewels to reflect its Selfhood back upon the one being focused upon. That's wholeness; a harmonious suspension of conscious participants boasting solidarity and flourishing as Life's sublime melody.

The Cemetery of Forgotten Books

Thus, you can rest secure in and as the One, with whatever you encounter. Every "thing" that your attention magnetically attracts (rather than "creating" it yourself out of infinite mystery's pool of possibilities by traversing the alchemical cycle of creation) enjoys a greater or lesser hearty prominence, depending upon the forces that item's consensus reality comprises. Now, I wish to share some passages, which beautifully present the importance of such consensuses of attention upon the gaggles of possibilities that your "own" consciousness congeals into what we so very loosely call objects. They are taken from Carlos Ruiz Zafón's novel *The Shadow of the Wind.*

Describing the Cemetery of Forgotten Books, the protagonist, Daniel's, father explains:

"Here is a place of mystery, Daniel, a sanctuary. Every book, every volume you see here, has a soul. The soul

of the person who wrote it and of those who read it and lived and dreamed[15] with it. Every time a book changes hands [whenever a person as an element of consensus perceives something], every time someone runs his eyes down its pages, its spirit grows and strengthens."[16]

Each presentiment ever brought about—in all eternity—retains its place in the *akashic* records, which Life populates as eternally conscious, inter-mirroring, interdependent, instances of the One, as Indra's web of unified jewels. The cemetery of forgotten books symbolizes *akasha*.

"...between the covers of each of those books lay a boundless universe waiting to be discovered, while beyond those walls, in the outside world, people allowed life to pass by in afternoons of football and radio soaps, content to do little more than gaze at their navels. [Every supposedly insignificant object is ultimately as boundless as any other.]

To grok anything—practicing the Presence—is to place yourself into the unbounded "confines" of *akasha*, where Reality pervades you. The outside world, beyond the cemetery of forgotten books, is the phantom realm of *maya* where the sense of separation is possible.

"His Father (his I AM Presence) gave Daniel the opportunity to choose the one book (his destiny) that would portend his whole life. Like all of Life's books,

"...the novel told the story of a man in search of his real father...[Every embodiment comprises our search therein for our I AM Presence.]...whom he never knew and whose existence was only revealed to him by his mother on her deathbed."[17]

This is a deceptively deep passage. Your mother, the divine feminine, is on her deathbed in and as your consciousness, many times per second. Her deathbed is the point in your awareness's cycling at which it is about to reenter the cosmic mean, the zero points of the sine waves composing the spectra of consciousness. That is the infinite "realm" where your Father dwells and where your Mother ever "goes" to rejoin Him. Twice in every alchemical cycle,[18] your feminine, outer consciousness dies unto the selflessness of infinite mystery. If you assume THAT resonance, living in self-surrender, All is well. If you don't, your criminality will have to return to the scene of its crime to balance its karma.

> **"The story of that quest became a ghostly odyssey in which the protagonist struggled to recover his lost youth [his eternal Selfhood], in which the shadow of a cursed love [identification with *maya*] slowly surfaced to haunt him [you have a little backpack of karma to balance each and every day] until his last breath. As it unfolded, the story began to remind me of those Russian dolls that contain innumerable ever-smaller dolls within [the spiritual Hierarchy]. Step by step the narrative split into a thousand stories, as if it had entered a gallery of mirrors [*akasha & antahkarana*], its identity fragmented into endless reflections." [Who/what are you, anyway, but the Presence of infinite mystery.]**[19]

That fragmented identity in the above quote refers to the piecemeal nature of a karmicly hampered life. But it also illustrates the insubstantial nature of the One's own ultimate Identity: infinite mystery. Again, every "thing," including your own Real Self, is not a stand-alone entity. It is a subset of the One set: the ALL, the One and only I AM Presence. **It's a proposal ratified by consensus.**

In *The Shadow of the Wind*, old man Barceló, a rare book collector, takes a profound interest in the book Daniel picked out. Barceló represents the Cosmic Beings of heaven, whose interest is piqued by the degree that souls can render their book of Life rare, i.e., unique by refusing to identify with *maya*'s phantoms as separate entities.

He introduces Daniel to his niece, who is blind (like Roerich's painting of the divine feminine: "The Divine Mother") and dressed immaculately in purity, from her radiant, porcelain-like untainted skin to the entire whiteness of her clothing. She reaches out and feels Daniel's face to memorize its form. This act portrays the divine feminine assimilating outer activity to the One's Real vision of the Real Image, by alchemically linking its outer formative facets to their white fire cores.

You Are the One Center Practicing Its Presence

Above, we have considered infinity transcending its Self through consensus. But there's another way. Each of us can foster infinity's transcendence by living every moment affirming and KNOWING and FEELING I AM actually THAT there I AM, way over there and "away" from me. THAT I AM, indeed. "I can feel it in ma bones." I can feel it in my center that's everywhere, focused in every point in all tarnation instantaneously, and focused nowhere, where I AM.

Identity nestles furtively in the mysterious nature of the Real Image, which has but one boundary, like a Möbius strip.[20] For only the One IS; so only One Real Image IS. (The Möbius strip has several curious properties. A line drawn starting from the seam down the middle meets back at the seam, but at the other side. If continued, the line meets the starting point, and is double the length of the original strip. This single continuous curve demonstrates that the Möbius strip has only one boundary.)

Like the Möbius strip, the infinitely mysterious One "touches" the entire manifest world all at once in the same "place." Your awareness is THAT one touch reproducing the entire universe each moment, taking no notice whatsoever of which handle your Christ/Soul's unique point of "contact" happens to "hold." Such awareness may be no-where/no-time, but it is more akin to keeping your nose to the grindstone—pulverizing the little ego—than to acting like a space case.

Now, don't get me wrong. Living in the radiation of 10,000 suns isn't easy for us pipsqueak humans. So don't get down on yourself just because every single moment of your life is not going off like Fourth-Of-July fireworks set secure in a placid Peace so serene that naught whatsoever can turn your head. Just knowing where you're headed is enough. Someday you'll be firing off galaxies and big banging universes the size of Alpha and Omega's here where we live now in your spare not-time. And if you really want to smoke your brain, think of what Alpha and Omega will BE then.

Foci May Intensify
But Has Anything Really Changed?

In and as the One, nothing really changes. Yet humans say that the only thing constant is change. Even so, that constant awareness, local changeability, never takes leave of mystery's grace, which frees the One's Great Unknowing from befuddlement. Unlike the human type, mystery's fathomless constancy relieves awareness of any need for handles to grasp Real bedrock NOWing.

Such "NOWing" is "knowing" sans time/space. That leading silent "k" is like the mathematical small "i," which egolessly renders value imaginary, virtual. In this case, though, infinity flashing its imagery is virtually Real. Real awareness stems the One as antahkarana's sans-I-thou observer, whose Peace fathoms infinity and whose serene, cosmic-mean, bare wire Love, maintains its crush on plus-minus flings. What's actually transcending Selfhood is not the objects of our perceptions, but our realization of All THAT I AM.

I Love You
Oh, Really?

Most Hollywood films contain a love angle. I guess producers mostly think there can't be much of a story without it. And most of those stories are thickly clad in some form of human outfit that doesn't compare very well to the styles of heaven. Compared to stylin' cosmic stars, at best an acting-out Hollywood pair is really just a couple a' swells.[21] So what's the story of bare wire love?

For one thing, it's unqualified, and that has little to do with mushiness 'neath the moonbeams or graduating simple preference into a profession whose text includes an "*I* love *you*" or two. Such emotive pleadings may seem a but diversion from proceedings in the court of absolute Truth.

Actually, such "I love you's would probably draw infinite mystery's defense attorney to ejaculate "Out of order, your honor! Strike that affront to the One from the record." Yet, the gracious One on the high court's bench may intervene: "Objection overruled, counselor. Endearment assuages in the space-time realm, where this court sits. Let the record show prosecution's intent to invite affection to the dance." And so it goes;

hands clasp and hearts meld midst the warmth of self-surrendering eyes. And the One has its day in the live-long end.

Bare wire Love enfolds forthright Life in surrender, for it controls only nothing even as it induces mystery to come out and play. "You" truly loving is nothing acting, and that's all you've got to lose. Dylan asks, "Are you willing to risk it all? Or is your love in vain?"[22]

Elsewhere, Dylan alludes to bare wire Love as a raven, at his window with a broken wing.[23] The broken wing of bare wire Love arises from your attention drawing it to a non-native grounding in the world of form. Nevertheless, that Love, even in its inhibited state, plays upon your innate compassion. Its soul stirring calling magnetizes you to grace's insubstantial vortex. Such Love would, if it were cosmically lawful, lock your eyes and all of your tendencies in a bracing infinite reunion. But your liberty is sacrosanct. God don't need no filthy badges.

Your only Real occupation, then, is to continuously heal your imagination of its involvement in *maya*'s mechanics, freeing it to soar as a night-side, Spirit, raven winging unhindered in wide open spaces and beyond.

Beauty in the Eye of the Beholder

There's no accounting for taste. You can walk down the street, and notice some things and not others; fall in love with some people or songs or this or that and not others. Besides your own internals, we've already seen how consensus raises some items into prominence. But where are your innermost magnets to be found?

Your high road carries you along as destiny. The low road, where human trial and error has tended toward error, brings about a multitude of stumbles over the likes of humanly disheveled Stones, crying, for instance, "It's just rock and roll, but I like it!"[24]

Such bad habits, unreinforced, can fall away of themselves. But you can accelerate the process by letting your angel roll away stones to release you from the whole sleepy-eyed ball of wax entombing you. Then your Deity ESTablished IN You will liberate you from your cladded finagling, and allow bare wire Love to celebrate the Great Central Sun Magnet in your heart.

If you can allow your Presence to pull that off, then there *will* be an accounting for taste. And you'll probably find it finger lickin' good. Not so much because it's scrumptious, but because every last syllable of its Word is predigested at the deepest core of your Being. Your Real taste in things ratifies and reflects your supernally sublime concurrence in and as the One: your unique intake, forgiving its masque even as it populates the plenum as your Beauty.

It's ever so easy to be flippant; even to flip off the scabs that blemish your basic immaculate *maya* (your yet-to-be-ratified Causal Body Patterns) in unguarded moments.

Don't.

Get serious.

You will be warded unto your ecstasy; rewarded in the throes of bare wire Love.

PART TWO

Setting the Stage Of Solar Evolution

Why?

Insubstantial,
yet seemingly substantial,
instants of consciousness are given
for a purpose.
That purpose:
to afford the One a skill.

That skill being to realize.
Realizing; not any supposed thing
but Self comprising All.

That Self may seem to exist,
that the One
about whom naught can be said
may know joy:
Joining the Om to You.

That individual union with All,
the One Individual Loving,
happily cascading haply,
spontaneously,
that solemn holiness
may fruit and disappear and

spacious emptiness withal resound

I AM.

A Cosmogony of Consciousness

My purpose here is to condense into a glimpse what could be (and actually has been) rightfully set forth extensively in many books. For instance, Master Morya, in the 1920s-30s published his Agni Yoga volumes. Madame Blavatsky's books evolved into the voluminous works of the Theosophical Society. Following that, the I AM Activity and the Summit Lighthouse released a plethora of expositions upon the subject of this, my abbreviated look at consciousness, its questing substance and structure.

My hope is that this bird's eye view of the subject will allow the reader to encapsulate enough of it as to carry it more or less in the forefront of remembrance even in one's daily busybody life. To do so will fertilize consciousness to grow apace, even as light begets its own racing, joy embracing plenum.

What's All the Supposed Stuff Out There?

Yogananda called this process of consciousness beholding its Self a Realization; and so it is, for nothing is new, or old. All so-called creation is but a picking and choosing from divine possibility. Consciousness is endowed with magnetics that can draw components into imaginative focus. The body can physically operate upon raw materials/possibilities to "create." But actually, the object brought together, brought into being, only exists as an inner realization of the One in any who behold it.

Notice that word "behold." It implies that being is actually "doing" the holding. The sensation of holding something in your hand is a compendium of perception which is at bottom no more real or factual than any inner meditative confabulation. Every bit of it is consciousness realizing a focused snapshot of infinite Allness wherein personal perception proffers a handle. (CB radio jocks and Rainer Maria Rilke relate to handles as names. Indeed, all our handling of the infinite One is but a naming that gets its number, its inner essence, its spatially capacious wavy vibe.)

This naming, this momentary taking stock of ourselves reveals our infinite inventory rolling on and on as our horizons give way to light's effulgence. That blooming is our fabled Selfhood, which is both worthless and priceless. It bears in its clutches the liberty that co-pilots the One's potential.

The Great Unknowing

Simply: Entering the Great Unknowing is to directly point consciousness into the infinite spaciousness within and without. Rainer Maria Rilke describes the conscious state of one who approaches it:

> **"Only he who can expect anything, who does not exclude even the mysterious, will have a relationship to life greater than just being alive; he will exhaust his own wellspring of being."**[25]

Master Morya refers to the childlike consciousness lacking preconceived notions, which Jesus so admired, as the Gates of Cognizance. I often use "the Great Unknowing" as an attempt to evince that mode of consciousness as the portal to illimitable possibility. Even recognizing that such a state exists lays down the red carpet for our formative outer awareness to give way, for our questing Selfhood to walk upon as an agency of the One's ever-new creativity.

It is super important to emphasize that seeking and achieving the Great Unknowing refers neither to going passively blank nor to ignorantly adopting some measure of imbecility.

Every moment, your perceptions receive illusory, often chaotic showers of energetic imagery. Nevertheless, the ultimate provenance of the imagery you encounter pertains to the Great Unknowing's infinite realms where Hope resounds fulfilled. William Wordsworth, so inwardly sensitive to that bourn recollects:

> **What though the radiance which was once so bright**
> **Be now for ever taken from my sight,**
> **Though nothing can bring back the hour**
> **Of splendor in the grass, of glory in the flower;**
> **We will grieve not, rather find**
> **Strength in what remains behind;**
> **In the primal sympathy**
> **Which having been must ever be;**[26]

That primal sympathy goes to the heart of your Real Selfhood. It is THAT within, which renders you human, which enables you to paradoxically run in tandem with infinite mystery. It is—though you be a soul in training—the opportunity to create largely unfettered instances of the One in consciousness. Your primal sympathy IS God within you, passionately enabling you to express divine Love right along with all masters, Archangels, Cosmic Beings and the Lords of the plenum of worlds, capable of representing joy in and as the One.

Synonymous with the Great Unknowing, Zen is the soul's relaxation in the potently persuasive flow of infinite mystery caressing Selfhood. You, the One's beloved agent, can validate its Great Unknowing as vividly as you refine our loved One's face. I love the poet Rumi's incisive suggestion, "Sell your cleverness and buy bewilderment."[27] Such surrender of the sense of separation evinces the courage to momentarily eviscerate the supposedly separative all from All and to subsume THAT All in ALL.

Thereby, Truth is called upon life's stage for soul to emblazon it in her cockpit of consciousness. Vital principles then can displace, fructify and render salubrious the energy formerly invested in a pipsqueak ego's grandstanding hubris, its strutting and fretting that so often sullies our Way.

Drawing upon the Great Unknowing, Morya encourages you to live the mantra:

GATE GATE PARAGATE PARASAMGATE
BODHI SVAHA

> **"The new is the oldest, hence, one should not fear something as being impossible. Everything is imaginable because everything exists. One cannot assume a poverty of creation. It is astonishing how easily science permits itself narrow limitations and responds to that of which it is ignorant. Children sometimes say, more correctly, 'I do not know.' A frank absence of knowledge [energized as the Great Unknowing] is regarded as the Gates of Cognizance."[28]**

Funny, how science's limiting laws, which only describe the interactions of secondary energy, are welcomed by so many to box consciousness into what spiritual masters call ignorance. That word is not used as name calling. It simply describes consciousness that ignores the Great Unknowing; consciousness that slams shut doors which smother the gates of cognizance. Indeed, the Great Unknowing opens your consciousness *parasamgate* to the ever present dawning, the rebirth that momentarily lights all the world.

In the following, Sadhguru Jaggi Vasudev uses "intelligence" to refer to the wakefulness of your entire Being in its encounter with the Great Unknowing, not to mere intellect:

> **"If you don't know, do you see, you have to use your intelligence. Let's say it's pitch dark. You Don't know how the ground is. Do you see how alert you will become? Every step that you take. When you do not know, everything becomes bright! It is just looking. Your intelligence is hyped up and looking. When you assume "I know," everything settles down and you go on with your stupid life."**[29]

"Just looking!" Simple enough, right? Find that Great Unknowing place within you; set yourself right there in the mood for that mode. You will brighten your outlook, your inlook, your Being. That Great Unknowing point of consciousness is not only never absent from you, it fervently presses unknowable Selfhood through your every pore.

Each moment of manifestation, at the inception of every alchemical cycle, your Higher Self is condemned to death. Yet, it is wholly within your power thence to choose Life, to ignore death's ignorance. You can wrench from the powers that be in their mechanized arena a pardon for the Lord, your interlocutor with infinity. Such pardon frees you and offers your very soul—your awakened consciousness—as joyous succor for the One. In such interplay, your every notion is a passion play.

Each time Jesus fell on His walk to Golgotha, he rose again and kept on keeping on. William Wordsworth passionately describes this utter refusal of our Higher Self to allow lazybones ignorance to rob us of the exhilarating color of our Sun/Son light. Yes. Yes. Yes. Delight's inner frenzy, if you take but a moment to look deeply within, will pounce upon your ignorant lapses into grayscale indifference, to which our mortal creature so easily succumbs.

In this passage, Wordsworth first remembers the joyous opportunities the past has left unsung. Then he opens our understanding to the precious cargo our bad karma freights abroad. He implores us to understand that in the dense substance of our mortal forms we can carry, "truths that wake, to perish never."

> "O joy! That in our embers
> Is something that doth live,
> That Nature yet remembers
> What was so fugitive!
> The thought of our past years in me doth breed
> Perpetual benediction: not indeed
> For that which is most worthy to be blest;
> Delight and liberty, the simple creed
> Of Childhood, whether busy or at rest,
> With new-fledged hope still fluttering in his breast:—
> Not for these I raise
> The song of thanks and praise;
> But for those obstinate questionings
> Of sense and outward things,
> Failings from us, vanishings;
> Blank misgivings of a Creature
> Moving about in worlds not realized,
> High instincts before which our mortal Nature
> Did tremble like a guilty Thing surprised:
> But for those first affections,
> Those shadowy recollections,
> Which, be they what they may,
> Are yet the fountain light of all our day,
> Are yet a master light of all our seeing;
> Uphold us, cherish, and have power to make
> Our noisy years seem moments in the being
> Of the eternal Silence: truths that wake,
> To perish never;
> Which neither listlessness, nor mad endeavor,
> Nor Man nor Boy,
> Nor all that is at enmity with joy,
> Can utterly destroy!
> Hence in a season of calm weather

> Though inland far we be,
> Our Souls have sight of that immortal sea
> Which brought us hither,
> Can in a moment travel thither,
> And see the Children sport upon the shore,
> And hear the mighty waters rolling evermore."[30]

Tap Latent Infinity NOW

Indeed, even the clanking chains burdening our commonly fateful walk bear in them proposals and infinitely capacious views that can leave even the All-Seeing Eye aghast.

With Great Unknowing as the coin of the Realm, Sri Ramana Maharshi would agree that we're left with the question "Who am I?" as the only Real slot in Life's machinery.

Consciousness carries the Great Unknowing about like a soft drink carries CO_2. It remains hidden until heat—a greater concentration of consciousness—is applied. Then it bubbles out into the open. Except that the Great Unknowing can express an infinity of possibilities, not just hot air.

But, note well, such energy transubstantiation must be consciously invoked through inner attentiveness, not by a phantom ego. Revelation of Selfhood may be spontaneous, but "you" must resonate in tandem with it. Sluggards will never take notice. Such alchemical processing is not on automatic pilot. Gautama says repeat after me: I AM AWAKE!

As an agent of the One, you are responsible for all of the energy that has ever flowed through you. Some of that, as awakened consciousness, has Artistically expressed divine virtue; some has not. The good news is that you have direct access to the healing grace needed to realign the spectra of your consciousness to divine Reality. But you—or a wonderful Being who is blessing you—must pick up the spiritual tools sitting there on your work bench and activate them in the here and now to assume your full Name I AM THAT I AM.

Four Simultaneously Operative Arenas

The Great Unknowing's creative salience complements its carrier's awareness in four major arenas simultaneously. Your spiritual flowering will accelerate as you are able to appreciate the magnificent scope of operation that your gift of consciousness partakes moment by moment:

- **Super macro consciousness:** Cosmic Beings ensouling and nourishing multiverses, universes, galaxies, solar systems, individual stars and planets. Herein we also find seraphim, cherubim, Archangels and angels, as well as other celestial choirs: Thrones, Dominions, Powers, Virtues, and Principalities. Believe it or not: These are all You!

- **Macro consciousness:** Your human identity along with all other sentient life in the arena where I-thou, secondary energy metadata largely holds attention's sway. This is a schoolroom where soul learns to realize Self Identity. But also way more than that: to derive joy from the Artistry of **Spirit's Own Union with Life.** That unitive consciousness is what enables divine Individuality: **IN-DIVIDed** Union of the **ALl's I TY** (eye tie) I AM THAT I AM. That tether lassos loved Ones and enfolds them in the secret places of the Most High to ennoble commonality as the One I AM. Thus, soul's stomping ground— the City Foursquare—is where you who is reading this currently focus most of your awareness. This realm provides the One with the laboratory where *maya's* magic is inculcated in soul. This magic, in turn, is so very becoming—like the bonnets in the Easter Parade—as it shares with All the One's beauty—the **Bright Energy of Alpha United To You.**

- **Micro consciousness:** Similar to macro consciousness, but on a much smaller scale, inaccessible to human perception. This includes cellular activity in the bodies of beings enjoying macro consciousness, as well as the mini lives of bacteria, viruses, super small insects, etc. In humans, this also includes the consciousness of the body elemental, the masterful being who manages the physical body. Just think of all the chemical reactions going on within you and the amazing complexity of intentional flows of energy and substance this being delegates as the CEO of your physical universe of personal operation. Flabbergasted I am, just attempting to imagine it.

- **Quantum consciousness:** Submicroscopic interactions of all the above arenas with the unbounded "arena" of infinite mystery. The lifeblood of this realm is the mysterious One's transcendence, which fuels imagination at all levels of awareness. While you may not consider a rock to possess any imagination at all, I would disagree. Some level of Elohim, as the builders of form, exists there and works imaginatively to eventually gain the mastery needed to graduate from the mineral to the vegetable kingdom. Life never slouches...except, of course, for beer drinking, pretzel gorging, NFL watchers.

I know...it's super hard for us humans to relate to ourselves as all that as we gad about our workaday worlds; much less truly appreciate it. But if you take a stab at it every once in a while, you will launch yourself into an n-dimensional, IMAX-style, in-your-face fervency that can, yes, leave you aghast. Then, you'll surely want it more and more. That's one addiction that one-handed clapping can applaud.

Only the One IS
The Far Off Worlds Abound Right Here

Easy to say. Impossible to encompass. For the One's provenance is infinite mystery. That Great Unknowing bares the beginningless-endless oomph that impels God's will and all of its ramifications.

In "The Eighth Letter" in Rainer Maria Rilke's *Letters to a Young Poet*, he muses about how we, in all of our supposedly variegated self-concern, must, if we be honest with ourselves, accept that we are ultimately alone; that only the One IS. None of life's fluff can ever displace that nagging hound of heaven apprising you of union. Here's Rilke:

"To return to the subject of aloneness: It becomes increasingly clear that it is basically not something

we can choose to have or not to have. We simply *are* alone. One can only delude one's self and act as though it were not so—that is all. How much better, however, that we concede we are solitary beings; yes, that we assume it to be true. Our minds will certainly reel at the thought, for all points on which we could heretofore focus shall be taken from us. There is nothing near and familiar left us; everything is in the distance, unendingly far away."[31]

Unendingly far away, indeed! Master Morya often speaks of the "far off worlds." And herein, we see that He refers not to particular planets or places. When Morya refers to the far off worlds, He is attesting to their Presence in the One's consciousness. He is citing Reality's inner nature as infinite mystery. Thus, each of the far off worlds is a mode of consciousness. Taken together, the far off worlds comprise the One's endless quest, which we call God's will.

Moreover, because of divine will's infinite provenance, even God—the agent, Him/Her Self, of the mysterious One—cannot Truly encapsulate the One's agents in preconditioned demands. The ultimate aloneness of which Rilke speaks is thus the bestowal of free will upon All.

God's will, as specific vectors directed to an agent's consciousness is not a boss giving orders. No, no, no...it's a bestowal of a beautifully crafted entry point to the One's infinite mystery. There's no God "over there" to do any bossing. There's no "God" separate from you. You are the one and only God realizing ongoing Selfhood.

Indeed, no member of the spiritual Hierarchy, however "high" their Being, is ultimately "God" to you. Every Individuality of the One—including the highest Cosmic Beings—is dependent upon the grace of the One's infinite mystery as the provenance of their Self realization: the centrality of their own BEness.

True, every Being and being has a guru (known or unknown) or a sponsoring master to whom is owed unbounded gratitude and obeisance. But that master earned their "rank" through humility, not by claiming some ungodly right to boss others around.

It is always up to a particular divine agent to make of divine direction THAT which the agent, themselves, freely chooses to bestow as Life in and as the One. Yet, your victory and victories are up to the Christ/Soul

You who knows that "of myself I can do nothing." Creative, momentary Self realization fuels divine joy's consonance with a far off world as a newly minted, unique mode of infinite Being. Every Real "THING" focuses an infinitely ongoing far off world.

The Mystery and Magic That Culminate in Joy

It seems that mystery and magic are first, kissing, cousins; as, magically, out of infinite mystery, THE Self realized Magician pulls the One and only I AM Presence out of the profoundly depthless black hat, which Kabbalists call *Ein Soph*.

That singular, one and only, I AM Presence knows *only* I AM.

That's it; period.

Not too exciting, huh?

But that uni-solar coherence also magically imputes grace to its unspeakable caress of All in ALL.

Even so, that One I AM Presence is so tremendously, unconditionally lonely that it doesn't even know it's bored out of its no-mind.

Wait...the magic gets even better.

The One I AM facets Selfhood...somehow.

Presence blooms as an infinity of I AM Presences, in-divided of the One, to take their precedence as divine Individuality.

But that solves nothing. The boredom would persist if that were some sort of end. For, these facets are still latent: all One. They are incapable of telling One from another.

But, have no fear. Joy is also latent in these great pretenders. These Presence"s" portend inherent union as both a noun and a verb, and behold, Love.

Twin Flames

Infinite mystery unmasks its potential in polarity as masculine and feminine I AM Presences—yet still One Presence: the scientifically disallowed mono-pole. They are fiery polar twins—called twin flames—sharing a common identity, referred to as the Causal Body of their single-Presence facet of the One I AM Presence.

As twin flames evolve in their masculine-feminine polarity, each is apparently endowed with their own Causal Body. Then, through their evolving Christ/Souls, they beautify these as Self realized Art. Each to the other, they partake of the complementary support and nourishment that blooms in them wholly to grace their One, unified I AM Presence.

Individuality Is All Important
Yet Way Beyond "All Important"
Only the One IS

Here's a first take on this. Being an Individual means that you are unique, that there are no more copies of you out there. But it is well known that a negative cannot be proven. There can always be something not yet considered.

The only way to certify Individuality is to lack any other places to check for duplicates. Thus true Individuality requires that each "Individual" BE all that IS and all that was and all that the future makes possible and ALL beyond conception. Your "Individuality," to be unique, MUST include infinite mystery. Thus, the question, "Who am I?" is not meant to be answered. It is meant to blow your block off.

Yes, your Individuality is sacrosanct; and right along with Muhammed Ali, You are the GREATEST. But don't bother looking to preen because there's no room left in front of the mirror.

So what's all that got to do with Twin Flames? Glad you asked. Honest...I was just about to get around to that.

Twin Flames Are Different—Yes, Unique
But They're One Individual

Each twin flame I AM Presence evolves as an Individual. That is, each evolves their joint One I AM by fashioning and accruing unique treasures of experiential Art to their own apparently individual Causal Body. The result is like a piece of living music realized through those two hands/Flames/Causal Bodies gracing the One Causal Body mansion of their One Presence.

The musical phrases of this Identity piece are the Akashic furnishings that their Christ/Soul has fashioned as living Art that draws upon the creativity of both Twin Flames. That is, the musical line played by each hand, say, in a piano piece, can be appreciated in and of itself as a beautiful expression. But the composer conceived of both the left and right hand lines together; and the piece comprises both equally, harmoniously.

So, as humans, we could look at each twin flame and find it easy to convince ourselves that they are independent individuals. Indeed, they act that way. But, again, they are no more separate from each other than, say, the right and left arm of an individual pianist. "They" are One I AM Presence.

Both Twin Flames Contribute To Each One's Evolution

I have not been directly told the following by any ascended master. I'm making it all up. But…I can't come up with anything else that plumbs my provenance and makes sense to me. In short, I am saying below that each twin flame enjoys and inhabits the Self-same Causal Body. I know that us humans get it into our heads that each twin flame has a unique Causal Body, different from their consort's. That's what I thought before writing this book. I no longer believe that. I now see each twin flame's Causal Body as a polar entry point to the One Causal Body of their One I AM Presence. Each may appear to be different; but "they" are One. Nevertheless, I've been wrong before about mostly non-spiritual stuff. So maybe I'm now also spiritually off kilter here. Yet, again, my deepest meditation on this leaves me in Peace. Don't take it from me, though. Do your own deep delving. So, here's what all this wondering is about:

So united are twin flames that my conception of them is that, <u>in both fact and activity</u>, they ARE a single I AM Presence. I would say that when either of them evinces light in a masculine mode, it is in fact the masculine I AM Presence who is expressing; same with the feminine. In other words, each twin flame evolves their One I AM Presence individually, but each of them uses both of their One's respective masculine and feminine modality to express their evolutionary path.

So when, for instance, Saint Germain expresses divine virtue masculinely, it is his "own" masculine twin flame Saint Germain's Causal Body that fructifies. When Saint Germain expresses femininely, it is the feminine twin flame Portia's Causal Body that fructifies. Likewise, when Portia expresses divine virtue masculinely, it is the masculine twin flame Saint Germain's Causal Body that fructifies. When Portia expresses femininely, it is her "own" feminine twin flame Portia's Causal Body that fructifies.

Don't feel Humanly Cheated

Most of us humans probably feel that the above statement somehow robs each twin flame of their claim upon their own unique mastery of their opposite polarity. That is, when Saint Germain displays feminine mastery, a normal human would say that he should "get credit" for that. That it somehow cheats him of his feminine attainment to say that whatever he accomplishes in a feminine light is actually Portia at work, not his own wholeness.

But I, in the One's final Truth, would disagree with that. Again, the union of twin flames is so complete that it is utterly impossible for either to "steal" anything from the "other." "Each" twin flame's I AM Presence shares the One's Reality and therein derives its Being. Indeed, "They" ARE one I AM Presence.

Bear with me...I think I need to say that again:

Both twin flames **ARE** one I AM Presence.

Yes, throughout all of its evolutionary activity, only the One I AM Presence IS: the ultimately inclusive One. Likewise, each twin flame assumes but a polar agency of "their" One Being—the One I AM Presence which each twin flame *entirely* IS. (I sure will not take offense if you now say I am spurting gobbledygook. The human brain we are stuck with is miserably intellectual bling that throws up its arms, shudders and collapses in the face of paradox.)

I interpret Ervin Laszlo's description of quanta as correlating this unity of twin flames:

"Quanta are highly sociable: once they share the same identical state, they remain linked no matter

how far they travel from each other. When one of a pair of formerly connected quanta is subjected to an interaction (that is, when it is observed or measured), it chooses its own "real" state—and its twin also chooses its own state, but not freely: it chooses it according to the choice of the first twin. The second twin always chooses a complementary state, never the same as the first twin.[32]

In other words, the Christ/Souls of each twin flame possess free will, each to the other, but neither actually acts separately. The "complementary state" Laszlo refers to is the twin flame polarity, opposite that of the twin flame's consort. No "act" of that I AM Presence in evolutionary mode can "exist" in manifestation without the masculine twin flame's proposal and the feminine twin flame's disposal. Again, this is the "complementary state" of unity Laszlo references.

Again, and again: Each of them ARE One I AM Presence.

Owing to the above ALWAYS complementary activity of twin flames, I must say that the Causal Bodies of both the masculine and the feminine twin flames are ultimately identical; their only difference being in the polarity of their viewpoint.

I have always, up to this moment, thought that the Causal bodies of twin flames are quite different in that they contain the results of markedly different Life experiences.

But now, owing to the above cited quantum physics underpinning and my own spiritual understanding of the identically equal spiritual nature of twin flame activity, I relate to their Causal Bodies also as identically equal, except for their polarity. In other words, Saint Germain's treasures in heaven find place in Portia's Causal Body even as they do in His own, and vice versa.

I can now envision the Causal Bod"ies" of twin flames as, in fact and actuality, the magnetic poles of a single sun magnet of consciousness— the One Causal Body of their One I AM Presence. To think otherwise is to ascribe to the word "One" a mighty weird definition.

Another view of this unity is the quantum entanglement of two elements of consciousness. Of course, you can't get "two" to tango more entangled than twin flames, however far apart they may find themselves. And so, quantum nonlocality applies in spades to them.

That means that they always share the same state. If the state of one of them changes while on earth, and the other is visiting aunt Vasipu on Venus, the Venus visitor's state will change accordingly. Nonlocality, then is the scientific language for saying that twin flames possess the same Causal Body state with complementary polarities as entry points to it.

I imagine that I need to assimilate a great deal more of alchemical knowledge re consciousness to understand how it can be that Saint Germain and Portia can appear so immensely different when they are actually One. I suspect that human brains will never have access to such knowledge; that only immortal levels of God's mind can put that together.

The Nature of In-Division
How New Divine Individualities Are Birthed

This section describes how a new divine Individuality comes to be, as an emanation of a Being's Causal Body. I include this section because it illustrates the amazingly far reaching work each of us do every day, every moment.

Let's say you're walking down the street, and you come across a little ol' lady shuffling along, trying to cross a heavily trafficked cross street. She can't get across fast enough to make it to the other side safely. So you take her along with you, helping her move a little faster; maybe even holding up your hand to oncoming traffic to stop it long enough to safely proceed. Finally, then, the two of you are on the opposite side of the street. Little old lady goes her way, and you go yours.

Know what you just did? You involved God's grace in an act of mercy and guidance. That divine virtue's energy "rises up" to your Causal Body to take its place there as an element of *maya*; of the primordially pure pristine awareness variety. It has become a living Being; a sphere in your Causal Body.

You may now be tendering a bit of a qualm at me because I called that act, that configuration of energy a cap "B" Being. But I suspect that by the time you finish this book, you will be completely on board with me about that.

So now let's say you are in the super market and at the checkout counter, someone is trying to pay for something and they need a few cents more, that they don't have. You fish their shortfall out of your wallet and make up the difference for them. Now read the same paragraph I wrote above, starting with "Know what you just did?"

I come up with lots and lots of the same sorts of examples in which you perform divinely virtuous deeds, and the same sort of spheres get implanted in your Causal Body, sittin' around up there just blazing away radiating their light out to all tarnation all the time. After a while, if you keep that up long enough, people will subconsciously realize that you are willing to lend a helping hand and heart, and they will choose to ask you for help when they need it.

Over a very long period, if you keep on practicing that divine virtue, such as mercy, a consensus will build up and up and up to such a level that its presence in you will be recognized as a unique divine virtue. This is what happened for the bodhisattva Avalokiteśvara. His practice of mercy became so intense and "fleshed out" to such a tremendously subtle panoply of nuance that it became worthy of becoming an in-division of his own Presence. In other words, the living Being that is the congregation of the living spheres of consciousness of mercy in Avalokiteśvara's Causal Body gestated there to the level worthy of being recognized as a Goddess and given a name that can be called upon for blessing.

Of course, I have no idea how the above alchemically came about, but it is universally recognized that the Goddess of Mercy, Kwan Yin, is an emanation of Avalokiteśvara. Thus, we can say that Avalokiteśvara "gave birth" to Kwan Yin by developing a divine virtue to such an extent that it was worthy of taking off on its own as an Individual Being. (As a matter of fact, Tibetan Buddhists consider Avalokiteśvara, Himself, to be an emanation of the Dhyani Buddha Amitabha.[33] That is a way the spiritual Hierarchy operates. It produces emanations of divine virtue over and over to in-divide and expand the consciousness of the infinite One I AM Presence.

You!!! are gestating possible divine Individualities in your own Causal Body every time you repeat a divine virtue. Maybe some will eventually reach the point where they can be recognized as a new independent Being; a new Individual; a new Divine Individuality. Then you and your twin flame will be beaming as you pass out cigars in heaven.

Incidentally, it is worth mentioning here, that the ascended masters have told us that the lady master Meta is a daughter of Sanat Kumara and Lady Master Venus. So the divine virtue that Meta represents had its start as a developing compendium of virtue in Their Causal Body. Eventually, it grew to such an intensity that Meta was born. Also Archangel Michael and His twin flame Faith concentrated so much on the virtue of unity that their Causal Body birthed their angel son Micah, the angel of unity. And so it goes...on and on...infinite consciousness transcends the One producing babes like the little ol' woman who lived in a shoe and just didn't know *what* to do! Seems she was right on key with infinite mystery.

Higher Service

A similar alchemy to an I AM Presence giving birth to a subset emanation, comes into play from the point of view of your own service here below. The higher—more inclusive—your consciousness becomes, the greater the level of divinity that you can inhabit and use as the One's agency. As you expand your consciousness, you can pick and choose whatever divine virtue you wish to focus from the Causal Bodies of Cosmic Beings without end. It may seem a bit topsy-turvy to say, but that is almost like you are giving birth to those Beings as your own Sons and Daughters because you are emanating them even as they enfold you. As the saying goes: "Drink me as I AM drinking thee." In fact, it is literally true that you ARE the God parent of every single solitary Being, for... sing it all together now: only the One IS!

I often find myself meditating upon being an agent of God's own expansion, immanently, this moment. The living wonder of this is so beautiful that I want revisit it here, regarding this and the previous section.

We often speak of the living Presence of God. But that Life also applies to the Causal Body. In fact, it's called the "Causal" Body because each of its spheres, each of its divine virtues, is capable of causing more creation. Every divine virtue you have activated and brought to Life as a treasure in your heaven world can grow into an independent actor. Even as Avalokita has delegated His divine mercy to Goddess Kwan Yin, each of your virtues can grow to the stature of a captain independently running the ship of some state of your own magnanimity. Each moment can be like a fulfilled Easter egg hunt with live eggs. The divine virtues you gather can hatch. Those Causal Body chicks will then go out and resurrect more, like unto themselves. And your Causal Body will someday host and nourish universes of life waves of evolving wide eyed goodness.

As Above, So Below

Right here in your everyday walk-around realm, you can realize your highest divine consonance momentarily. The union of any two elements of consciousness I AM THAT I AM radiantly ratifies All as the immanent Presence of God—the union of twin flames. And that living understanding keys right into a remarkable revelation I have supremely enjoyed regarding the nature of God's high flying Name.

OM I AM THAT I AM I AM THAT I AM OM
Saint Germain Spills the Beans

Jesus and Saint Germain posed for Charles Sindelar of the I AM Activity to paint Their portraits. Thus, those portraits were not just fanciful rendering; and it follows that everything in them expresses the masters' direction. In particular, the words at the left and right hand sides of Saint Germain's depiction, as well as the "aviator" wings at the top center certainly carry a symbolic meaning that the master wishes to impart to the viewer.

I have never been apprised of their intended meaning. Perhaps I am just ignorant of a given explanation, but I don't believe that one has ever been released. I even took a couple of hours on the Internet trying to find any mention of those symbols in the background of Saint Germain's portrait. No dice. So it is up to the viewer to make of those symbols what they will.

Personally, I have been trying to make even a modicum of a sense of those symbols for over forty-five years; since I first encountered that portrait in 1973. Again, no dice.

Until...

While decreeing, I sat for a long time right in front of that portrait of Saint Germain. I gave the master the eye. He twinkled back. I gave the master the heart. He suffused me with his all-knowing alchemical consciousness. His love flowed to me immediately and remained on the back burner for a long time as I decreed. I lost myself in service and in the vast universes of the master. Very often I would give Saint Germain a deep I AM THAT I AM glance and receive his I AM THAT I AM right back on the return current.

Then at one point it hit me...not like a ton of bricks...but like a greased lightning skewer that invested itself into my spine, rendering all the Lloyd meat and guts I was nested in a threefold flaming shish kabob.

I lit up. I realized, without even asking the question, what those symbols on the master's portrait are meant to convey.

In a sentence: They describe figure-eight flow and the winged, high flying consciousness it imparts.

Let me explain...

Figure-eight flow is called that because the flow of consciousness from your I AM Presence to your soul and back again, as depicted on the Chart of Your Divine Self, can be seen as a figure eight. The top portion of the eight is the Presence and the lower one is the soul. The Christ Self stands at the nexus/intermediary at the center crossing point of the figure-eight.

When your consciousness embraces/becomes that flow, you are identifying with Christ/Soul: the I AM Presence in evolutionary mode. You ARE God's agent; an agency enabling infinity to become more infinite. You are, as Brother Lawrence describes, "practicing the Presence."

Another way of describing this mode of consciousness involves becoming the Name of God I AM THAT I AM. This states that "you" ARE all "you" are perceiving in addition to the perceiver.

You, as an individual, occupy a seat of consciousness in your heart. From that point you sense yourself as an initiator of action. You feel like you are living your life by "doing" this and that to and with all that "out there" stuff, which receives your energy and activity. Simultaneously, you perceive what the "out there" stuff is emitting through your five senses and beyond. From your personal point of view, I AM THAT I AM is experienced as a masculine I AM initiator of awareness/action sensing THAT, which is received and expressed in and through the feminine I AM on the other side of THAT.

I AM (masculine) THAT I AM (feminine).

Now we need to get a tad subtle.

Above, I described the I AM THAT I AM from your own personal point of view. Now let's look at it from the "out there" point of view. From that vantage the "out there" stuff is also consciousness saying/acting I AM THAT I AM. In other words, as you act/perceive from the point of view with the first I AM being masculine, the feminine I AM "out there" is also assuming the masculine I AM point of view *from its own perspective*. In other words, that (to you) feminine I AM is also saying/acting I AM THAT I AM with the first (to itself) I AM being masculine and your own I AM (from its point of view) being feminine.

This is like the Eastern story of a master dreaming of a butterfly flying over him. And upon awakening, he really couldn't say whether he was dreaming of the butterfly or if he were the butterfly perceiving a man dreaming. We ARE both the masculine and feminine perceiver and perceived.

Now, back to the symbols on Saint Germain's portrait.

The only thing I could notice about them all these years was that the first/top of the lower three words on the left hand side is the same as the last/bottom of the three words on the right hand side. Similarly, the bottom of the left side is the same as the top of the right side. That is the three words on the left is simply the top-to-bottom reverse of those on the right. The middle word is the same for both sets of the three words.

The word at the very top is the same on both the left and right hand sides. Moreover, the shape is very similar to that of the well-known OM symbol (which is probably Sanskrit).

Now, I certainly do not know what language the words on the portrait are. But that's irrelevant. The big assumption that I am making here regarding that language is that it is capable of stating I AM with one word from a masculine point of view and that it uses a different word to state I AM from a feminine point of view.

So I read the words from the very top, going down, on the left hand side as OM I AM THAT I AM from the personal masculine point of view. And then on the right hand side, the feminine (to me) assumes its own masculine point of view to emit I AM THAT I AM OM, from the bottom up. In other words, the right hand side is responding (to itself) masculinely with me as its feminine expression I AM.

The result of this figure-eight flip-flop is resolved on both the masculine and feminine sides in the uppermost OM.

And when that OM becomes the all-One perceiver/perceived identity I AM THAT I AM, consciousness flies. It is not limited/contained in matter. It becomes the flying-eagle expression/agent of the One processed through the Maltese cross at the center of the wings. That cross is indicative of figure-eight flow simultaneously from both the Father/Spirit mode (vertical) and the Mother/Mater mode (horizontal) of consciousness.

In addition, behind the Maltese cross, are two layers of disks. The bottom layer contains seven disks, corresponding to the outwardly expressed Seven Rays. The upper layer contains five disks, corresponding to the inwardly expressed five secret rays. Together, their energy sustains the processing of consciousness as a Maltese cross flying as Father-Mother God's figure-eight flow.

THAT is Saint Germain's pictorial impression upon the viewer's subconscious. His goal, as I see it, is to get all who view His picture into at least a modicum of figure-eight flow with Him, at least subconsciously.

Kabbalah's Shin: The Crown

Kabbalah is a divine philosophy said to take lifetimes to master. Only mature, middle aged people, at the youngest, are supposedly capable of relating to it. Be that as it may, let me here strongly recommend the book *Kabbalah: Key to Your Inner Power* (See the bibliography) as an introduction that comes as close to a full treatise on the subject as most people will desire.

Kabbalists portray God as the consciousness of the Tree of Life comprising levels called *sefirot*. It is important to remain mindful that each of *Kabbalah's sefirot* is an alchemical processing of consciousness. They are not separate "things." The entire Tree of Life is One and each of its modes of Being contributes to every moment's Self conscious experience. That is, the *sefirot* are simultaneously acting modes of the One. "They" ARE the One.

The highest level, which is beyond all levels, about which naught can be said, is called *Ein Sof.* The top level within the Tree, the *sefirah Keter,* is referred to as the crown. The next two, *Hokhmah* and *Binah* are referred to as wisdom and understanding. These two relate to the mind of God, the flame of illumination. Taken together, the three *sefirot* are symbolized with the Hebrew letter *shin*. The central post of that letter corresponds to *Keter,* while the left and right posts correspond to *Binah* and *Hokhmah*:

I bring this up because I wish to relate to you a correspondence I find so useful as to have become a living foundation of my understanding.

These top three levels of the Tree of Life represent the consciousness from which divine creation ensues. Although the following is likely not strictly a part of Kabbalistic thought, I like to think of this creative trinity as aspects of the I AM Presence:

- **Keter:** The One and only I AM Presence, capable solely of realizing itself: I AM. It is BEING, beyond gender. But, since this Oneness is entire, it can very loosely be considered to be masculine. Yet the ability to be Self Conscious at all implies that the most ethereal feminine potential is also latently present. Moreover, being genderless, manifestation is utterly impossible to this One and only I AM Presence.

- **Hokhmah:** The One I AM Presence faceted—in-divided—into many instances of the One I AM Presence. Each One is endowed with Individual Self realization by receiving latent engrams of the Causal Body—each I AM Presence's divine personality in potential.

Although this level is far above the creation of humans, this in-division of the One and only I AM Presence into I AM Presence"s" is similar to giving Adam a rib cage, symbolizing the One's <u>potential</u> to manifest femininely as apparent "other." However, at this still wholly masculine stage, manifestation/joy is not yet possible.

Hokhmah is like my dog Rhua (Gaelic for red and also the second Kabbalistic aspect of soul, *ruah*), who becomes very quiescent when I or milady go away from the house. She lies in front of the glass, sliding doorway looking out at the driveway hoping beyond hope that the absent one will soon return. Sometimes she sleeps; sometimes just stares listlessly out. In other words, the I AM Presence of *Hokhmah* is an inactive, dormant STATE of divine potential, not yet brought to transcendent, evolving Life.

- ***Binah***: This is where things get really interesting. Here the masculine and feminine Twin Flames associated with each faceted, in-divided I AM Presence come about. (I am being careful to use supremely vague terminology here because I am entirely ignorant of how any of this alchemy happens.)

  It is so very important to note that *Binah* is identically the same as the I AM Presence Being of *Hokhmah*, but with some added attributes.

  Although this level is still far above the creation of humans, it is similar to creating Eve from one of Adam's ribs, symbolizing the One's Being encompassing **apparent** "other" as the One in-divided I AM Presence's twin flames. These flaming Presences are referred to as "twin" because they actually ARE the very same Presence and one Causal Body. As described above in the section "Twin Flames" those Presences are apparently different but they're One Individual. They just complement their unified Presence with their masculine and feminine modalities of consciousness, which us humans can conveniently envision as seemingly "separate" Causal Bodies for each Twin Flame.

The Creation/Birth of God

This is also where God—the **G**eometry **O**f **D**ivinity; the highest, subtlest format of relationship—comes into Being. (I find it quite amusing how so very many people speak of "God" as the highest, practically unspeakable divinity, when God is actually several steps down on the divine totem pole; the highest being *Ein Sof* or what Buddhists call Great Mother.)

Also, God here receives the Name I AM THAT I AM. That Name emphasizes not only the unity of Twin Flames, but the identical equality of Being of every single solitary element of manifestation even below the level of *Hokmah/Binah*. Mantra time again: Only the One IS.

Binah is also where the Spheres of the Causal Body come alive as the radiant Art fashioned by the I AM Presence in evolutionary mode: Christ/Soul. And Presence/God herein derives joy from THAT.

Further, *Binah* is the dais upon which God releases the fiat "Let there be light!" And God, the I AM Presence in evolutionary mode then comes forth as Christ/Soul and all the rest of the *sefirot* of the Tree of Life.

Finally, *Binah* is like my dog when both I and milady are present with her. She is Soooooo happy. Both masculine and feminine flames are present and accounted for. Kinda like "Elvis is in the house and there's a whole lotta shakin' goin' on." She jumps and plays and barks and talks to us in a voice that is nearly human English. She snappily asks that I throw her toy bone around for her to fetch, and right on schedule demands that I load it up with her jerky treats. Down a hall, she can get up almost to full speed and then jump high into the air, doing a full one-eighty, to sprint back in a jiff. This is a good way to envision the liveliness of *Binah* Being, compared to *Keter's* and *Hokmah's* states of BEING.

Look at that rascal, agog for action. Those back legs are ready to spring:

So Who Am I? What Am I?
That Depends

Your elevator-speech will vary tremendously depending upon who is asking and where and when the question is proffered. Obviously, you're not just a name. You may say you are a mother or father or a single twenty-something. Or maybe that you are a chemist or writer or sales person. Or that you're a long distance runner or a tennis player or.... Whatever you think you are, it is multiple, although your sane self is a far cry from the out-of-control chaos of multiple personality disorder.

Every activity and predominant state of mind or feeling you ever inhabit can fulfill your momentary identity's answer to who/what am I? Your current consciousness filter presents the image of who you seem to be right then. All in all, though, you are modified outwardly by the sum total of all of the filters you have ever accessed in all of your embodiments. In fact, the greater You is also colored with every exigent filter upon everyone and all that has ever been or will be in the multiverse.

At bottom, you are an agent, an active consciousness of the One. Even in deepest meditation, you are actively conscious on some plane.

Since this is more than a moniker can encapsulate, we just settle for a shorthand version of your current configuration—a descriptive name given to your momentarily active point of view. Your kids will call you mom or pop; your boss, your given name; a drill sergeant, your surname, etc.

People often adopt a religion as the baseline foundation for their identity. When asked what they "are," they'll respond that they're Catholic or protestant or Jewish or Buddhist or atheist or agnostic, etc. But that paints identity with such a broad brush as to be all but useless twaddle. Our Real identity has been so subtly refined over thousands of years that classifying it in Truth is utterly impossible.

One comes to BE what one IS step by ethereal step. For example, even restricting one's "home" identity to something within some religious doctrine is but to engage a foolish exercise. Our highly prolific outlook takes in and integrates many, many viewpoints, some of which are more fully assimilated than others. And efforts toward assimilation proceed over long time periods. So at any moment, who/what I am is quite a kaleidoscope. The following illustrates how people sometimes try to narrow down their identity to a particular spiritual teaching, but in actuality it can never be accomplished:

> **"[Each Buddhist doctrine delivers] views or philosophical understandings of the nature of phenomena that are specific to them. One speaks therefore of the Vaibhasika view, the Sautrantika view, the Yogacara view, the Madhyamaka view, the Dzogchen view, the view of the sutras, the view of the tantras, and so on. These views are keys to the understanding and implementation of the doctrinal system in question. Therefore, it is usually said that when one embarks upon the study and practice of a given teaching in the hope of attaining its result, the establishment of the view is the indispensable first step. For most people, the integration of any given view comes gradually, through the reception of instructions from a qualified source, through careful reflection on them in order to deepen intellectual understanding and remove doubts, and finally**

through meditation, thanks to which the instructions are perfectly assimilated, and understanding ripens into realization."[34]

Once such realization occurs, the given point of view falls away naturally and is discarded, like the raft of the Buddha. One's consciousness has then expanded to include that Way in the living energetics of the One I AM.

That previously distinguished doctrine/viewpoint then supports the traveler like an attained false summit on a mountain climb. It no longer positions itself in the realms of differentiated awareness. On each new "level" of the spiritual Hierarchy, one's attention is called upon to surrender its formative gradations to a more inclusive whole. There it complements all other levels of the individual's attainment and can act to bring about inspiration along with all that has gone "before".

An Exercise to Strengthen Your Spiritual Muscle

A well-known eye exercise involves focusing back and forth from very far away (infinity) to your hand very close to your face. You can choose several intermediate positions between the endpoints to soften the changes to the eye's lens curvature. This will help aging eye lens tissue by rendering it limber enough to more easily achieve flatter (for distance) and more curved (for close up) focusing.

If you're far sighted, at first, your view of your hand close up will look out of focus, perhaps just a blur. But after a few cycles of this exercise, it will become easier to see it clearly in fine detail, right down to your fingerprints.

Then you can do the same spiritually by focusing your attention meditatively from *Ein Soph's* Great Unknowing to the finest detail of apparent other. Like the eye exercise, you can soften the changes by visualizing and feeling your Presence, say, as the Great Unknowing, then at the Great Central Sun of our universe, then at a cluster of galaxies, then as the sun center of our own galaxy, then as the sun of our solar system, then as the entire planet Earth, then as a continent, a city and finally you sitting right there where you "are." Of course, you already know that you ARE alive and well at all of those levels of expression simultaneously in and as the One.

This exercise will accustom you to more easily find your Self living in and as the One throughout your day, no matter how focused your attention needs to be. You will find it easier in meditation to feel your figure-eight flow charging up your Individuality here and now in your human self. And, when highly concentrated on fine grained outer details—like writing a computer program or caring for very delicate plants in a garden—you can simultaneously find yourself at home in your House of **OM** Energy as an agent of the One.

Eight Chakras Nourish the Substance
Of Eight Bodies in Mankind

It is useful to envision the major chakras (etheric energy centers of consciousness) as spirit-mater pairs, the upper three chakras spirit, and the lower three mater. The middle pair are the spirit's secret chamber of the heart and mater's outer heart.

- **Crown ←→ Base of the spine**
  Father and Mother God are One, even as they evolve through the twin flames of One I AM Presence. Each of those twin flame I AM Presences plays the part of God the Father and God the Mother as they evolve through their humanity.

  The crown chakra focuses God the Father, resolving consciousness as the I AM Presence. The base of the spine chakra focuses God the Mother resolving consciousness in the physical body.

  Thus the highest spiritual energies of the I AM Presence as Father/Mother God find completion through their direct anchors in mater: the crown chakra and the Presence's activation in the physical body.

- **3rd Eye ←→ Seat of the soul**
  The 3rd eye chakra focuses divine vision, resolving consciousness as the Causal Body. The seat of the soul chakra focuses soul, resolving consciousness as the etheric body. Thus, the higher

spiritual energies of the Causal Body are anchored in mater and activated through the soul.

- **Throat ←→ Solar plexus**
  The throat chakra focuses the mind of God, resolving consciousness as the mental body. This is why speaking the Word of God out loud so powerfully configures the blueprints of apparent form. The solar plexus chakra focuses divine change, resolving consciousness as the emotional body. Thus, higher energies of thought, of God's Word, are anchored in mater and activated through one's emotions.

- **Secret chamber of the heart ←→ Heart**
  The secret-chamber-of-the-heart chakra focuses the threefold flame of divine love, wisdom and power (the living Presence of God), resolving consciousness as the fiery integration of all divine consciousness focused in the human body. The heart chakra focuses personal Christhood comporting consciousness as soul's consort as the Holy Christ Self, also known as the Logos, the Word, the Inner Buddha, the Higher mental body. Thus the higher spiritual energies of the threefold flame are anchored and activated in mater through the heart's focus of the Christ Self as a Christed one who walks the earth as a burning, shining light. (KJV: John 5:35)

The Cosmic White Fire Cross

Every point of consciousness focuses a Real Image comprising flowing energies symbolized by a white-fire cross. This cross's vertical bar refers to the Real Image's spirit form and its horizontal bar refers to its mater form. (Single-t mater is matter in figure-eight-flow mode; wherein, individual elements of consciousness are appreciated as differentiated yet experienced as One.) Consciousness perceives spirit form *as* the One. Consciousness perceives mater form *in* the One.

The crossing center point of the White Fire Cross positions it at every point of consciousness's Real Image. Therein, it harbors divine Life, arraying consciousness throughout the substance of inner (spiritual) and outer (material) realms. That is, apparent arrays of conscious awareness can perceive outer human perceptions and sensations *in tandem with* inner, unbounded divine Becoming. Since the cross of consciousness embodies all-inclusive white fire, it is directly tied in with infinite mystery's plenary possibilities.

Yes, Napoleon Hill rightly asserts that anything that can be conceived and believed can be achieved. Yet Lloyd is no Pollyanna. The level of "belief" necessary to achieve some possibilities may take thousands of years of hard work, *especially when it involves getting humans to cooperate.* (You can ask Saint Germain and El Morya about that one!)

The Substance of Consciousness
Spirit Form and Mater Form

As only the One IS, spirit form and mater form are not two different "things." Spirit form and mater form differ *only* as consciousness assumes one or the other's point of view upon the cosmic cross of white fire.

- **Vertical bar spirit form**: Spirit form assumes only the One, even while the act of perception facets THAT One.

  This is ultimately the Spirit of Selflessness witnessing joyous eruptions of its infinitely mysterious provenance. The Real Image appears All One, subtractively, as in sculpture. The One's prominence subtractively strips Reality of all semblance of relationship. Spirit form indescribably shines.

  Spirit form is perceived on the night side of Life, where awareness comprises formations that are only the perceiver's identity I AM.

  Spirit form's unique spectrum, a presentiment of the One, extends consciousness as unmitigated, creative Being. Spectra resound as all in All— indistinguishable from All in One—multiplies infinity's own potential. That omnipresent infinite potential frees "you" from exigent circumstance. Whatever the One has ever become, the One IS, and "you" ARE—even while karmic law temporarily aggregates you with space-time. Certainly, karmic bills must be paid, yet even in the paying, spirit form's coffers only multiply, never digress.

- **Horizontal bar mater form**: Mater form assumes the One's Individuality in a shapely mandala that includes all other participating identities I AM THAT I AM.

This is I AM Selfhood witnessing eruptions of its infinitely mysterious facets cascading joyously Real imagery. It appears positively variegated, as an artist adds to a painting. Selfhood's prominence I AM THAT I AM additively multiplies Reality's abundance. Mater form shines with heartwarming Loving grace.

Mater form is perceived on the day side of Life, where awareness comprises the perceiver's identity along with THAT which is perceived I AM THAT I AM.

Mater form appears upon a Hierarchical stage set, which partakes of the One's own unbounded Causal Body. Such a stage, a "level" of Hierarchy, is a living mansion furnished with props from the Causal Bodies of all actors purveying and partaking of that stage's play. Right here in our space-time City Foursquare, the lines we recite harmonize worlds without end as mystery's depthless piquancy; indeed, gifting the One with its lively arch charm.

In other words, spirit form presents BEING's unique recapitulation of the One. Mater form presents a Being's unique Artistry: a vision creatively amounting to the One's joy.

The White Fire Cross's Horizontal Bar Hosts Awe

Life's spiritual Hierarchy spans frequencies of consciousness trailing *akasha* even as *akasha*'s resurrected lively stones multiply potential. *Akasha* is generally taken to be the underlying substance of space— and very interestingly, by the Jains, also of time. Akashic records, say Theosophists, lie on the etheric plane and record all events that have ever occurred. H. P. Blavatsky says that they also depict the future. Since that would seem to obviate free will, I find myself needing to interpret her conception as a realm of infinity in which all possible "futures" exist—depending upon the karmic roads taken—and a lifestream can choose to incorporate any of those roads into their NOW's ongoing Art. Some quantum physicists have proposed such a "many universes" approach to relating to Reality.

Spiritual inspiration comes to us from our own Causal Body as well as from the Beings in the spiritual Hierarchy's higher frequency realms and others still karmicly confined to space-time. Indeed, since infinite mystery underpins all of Hierarchy's "levels," each of us—each One—partakes of the ALL in awe. We're privileged to partake of Life enrobed in unbounded gratitude for mystery's grace.

The I AM Presence in Evolutionary Mode

The foregoing discussion re twin flames has been somewhat deceptive in that it implies that twin flame I AM Presences actively perform work. This is not so. Any I AM Presence is a state of Being, at One with the ultimate one and only I AM Presence. (Trying to imagine any "thing" happening at that level will leave your gray matter in smithereens. Fortunately for us, you need not try, for that is not where the action is.)

The infinite I AM Presence, whose provenance is infinite mystery, is indebted to the grace of our old friend the alchemical "magic" for its enjoyment of Life. That magic produces somehow—out of a state that is only BEING—a level of activity that I call "the I AM Presence in evolutionary mode." That state as Being is BEING in action. The masculine personhood of that living grace is referred to by many names. I, as a Westerner, call it the Christ, the Word, the Logos. Its feminine aspect is Soul.

Christ: Universal-Personal
Soul: Oversoul-Personal

Christ, the Second Person of the Trinity, and His feminine consort, Soul, are twofold:

1. **Universal Christ:** Projects the space-time fabric/imagery comprising the basic immaculate *maya* selected from the One I AM Presence's Causal Body for the present moment of its entire multiverse. The One and only I AM Presence in evolutionary mode is God realizing joy through the Universal Christ as its masculine polarity.

   Oversoul: Ralph Waldo Emerson called the feminine polarity of the One and only I AM Presence in evolutionary mode the Oversoul. Of course, I know nothing of the inner workings of such a Being; how she manages to augment infinity by producing Art and by gestating unascended souls destined to join Her ranks in the endless spiritual Hierarchy.

   I feel that I can only contribute to your awe by disclosing my own upon hearing Gautama Buddha address a group of devotees, "O My soul." He thereby imparted His ultimate Love for us by informing us that He did not love us merely in the manner of human soul mates or lovers or even chelas, but that He had incorporated our "own" soul into the indivisible fabric of His "own." He nourishes us as cells in His own body. That simple affirmation, "O, My soul," lights the spiritual evolutionary way for us all. We are all destined to expand and to nourish lifestreams through our Oversoul consciousness worlds without end. It is precisely this concentration of universal attention that sustains individual cells, humans, planets, suns, galaxies, universes, multiverses.

2. **Personal Christ:** Projects the space-time fabric/imagery comprising the basic immaculate *maya* associated with an in-divided I AM Presence, a facet of the One I AM Presence.

   Personal Soul: Each Individual, in-divided I AM Presence in evolutionary mode contributes to and is One with the One I AM Presence. These Individualities realize joy through the personal Christ—One with the Universal Christ—as the masculine polarity, and your personal Soul producing Art, in tandem with her consort, as His feminine polarity.

The Daughter of God

Before I give my two cents on the divine feminine, I wish to share Mother Mary explaining how attuning to the mystery of the Motherhood of God can bring you into consonance with the feminine garment of infinite mystery, which is the flame of immanent, awakened consciousness:

> **"...understand the weavings of the threads of the form and the formless, that Spirit and Matter as Father-Mother principle, as the positive and negative polarity of being, commingle in and as the warp and woof of the whole of creation. Be it also known that the Matter which you observe has indeed other facets, other dimensions, and other frequencies which you have not yet experienced.**

> **"These are, as it were, the exalted manifestation of the weavings of the Cosmic Virgin outpictured through Omega—even the balancing factor of Spirit in what you have hitherto referred to as the planes of Spirit.**

> **"And so, you see, the exaltation of motherhood as the materialization of Spirit occurs in each succeeding level of God Self-awareness all the way back to the great central sun and beyond."**[35]

That is, the divine feminine brings about consciousness at every so-called level of the spiritual Hierarchy, from the incubator realm here, where our souls are aborning to immortality and all through the endlessness of the spiritual Hierarchy's rapprochement with infinite mystery. Most of us possess at minimum some sort of gut feeling for the nature of the Son of God as Christ. But the nature of Christ's feminine counterpart, the Daughter of God is not so easy to come by. Lemme tell ya, it's taken some deep meditation on my own part to come up with what I share below.

Some may see this section on the inner meaning of the term "Daughter of God" merely as semantic hair splitting; and, indeed, it is. But I have found it useful to my understanding of consciousness to clarify how the masculine and feminine polarities of the One relate to how the One expresses Individuality at all realms of Being.

Throughout this discussion, keep in mind that masculinity always denotes pure potential, while pure femininity denotes the expressive, active and formative fulfillment of potential.

This is subtle, so go slowly here.

All is potential at the core level of the I AM Presence. But active feminine expression still comes about right within that potential because the I AM Presence is surrounded by spheres of its Causal body. These spheres comprise the patterns of basic immaculate *maya* which bestow divine Individuality upon "each" I AM Presence. Those patterns partake of feminine expression simply because they are patterns: differentiable from "other" patterns in "other" I AM Presences in-divided of the One I AM Presence. This comes about by virtue of a single I AM Presence's masculine/feminine twin flame I AM Presences activating forms for the One; forms, which Buddhists refer to as empty, but apparent.

Then (and I sure don't know how it comes about) in order to realize joy, the I AM Presence focuses upon realms of consciousness that I call the I AM Presence in evolutionary mode. This is the Presence functioning as Christ/Soul, animated by the union of twin flames, which we also know as cloven tongues of the Holy Spirit.

At that expressive level—still focused in Spirit—Christ focuses the patterns of basic immaculate *maya* of the Causal Body in potential. Soul activates those patterns artistically to express/fulfill them as Art: as treasures in the Causal Body heaven realm. These are fully accessible/ viewable, capable of being experienced at the evolutionary Christ/Soul level as activated Causal Body joy. (Note well that human consciousness has not yet been alluded to at all.)

Now I wish to split hairs again.

Even though the active, expressing agent at this level is called Soul, She could just as well be called the Daughter of God because She operates in tandem with the Son to manifest patterned, fulfilling, joyful activity for the Son. Indeed, Soul is often referred to as the Holy Christ Self's consort.

Yet the elements of the Son's potential are, themselves, patterned. Therefore, the (femininely) patterned Son could also be called the Son/Daughter of God. That Son/Daughter is One proffered destiny of Living infinite potential patterned as the Presence's basic immaculate *maya*. Soul, then, conducts those keynotes as alchemical arrangements, arraying them each moment of Her Life's symphonic attunement.

The human soul achieving her immortality is referred to as her alchemical marriage with her Higher Self, the Son. So, I would speculate here that calling that feminine agent Soul instead of Daughter, might come about just to keep from insinuating incest of some sort. Saying Christ-Soul are married just sounds a bit better than saying that the Son and Daughter of God are married. But I have another solution to this supposed incest. And it's what I adopt in my writing.

The patterned energy that the Christ Self, Son, focuses is both masculine potential and feminine patterning, just like the basic immaculate *maya* at the Causal Body level. So I find it natural to refer to the Holy Christ Self as BOTH the Son of God AND the Daughter of God. In this wise, the Daughter of God can be viewed as latent "activity." In other words, the Daughter of God can be envisioned as the patterning inherent in the Son of God. And the Son and Daughter of God can thus be appreciated as identically the same agency of consciousness. That distinguishes the Daughter of God from Soul—the true activator of Son/Daughter—and enables us to envision Soul as the agent who brings about the fulfilled potential of the Son/Daughter of God.

Again, I know this is pretty fine nomenclature hair splitting. Indeed, the ascended masters often refer to the Sons and Daughters of God in their dictations. But I am not aware of any specific teaching regarding what they are really alchemically referencing when they refer to a Daughter of God.

I can even see how the term "sons and daughters of God" can (and often is) also loosely used to refer to male and female humans.

I have not taken a poll of ascended master students, but I believe most, if not all, would say that Daughter of God refers to a human being who has aligned their outer working soul consciousness with their Higher Self and who happens to be female. This may not be going too very far afield if "daughter of God" is written with lowercase "d." Such a reference would indicate a figure-eight flowing human female prior to their ascension to immortality.

Likewise, John writing "Now we are sons of God," (KJV: 1 John 3:2.) could refer to a figure-eight flowing human male prior to their ascension to immortality. However, in Truth, any figure-eight flowing human—male or female—prior to their ascension to immortality is both a son and a daughter of God AND a Son and Daughter of God by virtue of their identifying with their Higher Self, which is Christ/Soul, not exclusively Christ.

What's most important, though, is that we live in eternity NOW. And by virtue of figure-eight flow, we need not distinguish between before and after our ascension to affirm and BE our immortal One.

The Nature of Blessing

When your attention is focused inwardly, you are concentrating as Christ; when focused outwardly, soul is emphasized. Christ blesses souls by enfolding them in His inwardly flowing attention. This lends them His inward momentum and allows them to be less focused (blessed) on any sense of separation re the outer *maya* of false conception. Likewise, soul blesses Christ and the I AM Presence by enfolding them in her outwardly flowing attention. This lends them her outward momentum and allows them to be less in the Self contained state of Oneness, thereby to realize joy and to receive the Art of good karma.

Christ focused on the I AM Presence is not a blessing, per se, to the Presence. It brings about a broadcasting of All possibility expressed as the OM to all Life in space-time. That is a blessing to the outer space-time realm, though, for omnipresent OM increases the intensity of divinity, thereby displacing the temptation to treat the *maya* of false conception as separate entities. When such *maya* is perceived in consonance with OM union, it is no longer false conception; it is the Real Image I AM THAT I AM.

Soul focused on outer "things" as apparently separate entities in not a blessing. It amplifies the *maya* of false conception like Eve swallowing serpentine lies in the Garden, producing bad karma. The Tree of the Knowledge of good and evil—the *maya* of false conception—is not bad in and of itself. But new souls must establish a strong momentum of realizing divine unity in space-time before they can safely assimilate apparent separation and instantly transubstantiate it to its inherent union in and as the One.

So you can take it from Lord Maitreya, the guru in the Garden of Eden, with Lloyd's afflatus added, that you should not partake of the tree of the knowledge of good and evil until your consciousness is securely Present.

Don't get involved in all the name calling and baiting now so prevalent in the public arena. Keep your attention focused in and as the One.

Adam Kadmon: Our Original Soul Pattern

Kabbalists differentiate between universal soul and our own personal soul by pointing out the potential—through our everyday choices—for our personal soul to fall into illusory levels of consciousness:

> **"Before sin/karma descended upon us, our souls were bonded to the Universal Christ, [the *Sefirah*] *Tiferet*, and we were clothed in the original, etheric pattern of *Adam Kadmon* in which we were made. But through succeeding incarnations in an imperfect world, we descended to the level of the lower figure in the chart [of Your Divine Self] and lost the enlightenment we had. Today our Holy Christ Self sustains for us the blueprint of *Adam Kadmon*, which Kabbalists say we are destined to manifest again."**[36]

I will present much greater detail about your Holy Christ Self *Adam Kadmon* later. To preview that, simply understand that He focuses the intrinsic patterns of your divine personality from your Causal Body in the inner, time-space universe, presenting them to soul as the basic immaculate *maya* to be rendered Art in the everyday, outer world space-time universe we humanly perceive.

Going to an even deeper understanding of soul, Kabbalists explain:

> **"The Zohar says the soul has three parts: *nefesh, ruah* and *neshamah*. Each part comes from a different *sefirah*. *Nefesh* is the part of the soul that gives life to and sustains the body. Its source is the *sefirah Malkhut*. The Zohar says the *nefesh* stimulates the body to observe the commandments.**
>
> **"The second part of the soul, *ruah*, is the spirit, the seat of intellect and reason that allows us to transcend**

mere human existence. The *ruah* originates in *Tiferet*. It is 'the ethical power to distinguish between good and evil,' writes Scholem.[37]

"The third part of the soul, *neshamah*, is known as the spiritual soul, holy soul or divine spark. It is described in the Zohar as a spark of *Binah*, for it comes from that *sefirah*."[38] [39]

Christ Mediates Both Vertically and Horizontally

In Part Three, I will concentrate upon the interaction of the Christ Self with soul, symbolized by the horizontal bar of the White Fire Cross.

Here, I'll concentrate upon Christ's vertical mediation between the I AM Presence and the soul on the vertical bar of the White Fire Cross. Understanding this access to the infinite realms of God's (your) I AM Presence opens consciousness to an unspeakable sense of liberty, adventure, fulfillment and joy.

Kearney, a character in M. John Harrison's novel *Light*, wished to open himself to the great unknown world seemingly out there simply by taking journeys around town. He felt that this practice of often experiencing newness on these journeys would bring intimations of realms beyond the four dimensions of the human arena: "'...Mathematical physics was opening to him like a flower, revealing his future inside. But the future wasn't quite enough. By following the journeys as they fell out, he believed, then, he would open for himself what he thought of as a 'fifth direction'...[wherein] All...things can be redeemed and become for a time essentially themselves."[40]

Kearney is a soul like you and me, searching for the infinite revelation of inner, endless Selfhood embedded *in situ*. Be always open minded, in search of the miraculous; but not to the extent that depravity finds a welcome mat laid out for it.

Soul Never Disappears

Some people may quibble with me for supposedly elevating soul to an equivalency with Christ prior to her ascension in the light: the alchemical marriage that renders her immortal. But I take a longer view. I understand soul to be what master Morya calls the "spirit's own union with life," which provides the one I AM Presence and each of its twin flames with its feminine evolutionary agent at **all** levels of the spiritual Hierarchy.

Lacking such a feminine agency, individual ascended masters and Cosmic Beings would not be able to distinguish One another. But Morya certainly knows Himself to be personally different from Saint Germain. So the concept of soul is not confined only to the human level where we partake of earthly life's everyday comings and goings. Eternally, masculine/feminine polarity enables Life's divine expression throughout the spiritual Hierarchy.

Uppercase Soul Is Eternal
Lowercase Soul Is Maturing to Her Immortality

Thus, uppercase "S" Soul signifies that divine feminine after the human ascension to immortality, as well as unascended masters, as well as the immaculate purity of Soul for regular guys and gals. She is always the agent whose Life/Art/consciousness translates the Causal Body engrams of basic immaculate *maya* into Artfully expressive, radiating *akasha*. This becomes eternally primordially pure pristine, awareness, the divine personality of her I AM Presence, her treasures in heaven.

It just so happens that at the human, everyday level of consciousness in which we abide, soul can burden herself with so-called bad karma, which delays her freedom from that lower frequency arena. Nevertheless, she is also capable, even at the human level, of living in and experiencing in some measure the gracious Life of higher consciousness that she will evince after her graduation from the spiritual incubator in which she now finds herself.

That is why I use the term Christ/Soul to refer to the I AM Presence in evolutionary mode, independent of the level of the spiritual Hierarchy on which that activity occurs. I use Christ/soul—lowercase soul—to refer to the I AM Presence in evolutionary mode, but with soul still in its human, likely karmicly burdened, incubator. That is, anytime soul elevates consciousness to immortal levels, even for a snatch here and there, she thereby elevates her lowercase "s" to its capital "S." That capital "S" soul consciousness can always be encountered, even at the most concentrated focus upon outer things.

At all levels of Life, as James Irby writes:

"...movements toward and from immortality become one single approximation of universal impersonality."[41]

Each moment, in space-time and in the higher frequencies of consciousness of the spiritual Hierarchies, instantaneous approximations of the One bloom as joy. To engage figure-eight flow here below immortal realms is to partake of what Irby calls simultaneous "toward and from" so-called movements. My vision of so-called "from" movements in the higher octaves of light that may be imagined as "away" from the One, is that they never occur there. The spirit form in those realms of light is never perceived by creators there as any limitation of the One. Those "from" movements in eternal realms simply imply a choice to focus more intently upon the feminine pole of the Great Central Sun Magnet as more concentrated attention upon detail. But that never ever involves a loss of complete contact with the masculine pole as well.

The Zen of Soul
The Spirit's Own Union with Life
The Illusion of Separation AND of Union

The "Spirit's Own Union with Life" implies that soul is in no way separate from her I AM Presence. Soul, being the Presence's own capability to *experience* union can best be thought of as an attribute of the Presence, not as some part of Life controlled at some sort of a distance. Soul IS the Presence, which would have no ability to transcend its infinite Self without her.

Soul possesses her capabilities ultimately by virtue of the Presence's twin flames, which enable Life's entire appearance mode of consciousness: the illusion of separation which in turn enables the illusion of union. The illusory nature of ANYTHING seeming to be beyond the one and only I AM Presence explains why even the immaculate perfection of the Presence's divine personality—its Causal Body patterns—is a form of *maya*. That's why Keith Dowman translates the Tibetan Buddhist understanding of this extraordinarily subtle divine alchemy as "basic immaculate *maya*."

Both Christ and Soul partake of that same super subtlety. Even though they may appear to be acting independently in realms of constant apparent change, they are in fact activated *attributes* of the Presence, which can only realize a state of Being in and of itself. The paradox portending **all** consciousness is that their activity and the Presence's state of Being are One.

An H-Bomb on the Human Ego's Doorstep

The human's inability to reconcile THAT is the reason why the spiritual Path seems so difficult. It is the reason why "something" so intimately "you" as your soul cannot be ascertained in any way without a concomitant measure of Zen enlightenment. Even a smidgeon of a correct answer to the question "who am I?" is tantamount to an H-bomb set off on the human ego's doorstep. That explains why your little ego's dweller on that threshold sets itself in such unremitting opposition to the slightest inkling of your consonance with infinite mystery.

But you can also be unremitting. Setting your sails to catch infinite mystery's Holy Spirit winds momentarily will spell the end to the spells which that dweller on your threshold to infinite light casts in your way. Set your sails by invariably realizing your paradoxical identity:

- Universal Christ/**S**oul is the agency of the one and only I AM Presence in evolutionary mode.

- Personal Christ/**S**oul at all "levels of the ascended spiritual Hierarchy, as well as Christ/**s**oul at your current unascended prominence, is the agent of one of your I AM Presence's twin flames in evolutionary mode. (Never lose sight, of course, that both of your twin flames ARE your One I AM Presence.)

Does Literal Space-Time Really Exist
In the Spiritual Hierarchy's Higher Octaves?

An unanswered question sometimes arises in me. Since we know of space-time as an incubator for unascended souls, what would the soul-expressive feminine realm of consciousness be called after the ascension? That is, do ascended masters and Cosmic Beings retain an awareness of such temporary/creative realms as those that are referred to for unascended souls as space-time. Are such "outer" laboratories/realms applicable to the evolutionary work of immortal, Self realized lifestreams?

It may be that the ascended masters prefer to use the term space-time only to refer to the human incubator realm prior to the soul's alchemical marriage with her Holy Christ Self: her final ascension in the light. But, whatever the immortals call it, such a mode of consciousness must exist. So, for the sake of our human brains, I will continue to refer to that Soul-creative realm, even for the higher spiritual octaves of consciousness as space-time. My poor little brain just can't do otherwise.

When I try to imagine what ascended master creativity may be like, I speculate that a sort of "arrow of time" may exist up there, but it is more like an on/off switch.

Dr. Eban Alexander III inadvertently takes a stab at this question in his book *Proof of Heaven,* which describes his near death experience while he was in a seven-day coma. At the highest level to which he visited, which he calls the core, he experienced what he describes full waking consciousness but without any sense of his own selfhood. He could distinguish so-called objects, but was completely unaware of "who" was aware of them. He writes:

> **Up there, a question would arise in my mind, and the answer would arise at the same time, like a flower coming up right next to it. It was almost as if, just as no physical particle in the universe is really separate from another, so in the same way there was no such thing as a question without an accompanying answer. These answers were not simple "Yes" or "no" fare, either. They were vast conceptual edifices, staggering structures of living thought, as intricate as cities. Ideas so vast they**

would have taken me lifetimes to find my way around if I had been confined to earthly thought."[42]

The Spiritual Hierarchy Comprises "Levels" Of All Horizontal Expression

The upshot of the downdraft on this question of mine must be, then, that there is indeed some format for evolutionary form in the timeless/ spaceless immortal realms. After all, mighty Cosmic Beings who are capable of nourishing universes such as our currently realized one, can pop out galaxies and all that they comprise at will.

Thus, the convergence of the basic immaculate *maya* (innate Causal Body patterns) with the *maya* of primordially pure pristine awareness (radiant, Soulful Causal Body Art) is not confined to our human incubator realm where secondary energy *maya* can encumber Reality. Real creativity occurs in the higher octaves of Being, and this encompasses every "level" of the Spiritual Hierarchy.

Artistry in Immortal Realms

Like the passage from Eban Alexander, above, the ascended masters have illustrated the One's unrelenting creativity by relating how the master Paul the Venetian fashioned a finely crafted, exquisite threefold flame chalice as a gift for the master known as the Maha Chohan. If Artistic differentiated consciousness could not exist in the higher octaves of light where ascended masters and Cosmic Beings dwell, Paul's Arty creation could never BE.

The big question, then, that up till now had ceaselessly smoked my brain is how can "creation" occur in a timeless realm? In other words, there must have been a "time" when Paul's chalice gift to the Maha Chohan did not "exist." Otherwise there would be no point in His "fashioning" it. Then, after he completed it, well, there it was... something "new" in the infinite, timeless realm. Other masters even took the "time" to congratulate Him for his work.

The conclusion concerning this question that has given my weary brain a rest is that, as I mentioned above, creativity in timeless realms must be like an alchemical on/off switch. Artistic "work" would "proceed" with the building time reduced to zero for each step.

An ascended master artist would always instantaneously produce a completely finished product. This would be modified little by little as a series of such products. The work would involve a series of choices from among a plenitude of competed possibilities. That is, an artist or craftsman up there would not engage in sawing and filing and chiseling and sanding and putting on finish coats of this and that. The arrow of time that limits us humans in space-time would not exist. Again, each step would come about as a completely finished product. (I guess. I really *am* making all this up. But we *can* get off by meditating on it.)

I'll be returning to the nature of creativity found in all octaves of Being in Part Three.

Infinity Touching Time and Space

The ascended masters characterize the level of consciousness, above referred to as the Christ (universal and personal), as the interface between the Infinite I AM Presence and the finite, outer realm of soul. (I will be covering this in great detail in Part Three.) That is, Christ, simultaneously aware of both the I AM Presence and the soul, acts like an electrical step-down transformer. The channel of light "connecting" Presence-Christ-soul is called the crystal cord.

I have, since first reading about this, understood that there is an amazing bit of alchemy going on at Christ's infinite-finite interface. In M. John Harrison's novel *Light*, he refers to the crystal cord as the "Kefahuchi Tract." Chapter 17 opens the reader to the mind blowing nature of consciousness focused in the outer world of form as it approaches that interface with infinity. He sure does a good job of picturing what I would imagine life to be like where infinity "touches" finitude.

The first three pages of that chapter describe how the author imagines quantum level beings, elements of consciousness, becoming aware of that interface, how they might react to it. I strongly recommend this book for anyone who wishes to engage *Light*'s amazing rendition of spirituality, skipping back and forth between the macro, outer view of things and life at the quantum level.

I find it remarkable how well Harrison translates quantum science into the activities of characters living their lives at the quantum level, just as we do here in macro-land. Harrison describes those who ventured close to the crystal cord while remaining attached to their finite consciousness. Obviously, remaining attached to finite forms as one's identity when approaching infinity can produce calamitous results. The publisher Bantam-Dell declined my request to quote more than 300 words from the book, so I had to delete Harrison's description here. If you happen to pick up the book, look on pages 136-38 for Harrison's take on the violent discombobulation of ego centeredness as it approaches infinity.

Rainer Maria Rilke, in his Letters to a Young Poet, offers this insight on how a person who is firmly settled into an I-thou existence would react, even to a near proximity of the infinite threefold flame in their own heart:

> **"A person would have a similar feeling [lost, lacking touchpoints], were he, with practically no preparation or transition, taken from his home and placed on the summit of a high mountain. It would be a feeling of unequaled uncertainty—a vulnerability to a nameless something would nearly destroy him. He would think he were falling or would believe himself flung out into space or burst asunder into a thousand pieces. What a colossal lie his mind would have to invent to catch up with the condition of his senses and to clarify it. That is how all sense of distance, all measurements change for the one who is alone."[43]**

Perfecting Mater Vision Opens the Third Eye

Remember, each of us is one genderless BEING, one I AM Presence evolving as a facet of the One and only I AM Presence evolving through masculine and feminine sub-I AM Presences, called twin flames, evolving as Christ/Soul.

In our humanity, our third-eye chakra expresses this twin flame unity in that this chakra consists of two major petals, each with 48 sub-petals. Think of these as the twelve hierarchies of the sun applying consciousness simultaneously inwardly and outwardly (12 + 12) as figure-eight flow from the mutual vantage of your masculine and feminine approach (24+24). That is, activating both major petals amounts to living in the united wholeness of both twin flames as the 96 petals.

Thus, the so-called "opening of the third eye" enables consciousness to experience Life as the One I AM Presence through the expressed figure-eight flowing union of that Presence's polar masculine/feminine twin flames merging the night and day sides of Life.

Master Morya suggests that we practice exercises that will facilitate this mastery:

> **"Try to write different things with both hands at the same time. Or try to dictate two letters or conduct two conversations at the same time. Try to steer a motor car and carry on a conversation on complicated problems at the same time. Try to refrain from quarrels when the restless mood of your fellow conversationalist invites your irritation. Try numerous examples of dividing your consciousness. Try pouring your energy in several directions without losing nor weakening its flow."[44]**

And I would add, try playing piano, especially Rocky's Second.

Consciousness Includes Unconscious Perception

We consciously operate in space-time supposedly limited by our immediate awareness and outer perceptions. Even in our imagination, out-of-the-blue inspiration seems only to become operative as a behavior modifier when called upon to fill perceived holes in plans or to direct "thinking-on-one's-feet" responses to immediate demands. All of that is confined to consciousness processing and completing outer ideational urges in *maya*'s realm of secondary energies.

But the growth of consciousness proceeds both spiritually and materially in a twofold manner:

1. **Spiritually:** With inner awareness focused upon the current initiation while partaking of (standing upon) all the foundational levels of Hierarchy already attained.

2. **Materially:** With awareness focused on the exigencies of outwardly planning and executing those plans while partaking unconsciously of inspiration. This inspiration derives from the momenta of one's own mastery as well as the mastery and blessings of others whose resonance concomitantly complements one's intent. Vibrationally locating inspiration's portal in your heart and developing a momentum of assuming that mode will greatly facilitate its immanence becoming usefully apparent. Part Three of this book is intended to help you enhance this ability.

It's amazing where this concept—of consciousness operating from a base level of a Hierarchy of awareness—can show up, even in pop culture. In his 2001 interview with reporters in Rome, Bob Dylan was asked how he and his group go about doing concerts now as opposed to the early days. Has it changed? How much do they know what is going to happen? He answered:

> **"I usually play to the people in the back. I disregard the people in the front because usually these people have come to quite a few shows. They're gonna be there anyway. They're gonna like what they hear one way or another. So we're not trying to reach them. We're trying to reach the people in the back, who might not have been there ever before. We don't think about those people [in the front] because they're always there. We think about the people we've never seen."**[45]

Keeping your awareness on that "ever-new" that you've never seen is tantamount to Gautama Buddha's wakefulness. Its keynote is the Great Unknowing, which eradicates the sleepy-eyed been-there-done-that-have-the-T-shirt touristy slouch so many of us content ourselves with as we meander *maya's* patches, grazing on space-time bling and lazily chewing that stuff like cud.

In Amit Goswami's book *The Self-Aware Universe: how consciousness creates the material world,*[46] consciousness is said to be the ability to choose. It can include awareness; then a person is said to be acting consciously. It can be absent awareness; then a person is said to be unconscious. Conscious awareness limits the ground of being, while the unconscious is omnipresent, aware of everything, while waking or sleeping.

Conscious inspiration can draw upon past experience and even upon the unknown to provide a new outlook. It is common for us to concentrate on a subject and clear the mind to bring about inspirational help along a particular line. But it is also useful to understand that unconscious inspiration contributes much to our ability to cope with everyday demands. Unconscious inspiration is vital to Life's ongoing adventure. It provides pizzazz, serendipity and the feeling of peace that comes of knowing you are supported with unknown perspicacious forces.

You Act in Tandem with the One

You are the ultimate arbiter of your free will. Yet, Jesus emphasized that "Of myself, I can do nothing." It doesn't matter at all whether you or God are the co-pilot of your craft. You ARE God acting. Goswami emphasizes the universal nature of ALL consciousness in a more scientific way:

> **"I choose, therefore I am. Remember, also that in quantum theory, *the subject that chooses is a single, universal subject, not our personal ego 'I.' Moreover...* this choosing consciousness is nonlocal."**[47]

You ARE Consciousness at All Levels
Hence an Ultimately Responsible Being

Goswami's discussion of paradoxical unconscious perception concludes that not only has it been experimentally proved to exist, but that it influences thought and feeling.

It does <u>not</u> influence choice, however:

> **Apparently choice is a concomitant of conscious experience but not of unconscious perception. Our subject-consciousness arises when there is a choice made:** *We choose, therefore we are...*there is **a scientific basis for the emphasis that the Western tradition puts on freedom of choice as central to the human experience."**[48]

Yes, the ground, the essence of consciousness, always remains free. I see this as indicative of the law of karma's scales of justice being wholly warranted. We are always responsible for our acts since *human choice is ultimately self-contained.* Of course, our choices are influenced by everything we encounter, but in the end, every choice is our own; even for slum dwelling, single-parent kids. Remember also that Saint Germain has told us He earned His immortality by making two million right decisions. His emphasis on free choice as formative of immortal consciousness is well worth taking to heart. As a so-called "creator," you are actually choosing to activate potentials in and as infinite mystery. Grokking this is Zen...far beyond human intellect.

My, Oh My! I'm Soooooo Talented
What a Kaleidoscope of Viewpoints I AM!

I've said it often, and will be saying it again and again and yet again: only the One IS. But Life IS, too. And assuming diverse points of view, consciousness partakes of and operates within it simultaneously in many relationships. I certainly know that I am not just li'l old Lloydy boy. I am a plenitude; states of Being idiosyncratically expressing. I have taken it upon myself to think of as many of those archetypal, spiritual points of view as I can, off the top of my head, views which can be simultaneously assumed, consciously and subconsciously and, yes, unconsciously.

That exercise was quite an eye opener, which I share with you in the following list. Every one of these viewpoints is well worth meditating upon to enlarge your portion of conscious divine Reality. Many possible lifetimes of conscious endeavor is shown through the study and application of these viewpoints. And this just barely touches the possible.

- human chakras
- planes of consciousness
- The primary Seven Rays
- the Five Secret Rays
- The Eighth and Ninth Rays
- many undisclosed higher Rays
- vertical figure-eight flow
- horizontal figure-eight flow
- the cosmic cross of white fire
- colors of the Seven Rays and the chakras they're associated with
- Real imagery focused within *maya*
- the Catholic 14 stations of the cross as imagery describing the alchemical steps of precipitation
- "worldly" astrology
- "cosmic" astrology as the "cosmic clock" law of cycles
- personal karmic patterns
- group karmic patterns
- the quantum physical nature of elementary "particles"
- the holographic nature of the antahkarana
- acupuncture meridians as ley lines in the human body
- the caduceus flow along the spine
- Physical classes: chart of chemical elements
- all systems of yoga
- mudras divinely configuring consciousness with hands
- the Kabbalistic system's Tree of Life describing all levels of consciousness
- the Mandelbrot set, i.e., the fractal nature of divine imagery: as above, so below
- the inner and outer relationship between the three upper chakras and the three lower ones as well as the two heart chakras.

- whole map correspondences between areas of the body and the whole body in feet, ears, eyes, etc.
- the Tai-chi showing the inherent sexual polarity of all expression of the One
- Pranayama & other breathing exercises opening consciousness to greater levels of union, of inclusivity
- the Tai-chi with smaller Tai-chi's inside the yin and yang dots illustrating the beginning-less-endless spiritual Hierarchy
- mantras and the entire science of the spoken word
- the planets, which focus the chakras of the Cosmic Beings whose heart chakras are the sun centers of all systems of worlds
- time-space and space-time as arenas of parallel universes
- kingdoms of Being: Elohim and Beings of the elements; man/Christ; Angel/Archangel
- the seven bodies of Mankind and their correspondences in the seven major human chakras
- names of God; at least 215 metaphorical, descriptive names; 31 Hebrew names
- God's family: the Trinity of Father, Son, Holy Spirit; and Mother; and soul as inner child
- spirits of nature: fiery salamanders, sylphs of air, undines of water, gnomes of earth
- Gods and Goddesses of all religious pantheons, each a specialized divine point of view you can assume
- the Tibetan rainbow body
- the body elemental as the executive in charge of your health
- blessing, mercy and all divine virtues
- Chinese medicine, its precepts and pharmacology
- Indian medicine, its precepts and pharmacology: vata, pitta, kapha
- naturopathy, its precepts and pharmacology
- homeopathy, its precepts and pharmacology
- American Indian embrace of the Great Spirit
- Shamanic and all ethnic spiritual practices
- "Trekcho": mirror-like clarity that everything is a reflection of yourself
- all of the attributes of the Five Dhyani Buddhas

- I AM Tathagata: One who has thus gone beyond all transitory phenomena
- "Rigpa": knowledge of cutting through all tensions and rigidities
- clearance of ALL sense of separation
- writer's awakened awareness
- "Togal": releasing all fear and hope
- Seeing the sacramental nature of all things
- all forms of dance
- music: singer-songwriter; musician
- lives of saints

That's just a very few of Life's configurations that you host right now and which you could adopt as your ongoing life's work and viewpoints. There are, of course, many, many others that people are well aware of, which don't come to me right now, and an infinite number more that I'm not privy to. That's enough to make your head spin. I don't want to subject you to that, so in this book, I will be trying my best to convey the order of heaven, which leaves you in illumined Peace.

Incidentally, regarding hope and fear being associated under the "Togal" entry, above: students of the ascended masters, knowing Hope as Archangel Gabriel's twin flame, may be surprised to see hope associated with fear as a state of consciousness to eschew. I was alerted to this association through David Wilcock's talk on the Tibetan rainbow body. True hope is a state so pure as to become direct access to the infinite mystery foundational to all "things." Whereas, the human form of hope referred to here is tantamount to affirming that the item or state hoped for is missing from you, when in Truth you ARE all things and states in their divinely virtuous form already, eternally. Thus, humanly hoping is actively pushing something already yours away from you, and, along with fear, it emphasizes the sense of separation for your entire identity. Adopting the meme only the One IS obviates fear and human hope.

It's well worth meditating upon Real Hope to access the feminine nature of divine purity. Hint: start with it as an entry point to infinite mystery, the Great Unknowing. Arraying it at every point of your outer awareness will flood you with light.

Re spiritual experience, take it from one who knows for sure. It's easy to encounter frustration, finding yourself supposedly far, far away from some nebulous enlightenment wherein only the greatest masters abide.

Well do I remember my own thrown up hands and rolling eyes, when, in high school, I earnestly read deep Zen Buddhist texts that informed me that enlightenment was my goal. But if I ever thought I found it, that was proof that I was far from it. After reading that for about the millionth time, I quit.

Don't.

Every illuminating ray is infinite.

No master is ever "fully" enlightened. The spiritual Hierarchy is endless. Take it from the Elohim Arcturus, one of the Seven Spirits Before the Throne of the One. This is one of my all-time favorite quotes:

> **"...in the awful majesty of [God's] glory, the hearts of the Elohim throb with pulsations of divine love. We are sustained by his mercy, by his incomparable grace."**[49]

See? In a manner of speaking, they're just like us. Of themselves, they can do nothing. They've just been doing NOTHING with much greater, concentrated abandon, humility and a concentrated awareness of their cycling as beginningless and endless. I am tempted to say that they have been doing NOTHING so very much longer than any unascended Christ/soul, but since time is moot to them, any attempt at characterizing them like that must render me speechless. And I AM.

From the least to the greatest, All bow to the infinite mystery, without whose gracious care, no Life can Be. (Please be nice to me, and refrain from asking how mystery can "care," as there's nothing "out there" to care for. I only have words at my disposal here.)

It's God-Good to Be Awake and Alive

Every moment, unconscious perception lays new bricks in your identity. You are always infinity transcending its Self—like the expanding universe—just by virtue of your breath. You ARE the breath of Brahman, Self aware and suffused in candor. Your awareness of unconscious perception may seem to be but an absent adjunct to your outlook, but you can feel its afflatus as you use your conscious awareness as a catalyst to true growth. Thus Buddhists can expect a bit of a throttling from an overseeing observer if their meditation becomes sleepy-eyed. Indeed, such meditative wakefulness is to be encouraged for all of us throughout our waking life.

Consciousness Is Mudra

This book is all about configuring consciousness. Knowing about its buttons and levers and force fields, indeed, the whole architecture You ARE, is a primary step toward actively participating in the alchemy of spiritual growth. But acting as a catalyst to this alchemy involves much more than mechanical push-pulls. Understand that, at each moment, your consciousness is active on many planes and it projects your identity every which way simultaneously. That's much more than a puny human brain can handle.

So it's imperative that you relate to your entire consciousness as a mudra: a posture that aligns yourself to focus and maximize divine virtue. Such practice will contribute mightily to your wakefulness and encourage your busybody monkey mind to settle down.

Not to worry. This doesn't mean you need to think about your spiritual stance and consciously monitor yourself every second. It has everything to do with meditatively contacting your inner architecture and relaxing into it as the powerful, flaming peace commanding Presence I AM. And noting when you lapse from that as best you can.

Actually, every moment is a vacation. Your outer observations produce a house, so to speak. And you are instantaneously THERE always to pack up your attachments to it and to vacate it, leaving it to enjoy its emptiness.

Even if running a hundred-yard dash, straining physically with muscle and breath, the seat of your selfhood remains unmoved. Train your monkey-wrench ego to use your intellect, feelings, memories and physical skills to manipulate your outer world. But ALWAYS **BE**. Treat your perceptions as gift wrapping on the presents you momentarily offer to Presence.

Radical Dzogchen

In contrast to the paths of gradual study and practice is the view called radical Dzogchen, in which realization of the One appears in an instant. Of course, infantile humanity, engulfed in its own refuse, is not ready to instantly don infinity's garments and permanently sustain them. So both the viewpoints of gradual study and instant recognition proceed apace like two sides of a coin. In that way, the path of spiritual initiation can celebrate, a stepping stone at a time, when, through spiritual initiation, permanence can be attributed to each stage of solar unfoldment, as the aspirant cleans up their act.

El Morya's description of Agni Yoga (fire yoga) appears to be synonymous with radical Dzogchen:

"One can understand how greatly the ritual aspect of Yoga was demanded in ancient times, but now one should ascend by way of direct communion with the Highest World. The Yoga of Fire leads one upon this shortest path without abandoning life."[50]

Each and every focus of attention involves you in some point of view; and, of course, the diversity is infinite. That is why radical Dzogchen encourages aspirants to take up the mystery behind such a panoply and recognize themselves as indigenous citizens "there." Thereby, each viewpoint certifies all of them at once I AM THAT I AM, and the *maya* of everyday life magically sings an ever new song.

In his introduction to Jorge Luis Borjes' book *Labyrinths*, James Irby gives us a description of Borjes' fiction, which insightfully compares to the gradual and radical approaches in Dzogchen:

His fictions are always concerned with processes of striving which lead to discovery and insight; these are achieved at times gradually, at other times suddenly, but always with disconcerting and even devastating effect.[51]

Tibetan Buddhist Longchenpa (1308-1363) wrote a poetic trilogy that expounds the luminosity of pure Presence, which enfolds those who successfully impute to that radiance the magic in each and every moment. Keith Dowman translates Longchenpa's trilogy, book three, titled *Maya Yoga: Finding Comfort and Ease in Enchantment.* It is my hope that my own offering here will encourage you to find such comfort and ease in what Dowman calls:

> "cool contemplation, [which] provides the sense of vast mystery, exhilarating and uplifting, that allows us to recognize our momentary release from the heaviness and density, the confusion and pettiness, of samsaric existence."[52]

I love Dowman's translation in which he implores us to

> "...chill out behind enchantment. This is the skillful means of atiyoga and allows the Dzogchen dialectic to perform its magic."[53]

Fortified Forgettery Festers
Find Fire and Fly

After death, and before our next birth, the clear light of Oneness I AM can be most easily perceived. Those impressions remain in young children until they are trained to live more reactively and buy into dense outer world hype. Gradually the forgettery is fortified, and Man becomes more me, me, me; yet the unitive spark always remains. William Wordsworth describes this process and encourages us to find and live its immanence as "nature's priest."

> Our birth is but a sleep and a forgetting:
> The soul that rises within us, our life's Star
>   Hath had elsewhere its setting
>   And cometh from afar:
>   Not in entire forgetfulness,
>   And not in utter nakedness,
> But trailing clouds of glory do we come
>   From God, who is our home:
> Heaven lies about us in our infancy!
> Shades of the prison-house begin to close
>   Upon the growing boy,

> But he beholds the light, and whence it flows,
>   He sees it in his joy;
> The Youth, who daily farther from the east
>   Must Travel, still is Nature's Priest,
>   And by the vision splendid
>   Is on his way attended;
> At length the Man perceives it die away,
> And fade into the light of common day.[54]

That light of common day can be melodic or hypnotic. It can intimate freedom's holiness or numb one's every step "As if his whole vocation were endless imitation."[55]

Nondual Maya Can Grace
The Maya of False Conception

Some people discount their everyday existence because an aspect of its *maya*—the sense of separation that accompanies the outer substance—is illusory. Others, realizing that only the One IS, treasure *maya*'s Presence as a precious gift, and understand their role <u>and</u> *maya*'s role in gifting infinity with ever new versions/viewpoints of its Self. Even the natural world "out there" pertains to the I AM Presence of the Elohim—Who ARE You.

In Dowman's words, this:

> "...nondual reality, the reality of *maya* [is] magical illusion, happiness...[this is] 'the basic immaculate *maya*' that is our original, natural disposition. It is this nondual *maya* of our self-illuminating awareness that constitutes our innate three-dimensional Buddha-being inseparable from its primal awareness. This unitary reality presents itself spontaneously and perfectly in every instant of the here and now as an integral part of the cosmic whole, like a hologram. This is the *maya* of the Great Perfection and in its nondual awareness it lies beyond the intellect...

"The second aspect is the delusory *maya* created by the intellect, known as the '*maya* of false conception'... [The] *maya* of our ordinary experience rests upon the structure that our intellect imposes. This is a diverse and complex system of concepts and beliefs that not only determines the quality and nature of our experience but also of the natural—seemingly external, world. <u>This belief system and the *maya* of experience that it manifests, however, is never cloven from the vast expanse of compassionate clear light in which it arises. The '*maya* of false conception' and the 'basic immaculate *maya*' of the natural dispensation [the Causal Body patterns] are one</u>" [56] (My underline emphasis)

Thus the *maya* of false conception—usually referred to as bad karma—is part and parcel of the spectrum of consciousness. There is only one spectrum, so bad karma is not something separate from you. It is modification of the frequencies and phases of the waves composing consciousness at any moment.

The yogi Vasiṣṭha gets deep as deep can be in his description of infinity's "relationship" with the outer world:

"The infinite (space of) consciousness is even purer than infinite space; and the world is even as that infinite is. But, one who has not tasted capsicum does not know its taste; even so, one does not experience consciousness in the infinite in the absence of objectivity. Hence, even this consciousness appears to be inert or insentient, and the world is experienced as such too. Even as in tangible ocean tangible waves are seen, in the formless Brahman the world also exists without form. From the infinite the infinite emerges and exits in it as the infinite; hence the world has never really been created—it is the same as that from which it emerges.

> "When the notion of self is destroyed by the withdrawal of the fuel of ideas from the mind, that which is, is the infinite. That which is not sleep nor inert, is the infinite. It is on account of the infinite that knowledge, knower and known exist as one, in the absence of the intellect."[57]

That meditative jumping off point will probably need to be read more than once to get it in the belly. Then, taking the plunge into the Great Unknowing, the merged you and not-you can rehearse delight.

Ervin Laszlo explains that quantum physics closes in on this unified consciousness when it realizes:

> "The classical view insists that, even if particles themselves are weird, the whole made up of them is a classical object: The quantum indeterminacies are canceled out at the macroscale. But this is not—or at any rate not entirely—the case. Instant, multidimensional connections have come to light between the parts of a living organism, and even between organisms and their environments.
>
> "Cutting edge research in quantum biology finds that atoms and molecules within organisms, and entire organisms and their environments, are nearly as 'entangled' with each other as microparticles that originate in the same quantum state."[58]

The ascended masters refer to living nondual *maya* as "figure-eight flow." I often use that term synonymously with the "Real Image." That communion is what Laszlo points out above. The Reality IS that consciousness and its perceptions can be so perfectly entangled that even in the macro world their up close hug is tantamount to divine Love.

My goal in this book is to so elucidate how the structure of the *"maya* of false conception" can be understood in such a way as to liberate it from its illusionary moorings so that your everyday life can sing in and as the One in its midst. Krishnamurti suggests:

**"The soil in which the meditative mind can begin is
the soil of everyday life, the strife, the pain, and the
fleeting joy. It must begin there, and bring order, and
from there move endlessly"**[59]

Basic to every self-help notion is that it behooves us to envision
Life as a bottle half full by concentrating upon the spectrum of our
consciousness through the lens of its basic immaculate *maya*. While it is
counter-productive to spiritually ignore bad karma's half empty bottle—
the *maya* of false conception viewed through the sense of separation—
be certain to consistently tailor your outlook to the ascended master
declaration "Evil is not real, and it appearance has no power." The evil
referred to there is the sense of separation, not the formative outer world
essentially reflecting its basic immaculate *maya*.

Finding the Order of Heaven
Right Here in the Chaos

We know order as the first law of heaven. Maybe so, but the first item
on our everyday, outer world to-do list is to translate heaven's order to
space-time's matter and our perception of it. This isn't easy for your run-
of-the-mill human. For them, ascribing the infinite meaning deep down
within themselves to the outer miasma is all but impossible.

But it can be done by Life's willing participants: those who insist
upon delving deep enough to find heaven's own provenance even in the
face of the most viciously depraved evil Earth has to offer. (I'm definitely
not there yet. I abhor a lot of stuff out there. I can get moved to tears
by some activities I become aware of that make me ashamed of being a
human.) I suppose that real, honest-to-goodness embodied masters of
light can remain unmoved from their heavenly perch in the face of the
most malignant hearts roaming about. Jesus is said to have done it, as
he preached to the deepest, darkest blackguards in the lowest planes of
hell prior to His ascension.

The highest to the lowest among us enjoy equal inner opportunity
to encounter the white-fire-cores of heaven's open portals to unity
in everything we encounter. The many overlays upon heavenly
consciousness may convince us that our life's supposedly raw material

comes to us ready made for good or ill. But ultimately we make the final choices about how our soul will qualify every bit of it. We can disparage it or sing along with that old song, "Everything Is Beautiful." It's truly up to us. Here's how Kearney, a character in the book *Light* describes it:

> **"'It doesn't look like anything....there isn't really anything there...Any day now...all this—' he gestured at the TV, the shadows in the room '—will mean as much to us as it does to a photon.'**

> **"'How much is that?'**

> **"'Not much.'**

> **"...'Space doesn't seem to mean anything, and that means that time doesn't mean anything.' He laughed. 'In a way that's the beauty of it.'"[60]**

Don't let intellect's emptiness get you down. Yes, indeed. It's all up for grabs. You are a creator in apparently disordered space-time as your intellect masticates it. It's for you to exert your free will to let it BE where infinite "meaning" resides. You're in charge of proclaiming the beauty of it by practicing the Presence. THAT beauty is God's ultimately ordered will riding about as "You" in and as infinite mystery.

Black Holes

In the book *Light,* the character Kearney mentions some newly discovered X-ray object. Then he goes on to mention someone from Cambridge talking about Penrose and the idea of a "singularity without an event horizon." (An event horizon is a spherical location around a black hole. Light going into the black hole beyond that sphere will never emerge again due to the tremendous gravitational pull therein. That's why it is called a black hole.

> **"...[Then he thought of] Penrose's definition of the event horizon not as a limitation of human**

knowledge but as *protection* against the breakdown of physical laws which might otherwise leak out into the universe."[61]

That's a very imaginative way to think about "who/what I AM": a singularity without an event horizon. That is, an open universe.

A singularity is a point at which space-time "touches" infinity, which is mathematically considered to be simply undefined. A "place" to which thought cannot go. And it's true. Your infinite Reality, a singularity, denotes a breakdown of physical laws; and the conservation-of-energy-style physical universe is protected from the likes of You. Only your own God realization flaming in your heart can safely interact, worlds without end, I AM THAT I AM. I mean, heavens to mergatroid! We can't have that infinitely powerful You—a breakdown of physical laws—sporting your mystery like a letter jacket, leaking out into the precincts of secondary energy's scientific befuddlement!

I believe that we can actually go so far as to say that the white fire core of every "atom" is a black hole, of sorts, because it is an entry point to Spirit's night side of Life—be that "side" the time-space realm of the horizontal bar of the White Fire Cross or the Spirit realm on the vertical bar of that Cross. (Pardon me, if those terms don't mean much to you yet. They will later, in Part Three.) Thus the white fire core's event horizon guards the Individuality of its focus of the infinite One. And, on the macrocosmic scale, it guards the Individuality of the indivisions of the One I AM Presence—the so-called individual I AM Presences. A singularity without an event horizon, then, would signal the transmutation of an instance of consciousness from mater form—an array of white fire cores producing holographic imagery—to the One's consciousness as Spirit form.

It's Easy to Let the *Maya* of False Conception Get You Down If You Don't Consciously Address Your Self

I just, for the first time, read the lyrics to Bob Dylan's song "It's Not Dark Yet." I would include all four verses here, but I don't want to deal with copyright issues on that. So I won't. Each verse ends with "It's not dark yet, but it's getting' there." Getting dark refers to Dylan's soul returning to the night, Spirit, side of Life. Here are a few lines taken in order, but with many lines left out:

"Feel like my soul has turned into steel...

"There's not even room enough to be anywhere...

"Well, my sense of humanity has gone down the drain...

"Behind every beautiful thing there's been some kind of pain...

"I've been down on the bottom of the world full of lies...

"I ain't lookin' for nothin' in anyone's eyes...

"I know it looks like I'm movin' but I'm standin' still...

"I can't even remember what it was I came here to get away from....

What he came here to get away from is the karma he still needs to balance. This song is the plaintive sighing of a soul who needs to get it, and get it STRONG: **"The '*maya* of false conception' and the 'basic immaculate *maya*' of the natural dispensation are one."**

DON'T swallow the lie that the chaotic, meaningless-in-itself-*maya*, is a useless Neverland. You ARE moving forward, balancing karma, fulfilling your divine plan, as you find and evince the Great Unknowing portal to your infinite light Being. And by learning to decree (practicing the science of the spoken word), and using that spiritual instrument, you can put on ten-league-boots and put a stop to Dylan's stuck notion of "standing still."[62] You can ride the coat tails of the Cosmic Being Maximus to accelerate your acceleration unto the Summit of Being.

God's Karma

I conceive of *maya*, not just in the sense of its bad karmic space-time sense of separation, but as the feminine differentiation that enables BEING to recognize faceted Selfhood. Thereby ascended masters and Cosmic Beings can appreciate each other, all the while KNOWING each other as One Another.

This faceting alchemy is called "in-division," whereby differentiated vision never loses sight of the One. In-division can be thought of as a word with no Real opposite, in that "out-division," portending the sense of separation, is but illusion. It seems to me that there ought to be a short word like *maya* to refer to spiritual differentiated vision that never loses sight of the One, but I am not aware of one. The term figure-eight flow does refer to that, but I'd like a shorter, single word; maybe something like "spirimaya," for spiritual *maya*. I like it. It has a wonderful flowing, mystical gist.

Individuality, God's own storehouse of magic, resides in the Causal Body: spheres of light surrounding the I AM Presence. Each Causal Body engram first and always exists as possibility to be enacted and acted upon as Christ/Soul. That evolutionary realm of consciousness—Brahman breathing—serves up the One with soul's unique secret sauce. Fast food never had it so good: no-time service in a satiated plenum can't fail to put a smile on God's face.

No wonder God's gratitude enshrines "your" soul as an evermore item on the One's menu. (It must be mentioned, however, that soul can also delete herself from God's menu by repeatedly ignoring many, many opportunities to choose Life, by most always cleaving to secondary-energy illusion.)

Won'tya Gimme a Kiss, Big Boy

Spiritual inspiration's latent stories complement mystery's infinitely untellable wakeup calls. They challenge even the highest Cosmic Beings: come find me, I have a kiss for you. I like to think of "kiss" here meaning: Karma Is Something Special. (Karma refers to all action, works or deeds.) Divine Love sings God's karmic melody. Karma is God's own *raison d'etre*, for karma's capacious Art testifies in God-Justice's witness box as it evinces divine Love's lively, All enfolding joy.

Going about our commonplace business, we karmically arrange *maya* with repercussions outwardly in our awareness and inwardly all the way to *akasha*'s precincts. And that's sure saying a lot, for *akasha* is the primordial substance even preceding THAT of light.

Theosophists and Hindus consider *akasha* to be the sound God uses to bespeak the creation of worlds: "Let there be light!" Such releases of light flavor the One's joy, even as our attunement with our Real Self and our higher frequency Sponsors bequeaths I AM THAT I AM fleshed out Individuality—God's own karma as Art and Beauty—to the nameless, faceless One.

The Nature of Bad Karma
Dyes of the Human Consciousness

More anent this will be discussed later, but here I wish to illumine a very subtle misconception re karma. Assimilating the oneness of the basic immaculate *maya* and the *maya* of false conception, will shed light upon what we usually call bad karma. Their oneness correlates to a teaching from master Serapis Bey, which describes bad karma as "dyes of the human consciousness."

That is, this bad karmic "substance" is indelibly mixed in with the good stuff. It is not some sort of standoffish separate gobbledygook. That is, bad karma doesn't just overlay a spectrum of God intent; it mangles it. That is, the amplitudes and phases of the infinitude of wave frequencies composing the soul's expression of consciousness are modified in a manner that obviates divine virtue to some extent. "Balancing" bad karma involves modifying a spectrum of consciousness so that it can fully resonate with a spectrum of divine virtue.

God Wills or Allows All Expression

Darkened karmic substance could not "exist" even as illusory perception if it were not supported by the One. Remember the old saying that everything exists because God either wills it or allows it. For a time, God allows soul to push Him onto the dance floor of whatever masquerade ball she wishes to attend.

The ascended masters also put it this way: everything has a white fire core. That is, everything is *expressing* God's Reality—expressing it beautifully well, poorly, or pitifully poorly. Yes, God's energy impels even the spectra of consciousness purported as bad karma, which is ultimately unsustainable and whose spectra will eventually disappear.

White fire cores energize all of the manifest worlds. Nicholas Roerich—in his "Mother of the World" painting shown below—illustrates God's willing or allowing all of soul's manifest action by portraying the Divine Mother with covered eyes. Just as impartiality is attributed to divine justice by portraying Her as a blindfolded Woman holding the scales of justice, so also Roerich's Divine Mother is unbiased in the opportunity She provides to souls learning to create as God. Of course, neophytes will make mistakes, and sometimes quite dramatic ones. But when necessary, spiritual growth can proceed along the lines of trial and error.

Courtesy of Nicholas Roerich Museum, New York

Surely, a great deal of all of the energy soul has ever qualified must be cleaned up, be transmuted to align/resonate with divine virtue. The substance, itself, which soul may malign with misdirected consciousness is ever inherently in the One and it can never forsake its provenance as the One, however grotesque it may illusorily appear.

Each moment that the sense of separation is forsaken, illumination, enlightenment comes of soul re-cognizing THAT: figure-eight flowing Selfhood. The bad karmic patterns are, indeed, illusion; and they will never in their grotesquerie reside permanently in the Causal Body. But, again, for a time, they are allowed to teach soul her divine Love lessons by rubbing her nose in their *dukkha* (pain/sorrow).

I find it best—to maintain a Zen awareness, as much as I can—to consider bad karma to be a **misapprehension** of the divine Real imagery that I AM intending as divine virtue. Of course, I visualize and feel the Violet Flame in places all around the world when I decree (use the science of the spoken word). But my internal feeling upon giving Violet Flame decrees to transmute my own bad karma is that *my entire Being* is reforming itself simultaneously on many planes and outposts where my consciousness converses with awareness. I feel this realignment not just confined to some pimple of bad karma, but to extend throughout my entire consciousness as it more closely aligns with my Causal Body.

Don't Entertain the Sense of Separation
!Period!

I find it counterproductive to consider that bad karma substance is ever stripped from me. That would condition me to entertain the sense of separation—the primary no-no of spiritual life. Let me repeat: ridding myself of bad karma is a realignment, not a skinning. So I do not visualize, nor do I conceive of, the flames of God to be plucking out some amount of bad karmic substance from a vat "somewhere" so it can be carried over to a furnace "over there" to be burned up. I'm no chicken that needs plucking to fit me for the supper of the Great Lord. No, no, no! I AM THAT I AM surrendering jive for Siva's cosmic dance.

It is all of me that is experiencing a realignment through and through, for the dyes of the human consciousness have more or less apprehended me (taken illusory hold of me) through and through. That misaligned bad karmic energy will never make it "up there" to the Causal Body until that energy invests God's good karma. Then it can "thread the eye of the needle," as I shun and accelerate the frequencies of densely clogging awareness.

I embrace this responsibility because—need I say it again?—only the One IS. The mangy magnetism that attaches me to false conceptions is still magnetism, and that is no different in its operation from any divine or human magnetism. It's a change of consciousness and my active awareness that must change and then its magnetism follows right along. Cease feeding the human ego; direct it merely as a tool. Then spiritual Victory will have its Day/Night.

The Purpose of Our Embodied Being

The awareness of Oneness in all perception is so important as to inspire Dowman to write:

"...the *purpose* of our embodied being is to recognize the unity of our basic immaculate *maya* and the *maya* of false concepts."[63]

If you read and meditate upon that quote often enough to fully grok it, you will relieve some Zen master of the need to bop you on the bean with his/her staff. (If you think that I'm claiming to have accomplished that, be disabused of that notion right now! All I can say for myself is that besides my more formal spiritual practices, multiple times a day I catch myself engaging the *maya* of false conception as separated entities more than I wish to tolerate. When I do notice such misapprehension, I sashay over to the Great Unknowing and reignite my perception of identity as infinite mystery.)

There's a Whole Lot 'a Shakin' goin' On

The consciousness of surrender is synonymous with divine Love. Both are the inner ground out of which your personal recognition of the above unity blooms. All that "stuff" seeming to populate everyday perception seemingly out there and appearing so hard and real is but consciousness processing energy. THAT *maya* of false conception is what you have made of You. Your identifying with the unitary *maya*, which deconstructs outer false conception's sense of separation, is also You. You ARE both and "more." You are infinite mystery apparently "bursting the seams" of your awareness as the Great Unknowing's Oneness that doesn't displace time or space.

Obviously, some physical interactions can hurt like mad and some can provide great pleasure. But if you want to be a smarty pants, walk the middle way, and render yourself riveted with Peace.

That Exasperating Amateur

W. H. Auden knows all about life's play by play. In his "Detective Story," he describes the outer accidents of everyday life carrying along infinite mystery, how we cling to them and think they're real. But there comes a time—perhaps right now or in a future embodiment—when the piper must be paid with the only coin of value in the outer realm: surrender:

> **What follows is habitual. All goes to plan:**
> **The feud between the local common sense**
> **And intuition, that exasperating amateur**
> **Who's always on the spot by chance before us;**
> **All goes to plan, both lying and confession,**
> **Down to the thrilling final chase, the kill.**

Oft given advice to writers is that they must be willing to kill their darlings—to not be attached to the worded babes they create. That is equally applicable to everyday life, for the Word of God, your masculine Higher Self, comprises the imagery you surmise momentarily; each letter and syllable of a moment's Word a satchel bearing your identity. Those formations infuse consciousness. They draw light through their live wires. Surrender strips *maya*'s circuitry, transmuting "local common sense" into bare wire Love.

What a telling phrase Auden uses: "that exasperating amateur." Intuition, the agency of the Higher Self, aka the Holy Christ Self, the

Son of God, is the essence of that wide-eyed amateur, as His Presence in space-time, a focus of eternity, is brand new every cycle. Indeed, master Godfre reveals an alchemical key: "Eternity flows as the dawn." Your Christ Self is so "inexperienced" that our outer habitual sense of duration, the "local common sense," can't touch Him. He exasperates because He defies logic and often pokes unexpectedly into our awareness with confounding Truth.

Each invited visitation of this infinite One into your outer busybody realm signifies the coming of age of the heart: courage. Christ in you comes like an angel and, as Rilke says, "Every angel is Terrifying."[64] Terrifying to the outer ego who knows his end is nigh for that cycle every moment that you look to your higher realm to invite blessing—be-less-ing—upon your creation. Be-less-ing: the kill that IS the Life: eternity rending the space-time impostor veils to impute to You the Holy of Holies. Yes. Yes. Yes. the kill; recognizing the *maya* of false conception as Reality so it can resonate and shine in Another Country.

As we will be examining in detail later, all indeed goes to plan, and God's plans, as Auden says, work out as "lies and confession." Waves of consciousness comprise a masculine positive portion thrust above the cosmic mean, and a feminine negative, return current, portion below the cosmic mean. This apparent form professes *maya*'s lies. The confession/surrender involves the waves of created form returning periodically to the infinite cosmic mean, even as their energy is ensconced as Artful treasures in the heaven world of the Causal body: the *maya* of primordially pure pristine awareness.

So-Called Hard-and-Fast Tinsel Matter

A perfect cycle of creation ends physically with what Auden calls "the kill" and what the Catholic Stations of the Cross refer to as "Jesus dies on the cross." Thus, perfectly created Real Images are completely not-of-this-world, leading Buddhists to call them "empty." This emptiness is the living Presence of God, the perfect Peace that passes understanding. Contrasting Auden's "local common sense" to that shows that it comprises naught but the illusory secondary energy relationships idolized as the fatted calves that science gets so caught up in.

All that stuff out there that seems so hard and fast to consciousness is but an after image. When anchored in and as the One, it is left behind as trailing clouds of glory, as the wake of Maitreya's clipper ship apparently passing through. True, Real imagery bears and bares the fullness of God's willing Presence, yet even their Reality is "empty" to space-time observers by virtue of their essence being "rooted" in infinity, which is, shall we say, ultimately orthogonal to their perceptions.

The imagery purporting the *maya* of false conception is also empty simply because it takes its cues from secondary energy whose relativity can produce only meaningless, idiotic tales and dust storms. That is, outer perception that is attached to the *maya* of false conception's seemingly separate entities can't tune in to infinite provenance any more than a person can watch TV shows burdened by a preponderance of static.

That's an interesting correspondence, isn't it? The hard and fast, outer world, secondary energy stuff is static. It's standing still compared to the infinite "speed" of Oneness. And that static stuff is what produces adumbrating static in consciousness. But, we have already seen how the *maya* of false conception is not to be castigated because, in and of itself, it is one with immaculate Reality. It is only when consciousness embroils itself in secondary energy's ignorance that it incites soul to perceive and act like brawling, drunken sailors to land herself in karmic jail cells. The Real Image will appear in consciousness when the *maya* of false conception assumes its place as unitary, light speed *maya*.

Dada Got Stuck in *Maya*'s Quicksand

Just in passing, I wish to mention how easy it is to fall into the trap of resentment, of castigating *maya* for its emptiness. A blaring example is found in the nihilist, anti-aesthetic Dada art movement, which came about during World War I. Its manifesto—written in 1918 by Tristan Tzara—is a diatribe against the meaningless outer world of everyday experience which reads like existentialism on steroids.[65] It emits such down-in-the-mouth disgust with life that I find it painful to read.

It seems that its author is so utterly attached to the *maya* of false conception as the sense of separation that he makes it his life's work to rail at the raw deal his gambler's heart has received. He appears to have dissuaded his consciousness from ever approaching anywhere near the sure thing to be found in the cosmic mean. Yet infinite worth, infinite meaning, infinite Love, infinite Selfhood was right there at the tip of his nose. Still, his self-righteousness blinded him to all THAT. In the last word of his manifesto, he summarizes down-in-the-mouth Dada as LIFE, though his manifesto's entire vibration is anti-life.

A Side Note on Science

Deep thinking scientists want to know how matter was first created; how life began. They ardently search for the irreducible building block. (Heaven only knows what human madmen "leaders" would do with it if they could ever discover such a thing.) They would do better to chase their tails and acknowledge their glee in doing so.

The mental arena to which so many of them confine themselves leads only to counterproductive energetics. They consider the notion of beginningless-endless eternity to be woo-woo. By their confined, authoritarian mindset, they think that they are worthy to poo-poo that. And that brown (not Brownian) motion is all they will ever find in the cat box of their intellectual purview. They have the gall to believe that their speculations have a ghost of a chance to reveal Life's meaning, when all it can uncover is the shenanigans of their inflated hubris. The only ghost that can reveal Real meaning is the Holy One that they reject out of hand. As Morya puts it:

> **"One may prosecute ignorance, but one should especially chastise superstition and hypocrisy. Like a leprous film, superstition covers weak brains. [Lloyd would add that the entire illusory "matter" point of view is purely superstition—misguided consensus.] We are not against laboratories and Western methods, but We demand that honesty, efficiency and the courage of impartiality be added to them."[66]**

Searching for ultimate meaning in circular, self-referent fluff balls is laughable, yet material scientists like Steven Weinberg persist in thinking that human intellectual mentality encompasses all of life's meaning. He writes:

"I believe that what we have found so far—an impersonal universe which is not particularly directed towards human beings—is what we are going to continue to find. And that when we find the ultimate laws of nature they will have a chilling, cold, impersonal quality about them."[67]

If I were to be allowed but one assumption re Weinberg, it would be that his mother withheld her teat from him, kept him in a cold crib, and neglected him. On the contrary, El Morya's heart warmly enfolds us:

Truth is the same, but combinations vary, according to consciousness. How much of the beautiful is destroyed, owing to the ignoring of the temple—the heart! But let us irresistibly strive to a realization of heartfelt warmth, and let us begin to feel ourselves as the bearers of the temple.[68]

Further, Morya advises:

The sun is the heart of the system; so, also, the heart of man is the sun of the organism. There are many sun-hearts, and the Universe represents a system of hearts; therefore, the cult of Light is the cult of the heart. To understand this abstractly is to leave the heart cold; but as soon as the Light of the sun-heart shall live, the need of the magnet's warmth will begin to shine forth like a true sun. It is said, 'Cross Santana with the aid of the heart.' Thus one can come closer to an understanding of the heart. The heart's rhythm can be regarded as the rhythm of life. The Teaching about the heart is as bright as the sun, and the warmth of the heart speeds as swiftly as a sunbeam. Everyone has wondered at the instantaneousness with which a ray of the rising sun warms all things. The heart can act likewise.

"I speak of the warmth of the heart when it is especially needed. The striving thought kindles space, but the warmth of the heart is a constant hearth. **Courage dwells in the warmth of the heart. This must be remembered. The appearance of the dark forces is like a frost to the sowing. Only the heart's warmth provides a glowing shield. But, as we delicately test light-waves, so solicitously must one approach the heart."**[69]

All Energy Is Consciousness in Motion
Reaching Out, Seeking Resolution
In and As Divine Love

Theosophy teaches that the laws of nature are the habits of a Cosmic Being. That is—and this must be the keynote of all spiritual *and* scientific inquiry—all we perceive "out there" reflects and embodies the consciousness of a person, a cosmic, divine Individual.

When we notice that the Individual in Whom we live consistently repeats a configuration of energy, an interactive potential for processing, we call that a chemical element. Even inert elements hold a unique place in Life's matrices. When we notice a repetitive activity, it's said that a law of nature has been discovered. Yet if we fling ourselves so far afield that we find ourselves living in a different Cosmic Being, we may find that that One likes football better than basketball, and that all the rules, all the so-called "laws" we have grown accustomed to have changed.

In other words, the "laws" of nature are a fickle as Lucy Ricardo or Gracie Burns or Mork (of the Mork and Mindy TV series). All is unique and changeable, no matter how macrocosmic the focus of our layout may seem.

Physicists spend their lives attempting to understand, to pin down, the laws of nature scientifically. But many, if not most, today, are barking up the wrong tree. They regard nature as a system of cold, unconscious repeatable reactions, as an impersonal, heartless, episodic series of interactions, a meaningless menagerie of dead substance which somehow has come to form a chemistry purported as what they call life.

They believe what their senses and machinery report to them about consistent, repeatable activity that they classify as phyla, species, the table of the elements, etc. Such meaningless life, as they call it comprises the vegetable, animal and human kingdoms. But they ignore as life the living beings of the mineral kingdom, consigning it to populate a realm regarded as dead matter. They have taken patterns of nature as the idols of a dead religion, a science which is but a conglomerate of chemical equations and mathematical formulae.

The correct Tree to be barking up is the Tree of cap "L" Life. Up that One is found the critter they seek: Life's Real meaning, which is infinite mystery.

I can see you there, down on your knees, begging my pardon for not quite getting how a thingy noun like "Life's Real meaning" is something unknowably open ended: infinite mystery. How, it may be asked, can we ever get our final Truth answer, then? Well, it turns out that the answer is how you adjust yourself to **find comfort in the Great Unknowing**. Make that adjustment, and you will find yourself to be a know-it-ALL. All knowledge is but a gaggle of navigational devices enabling you to tour about your far flung farm to find what's harvestable NOW as joy.

Physicists will find the personal homeostasis that their science restlessly quests when they finally wake up to *all* Life as personal Being.

Our entire universe, a mere bubble in an infinitely unbounded multiverse of multiverses, is nourished through the heart chakra of a Cosmic Being Who has gifted us with some measure of access to their personal Selfhood. They accomplish this magnanimous outreach by disclosing nomenclature imbued with the power to resonate with them intimately. The name we can use to personally engage our universe in divine Love is Alpha and Omega.

This twin-flame Being has consented to a "getting to know you" relationship with the unascended mankind of Earth. They want to go steady with us. But with so many of our set down here treating them like an old, dead-matter shoe, they can be forgiven if they have misgivings about even inviting us to the junior prom. I mean...the least we could do when they ask us out—and, they're continuously doing that—is to become living, breathing flow-ers so that we can present to them as a corsage in their multi-galactic bouquet.

Then, perhaps on the dance floor, waltzing to the music of the spheres, they might just whisper sweet nothings in our ear. They might introduce us anew—and ever anew—to the no-thing: the infinitely mysterious provenance that sets their very own heart afire. Together, then, we might swoon and croon our Love all through the spirit's night till the rooster crows at the break of day.

That will charge us with an afflatus sufficient to shake Life's Tree and reap abundant harvests of fruit. Fruit pregnant with enough of infinite mystery's meaning to re-solve mankind's problems out of the box in which misguided scientists and bipeds of all stripes have deadly, hypnotically confined us—consensually, I might add.

But encouragingly, not all of today's scientists subscribe to the commonly accepted ignorance. Quantum physics leads those who dare pursue it, along a path that deposits them in a quandary that at least points them in a useful direction: inward. As the old blokes die off, their replacements will eventually come to accept that consciousness is the seat where all of their answers reside. A significant number of scientists have already arrived there, but a quorum has not yet been reached.

As I pointed out above, Steven Weinberg incorrectly posits human thought as a useful point of view to adapt when searching out Reality. But his off key position is not entirely far afield. Humanity—its Being, *not its intellectual miasma*—is, according to Morya, is capable of Self awareness as a prime actor in infinity's evolutionary play:

> **"How powerfully the cosmic energy is reflected in the human organism! Each cosmic fire meets consonance in the human organism. How much may be learned by a spiritual approach towards the investigation of all manifestations of the centers [chakras]. If one would consider the human organism as the reflection of the manifestations of Cosmos, how many consonances could be perceived; and the centers would evince to science a fiery expression. Only a spiritual approach will reveal the significance of all cosmic correspondences and their human reflections."[70]**

So much for the Rinky-Dink atom!

More and more, scientists are coming to terms with the sort of merger of spirit and science that Morya speaks of. Modern "emergence theory" postulates that everything in 3D is composed of very small tetrahedrons: four sided pyramidal objects. These create what is called the quasicrystalline spin network: QSN. This network emerges from the mathematics describing a 3D point space—each point surrounded by a tetrahedron—comprising the closest packing of "spheres" in eight dimensions. This space is called E8. A quasicrystal is an asymmetric projection into a lower dimension of a crystal structure in a higher dimension. Like casting the shadow of a 3D cubic crystal lattice onto a sheet of paper. To define the substance of our reality, an 8D crystal is mathematically projected down onto a 4D structure and that is then projected down to 3D at a specific irrational angle to form a theorized fundamental substructure of space-time.

Two of the chief scientists working on this emergence theory are Garrett Lisi and Klee Irwin. They explain that when these projections are made, the resulting objects become a language: a set of structures (letters), rules on how you can arrange those letters, and freedom within those rules which allows you to express or encode information.

So, this 3D quasicrystal is essentially a geometric code. A code composed of symbols, which express meaning. And this meaning is reality, itself. (Remember Keith Dowman using Tibetan Buddhist terminology to state the same thing: "The *'maya* of false conception' [the forms of our outer space-time world] and the 'basic immaculate *maya'* [the inner time-space Causal Body patterns] of the natural dispensation—of Our infinite Selfhood—are one.")

In this approach, we never have to introduce the higher dimensions because we get the same information of the higher dimensional math encoded in the 3D quasicrystal language. That is, all the information of E8 exists in its "shadow." Mathematically, one can recover the information of the E8 lattice that encodes unification physics from the lower dimensional quasicrystal.

The scientists working on this theory believe that if they can discover the very workings of the pixelated sphere of reality, that should open up a treasure trove of new technologies, and perhaps even new philosophies relating to the "strangeness" of quantum mechanics that allow things that we couldn't imagine. They believe that reality is deeply related to higher dimensional objects.[71] Again, those higher dimensional objects are the inner time-space Causal Body patterns, Dowman's basic immaculate *maya* referenced above.

I have included this little side note on science to set what I am asserting in this book apart from both cold, calculating schemas and from equally idolatrous religious detours. Truth partakes of an infinitely ongoing inner science wedded to consciousness; yet it embraces warmly the divine Mother's tender nurture in league with her unflinchingly protective cover and the Father's encouraging, directing, supportive fortitude.

Humanity as we know it carries that consciousness to its apex in mortality, at least in our small portion of our galaxy. Thus, it's worthwhile to examine how our human consciousness is configured to allow God's grace to enable pulling ourselves up by our bootstraps by enacting our immortal Identity.

The Divine IS Consciousness
And THAT is an Infinite Open System
The Super Additive Viewpoint

Consciousness is not confined by the 3D space-time realm where humans express and learn to tailor themselves to divine Love. Consciousness "grows," without beginning, without end, unperturbed by the constraints—such as conservation of energy—of the 3D tools it uses to prepare soul for her alchemical marriage with her Christed consort. The super additive effect hints at the limitless freedom consciousness can enjoy.

A super additive sum occurs, for instance, when $1 + 1 = 3$. That is, just the action of performing the addition alchemically multiplies the substance. A Hierarch imparting a blessing, for instance, may appear to be giving energy/consciousness away to a deserving recipient. Yet, the Hierarch knows full well that Life is not a zero sum game. He/She knows that only the One IS. So "giving energy away" is tantamount to giving it to Him/Her Self. The energy "given" is exactly the energy received by another facet of the One's own consciousness. With every transmission, consciousness is, then, doubled I AM THAT I AM.

But then the super additive effect kicks in because the receiver is going to utilize that energy, and that alchemy also multiplies that same energy in consciousness I AM THAT I AM again.

In fact, the super additive effect in consciousness rises as the square of the number of participants in a shared experience (assuming they are all of approximately equal power and that they are attuned and participating I AM THAT I AM).

This is especially true for people decreeing together, i.e., using the science of the spoken word to direct light. That's because each one reaffirms their unity holographically with each of the "others," and each one is an independent source of energy tapping into the infinite One.

Here's how it looks for two people decreeing together. (CW is used here to mean "Connects With")

#1 CW #2 = 2 units of energy
#2 CW #1 = 2 units of energy

—

4 units of energy

So two people decreeing together experience four times the power of a person decreeing alone.

Here's how it looks for three people decreeing together.

#1 CW #2 and #3 = 3 units of energy
#2 CW #1 and #3 = 3 units of energy
#3 CW #1 and #2 = 3 units of energy

—

9 units of energy

So three people decreeing together experience nine times the power of a person decreeing alone.

And so it goes ad infinitum. This multiplication of consciousness occurs as an unlimited open system. Many of today's scientists stifle themselves by confining their attention to the closed system of the *maya* of false conception comprising the outer relative world of secondary energy. But consciousness exists outside of that realm. It can direct outer energy but its power is not confined to the realm where Newton's laws apply.

You ARE an infinitely open system. God's Name proves it.

Divine Standard Equipment
Our Vehicles of Ascent
Humans Entertain Eight Major Points of View

The I AM Presence in evolutionary mode expresses through many modalities. In humans these coalesce as chakras—focused divine energy centers. The ascended masters teach that the human body comprises 144 chakras focused in the etheric plane of divine fire. The chakras expressing the eight major modes—or Rays—are situated along the spine, and they anchor the infinite One right here and now as inner foci directly nourishing our consciousness as we direct our awareness either to our inner world in meditation or our outer busybody world, or, preferably, an awareness figure-eight flowing to both our inner and outer world simultaneously as One.

Since only the One IS, our chakras are simply points of view. In no way are they broken up segmentations. They act on behalf of the One, anchored in a cognizant matrix that may seem to be diverse, but that apparent diversity only arises because human perception and thought arrange them categorically. Again, the experience of each instant is in Reality indivisible.

Spatial Form

Spatially, any shape comprises an infinite spectrum of component wave shapes. For instance, the shape of a washboard would consist of a preponderance of waves bearing the frequency of the washboard undulations. The shape of a tree would comprise a much greater variety of frequencies, what with all that fine detail needing to be portrayed.

The component spatial waves composing any shape vary in **amplitude** (how bright they appear) from zero (black) through the shades of gray to white, whose brightness is essentially limitless. (Not that any of us could actually do it, the immortals encourage each of us to visualize the light we wish to focus on Earth with the intensity of ten thousand suns.)

Different waves also present themselves in space at different **frequencies**. That is, whatever a wave's amplitude may be, the peaks and valleys of that wave's amplitude could regularly appear spaced widely apart (low frequency) or very close together (high frequency).

Moreover, when comparing one wave to another, their starting points relative to a point of origin, can vary. Two waves are said to be out of **phase** with one another when this occurs. That is, when adding two waves of the same frequency and amplitude that are in phase with each other, the result will be a wave varying between zero amplitude and twice the amplitude of one of them. When these waves are ninety degrees out of phase, adding them together will produce a constant "wave" with a constant amplitude of one of them. When these waves are 180 degrees out of phase, adding them together will produce a black absence of any amplitude because they will completely cancel each other out.

These amplitude, frequency and phase variations superposed posit the shapes of things spatially. Stuff appears to awareness as more or less grossly or finely separated detail. Different optical systems or consciousness in different people can be said to be capable of resolving detail more or less finely. The higher the resolution, the finer the detail that can be distinguished. For instance, some people are said to be gross individuals, and others highly sensitive or finely tuned. Thus, although Reality's images comprise an infinitude of frequencies, different people are capable of tuning in to more or less of their charm.

Thus, even though every shapely thing consists of an infinity of wave frequencies, the potential to increase the strength of the higher frequencies an observer can reproduce is proportional to the attainment of higher consciousness (humility) that observer has instilled within. The smaller be the bull in the china shop, the finer will be the china that one can appreciate without bumblingly breaking it to chaotic bits. And the availability of such attainment is limitless.

The Beauty of BEING Over the Top
The Peter Principle Peters Out

The "glass ceiling" refers to an invisible barrier placed upon a class of people, which keeps them from rising higher. For instance, feminists balk at the limits to advancement that well qualified women often encounter in the work place. Another artificially imposed barrier, the Peter principle, says that people rise to their level of incompetence. While both of these impediments to achievement may indeed exist in consensus reality realms, Self Identity imposes no such limits.

I sure do know how easy it is to feel oppressed by one's own supposed limitations, to assume that you've topped out. But, just as glass ceilings have been shown to be breakable, the Peter principle is also known to be a moving target. I wish to end this part of our Self examination by encouraging you to adopt the Great Unknowing's attitude; live a life that's always over the top.

You ARE. You are fit to inhabit the far off worlds that are over the top for whatever world your current consciousness defines. So leave your little self in the dust as you invite the Cosmic Being Maximus to help you accelerate false summits of acceleration at which you think your consciousness must settle. Pedal to the metal. Vroom-vroom! Ten thousand suns are but a pittance of the light I AM.

Master Morya gives us an experiment in consciousness that we can use to more closely encounter the endless spiritual Hierarchy of light:

"Accustom yourselves to see without looking and to hear without listening. In other words, to this degree encompass the vision into the spiritual region that despite your open eyes you will not see that which is before you. Or, in spite of the evident noise not to hear it through open ears. Through such physical tests one can greatly progress in psychic vision and hearing. For this it is useful in imagination constantly to hold before oneself the Image of the Teacher [your I AM Presence and Holy Christ Self and spiritual guru] as That Which is the most precious to bind you with the Supreme.

"Now, imagine for a moment that you have succeeded with the help of chemical reactions in creating a complete microcosm; for this microcosm you are the creator! Why is it then so difficult for people to imagine an endless chain of Creators from the lowest to the Highest, up to the Inaccessible? Therefore, speaking of the Infinite, we will not imagine it as something void or measureless but as something integral in its incessant ascent. And is not the entire Infinite expressed in your consciousness, since the measure and boundaries of the consciousness are limitless? Thus, from the smallest to the Greatest, proceed by steps, each link being visible and sensed and tangible. There the indicated experiment will serve you in seeing the invisible through the physical, impenetrable forms which stand before you. From

the evident, proceed to the reality which will enrich your path."[72]

Further, Morya invites:

"Let us calmly discriminate in all the details of life— not for self-vindication but for the investigation of our nature and the assimilation of the measures of perfection."[73]

PART THREE

Manifest Action: A Closer Look at
the Horizontal Bar Of the White
Fire Cross of Creation

El Morya delivers the keynote of this part:

People give very little attention to the Invisible World. It is necessary to consciously learn to understand its presence in everything. One can look upon space as upon the passageway to invisible worlds, which are observing us.[74]

Parallel Time-Space and Space-Time Universes

In his book *The Source Field Investigations*[75], David Wilcock examines in great detail the reciprocal relation between time and space. He postulates that each realm portrays simultaneously progressing parallel universes:

- the space-time universe our normal perceptions deliver to us
- the time-space universe of divine possibility, "the space where all experience remains in potential"[76]

Let's get Sexy
The One's Parallel-Universe Expression
Hosts the Masculine and Feminine Aspects
Of the I AM Presence in Evolutionary Mode

- **Time-space** is the masculine realm of infinite possibility. It resides at the consciousness realm/level that the ascended masters call the Holy Christ Self. This aspect of our Being comprises infinite possibilities drawn from our Causal Body and from the gracious blessings of other Beings of light. Here, God's arbiter of consciousness in league with the Soul, chooses shape/form spectra to be outpictured. These are translated through the substance of the time-space/space-time interface. Outer consciousness can then access them holographically at each of the infinitude of points in space-time.

- **Space-time** is the feminine realm of *akasha wherein* building and completed choices come about. In this everyday realm of outer activity, consciousness is meant to express Selfhood as Art. It provides the arena of Artful soul craft. Her inspiration and creativity arise as she accesses her Christ Self's time-space realm through the time-space/space-time interface.

The "normal" world we perceive is called the space-time continuum because it comprises three dimensions of space and one of time. Each moment, a three dimensional spatial image flashes through our senses. Indeed, it's our entire spatial universe that's flashing on and off like that.

With actions performed in space-time, we are at liberty to resonate with God's blueprints, whilst adding in our own artistic fillips to co-create beatific visions. We can harmoniously robe ourselves in beautiful garments that impart freedom to our outer awareness and joy to our everyday and eternal consciousness.

That interchanging divine intercourse—I AM THAT I AM—sings the One through your everyday awareness in and as THAT.

THAT is your infinite confluence.

THAT is joy.

THAT resonates as the One's only opportunity to grow.

THAT takes your hand upon a perp walk to a lineup, where you are in all ways identified as the fire blossoming One.

Thusly, we run in tandem with God's own good karma as it furnishes the Causal Body mansion.

God's will is consciousness sweeping infinite mystery across a field of possibility. How a particular possibility field comes to be selected and Who is selecting it is way beyond my insight. A true divine alchemist is one who can consciously activate manifestation and precipitate substance, by virtue of that knowledge. But a true alchemist's goal is not to produce space-time end results. It is the expansion of joy as the One's conscious opportunity. I know how paradoxical it is to say that the One—already everything—needs open portals to unity. But, again, it is not any end product or any unity that the One needs; it's the open portals that the One cannot conceive. That's where soul, time and space come into the play.

So-called particles of consciousness bring about outer perception. But the infinite One plays quite a hide-and-seek game.

Where Is the Electron Between Observations?

Dr. Amit Goswami explains that the electron only exists in potential while unobserved. He writes:

"Since the electron's wave collapses immediately upon observation, potential could not be within the material domain of space-time...[You can't have a little bit of observation any more than a woman can be a little pregnant.] Between observations, the electron exists as a possibility form, like a Platonic archetype, in the transcendent domain of potential ('I dwell in possibility,' wrote the poet Emily Dickinson.)"... The important new element is that the domain of potential also exists in consciousness. Nothing is outside consciousness. This monistic view of the world is crucial." [77]

This perfectly corresponds with our notion of your Holy Christ Self holding forth transcendentally in time-space, serving up basic immaculate *maya* to soul for her to exult and bloom it in her cascading space-time instants.

Quantum Strangeness Is a Koan

Quantum physicists are people whose inquisitiveness has brought them smack up against the time-space/space-time interface. They must come to terms with a particle appearing as a piece of something when flying through a cloud chamber, leaving a straight line wake behind. Yet the same sort of particle will act like a wave when traversing two closely separated slits in a barrier.

These poor physicists have spent countless hours focusing their attention upon matter and mathematically describing it in fine detail.

They bury themselves deeply and ever deeper in interconnected layers of the *maya* of false conception, which their fantastically expansive brain power cloaks in highly abstruse math. Then they must reconcile observable opposite behavior.

Dr. Amit Goswami likens this to a pair of Buddhist students confronted with a koan. Zen master Basho replied to them when asked what is Buddha? He said, "Buddha is mind," to the first; and to the second, he said, "Buddha is no-mind." The perplexed students couldn't "get it" while dwelling in the world of opposites, for that realm doesn't hold the answer.

But...it does *host* the answer, which is always some flavor of united twin flames. The key to busting through to the other side of a koan is to translate opposites into polarities of the One. That doesn't mean that the two opposites are redefined to be poles with consciousness plopped in between. No...not at all: Each of the apparent opposites can appear because each of them are, in themselves, both polarities of the One. Each apparent entity is a union; each is the All.

Sustaining time-space consciousness as the One while awareness is focused upon space-time in the One: that's the koan key. Buddha IS entirely no-mind. Buddha IS entirely mind. Quantum physics, still in its infancy, awaits the arrival of a science oriented populace of figure-eight flowing rascals.

A speculative Note Re String Theory

This thought just came to me out of the blue. I think that it will do little more than illustrate my ignorance of the particulars of the string-theory TOE (Theory Of Everything). But I find it useful, so I'm of a mind to share it with you.

I can imagine that the vibrating strings that string theory proposes as the underlying building blocks of everything correspond to the Causal Body patterns made available to consciousness as its evolutionary forte. Those are the patterns of basic immaculate *maya* that populate time-space. These strings found then in soul's province are pressed into action as her mission to marry them and bring each of those wild rascal proposals out for the time of their Life on a spontaneous joy ride.

String theory, if I get this right, proposes that there are either 10^{100}

or 10^{500} alternate universes that consciousness has available to play in. I don't take any stock in any particular number. All I can relate to is that consciousness's playpen is one heck of a panoply. The immortal masters of wisdom probably know what the number of these universes archetypally is, but not knowing this number is not going to keep a tenderfoot like me up at night.

What does keep me up—day and night—is my wide eyed wonderment at the comprehensive content of the TOE this book you're now reading points out. By riding on the wagon it purports, your brain is enabled to grapple with consciousness enfolding Spirit and spirit; matter and mater; infinite mystery; God; Gods and Goddesses; Sons and Daughters of God; free will's possibility of error—bad karma; free will's possibility of perfection—God's own good karma, your treasures in heaven; the translation of basic immaculate *maya* into the *maya* of radiant primordially pure pristine awareness; ever present growth in Reality and its antithesis, the second death; re-embodiment; laws of nature as the habit patterns of Cosmic Beings; death as a changing of the guard and our endlessly cycling opportunity to express the One as a clean slate; the law of cycles; expanding and collapsing universes; ultimate purpose; consciousness as the building block of All; spiritual white fire cores as antahkarana unifying the *maya* of false conception with the God intent embedded in basic immaculate *maya*; resurrection ratifying the fractal nature of consciousness as above, so below; mortality paradoxically expressing eternity; perception modifying absolute mystery. And on and on and on it goes.

I'm sure master Morya could add many pages of subjects to this list. Such topics as the above are the real province of a science headed in a direction that would enliven knowledge and fructify it as wisdom.

Time Bridges One Illusory Dream Setting To Another: Time is not; Space is Not

Time's cascading outer-world tale told by an idiot indeed signifies nothing. The "meaning" undergirding our workaday space-time realm resides in the attunement of consciousness to the infinite mystery equally suffusing both the parallel time-space/space-time universes.

Yet time-space's immaculate conceptions provide the raw material from which space-time Self Realized Art is destined to grace the Causal Body: God's own personality. The "time" we "experience" in our everyday world just allows us to bring order to the everyday transactions carried out in space-time. Moreover, it offers some degree of intellectual comfort for our encounters with apparent macrocosmic movement, such as our Earth's rotation and its path along with our sun around our galaxy.

But always keep in mind Gautama Buddha's declaration that "time is not; space is not." The entirety of the space-time training ground in which we prepare for our immortal birthing is fictional (that idiotic tale).

But don't deride it just because of that.

It is a necessary catalyst to unascended soul's Self realization. It imputes God's archetypal habits (the "laws" of nature) to our consciousness. Our everyday life gets us into the swing of "things" to prepare us for the Life where "all this swing both to and fro alters not a jot of Cosmic Purpose I forgot."[78]

Time's Illusion Is Like a House with Many Rooms

Jesse Elder describes time's illusion as a house we call the NOW.[79] In that house, someone might be in the kitchen, another in the den, and another in the bedroom. Our outer consciousness may create a path for one of time's arrows by making breakfast in the kitchen, eating it in the den and then going to sleep in the bedroom. But it is always in the NOW house where/when we perform each of those activities. All of them coexist in the same unitary quantum field encompassing what we call past, present and future.

Giving *Akasha* Legs to walk

The crux of our timely illusion is imagination's creativity. When you remember a past event, you are re-membering it, giving it legs, bestowing upon it a new active life in the NOW. Indeed, Elder points out that it is possible that what you call your present actually outplays a future you imagined in the past. When you imagine a future, you are acting as a catalyst to bring that possibility to birth in the NOW. Elder says, when you imagine a future, you are simply focusing upon the memory [the etheric pattern, the *Akashic* record] of that version of you. It all exists right NOW. That activity of concentrating upon desired futures is the essence of what has come to be popularly known as the "law of attraction".

In fact, the present is just as illusory as the past and future in that it occurs within the same relative realm that they do. Such relativity reminds me of the old question, "Am I presently a butterfly imagining a dreaming man, or am I a dreaming man conjuring a butterfly?" Consciousness never finds wholeness in and as the One in the present; only in the infinite moment NOW.

The timeless quantum field, which Wilcock calls the Source field, eternally encompasses all possibilities, which can only be expressed in Reality NOW.

I actually have a bone to pick with Wilcock for calling the One, the I AM Presence, a Source field. That's because "Source" implies an associated object, which relegates the I AM Presence to no more than another element deriving its being from the sense of separation. The ascended masters obviate this mistake by proclaiming "individual" I AM Presences to be "in-divisions," i.e., facets of the One I AM Presence; not really divided. Only the One IS. There is no "Source" in Reality expressing infinite mystery. I AM THAT I AM. Both I AMs of God's Name are co-equal. Quantum physicists, grasping the non-local nature of Reality, appreciate the One's omnipresence. Perhaps a better version of Wilcock's book title—as uncatchy as it is— would be "Quantum Field Investigations."

When non-local THAT is expressed as the soul's living Art, eternal possibility becomes a radiating sphere in the outer seven spheres of light of the Causal Body. May I incite you, then, to forthwith shred the past/present/future mindset, which inflicts consciousness with—let me blare it again—tales told by an idiot, signifying nothing. Live above all that in THAT.

The Holy Christ Self as Prisoner and Liberator

Also beyond our scope here is consciousness that fails to resonate with divine intent, producing the illusory realm called bad karma. But it's useful to note how the Celtic God Mabon exemplifies the tradeoffs that evolving deity (us) must endure on the Path to permanence in divine Love:

> **"The young Son of light, Mabon or Maponus, [is] the Celtic god of liberation, harmony, unity and music. He may have been one of the most universally worshipped deities in the Celtic world, and was at the center of the Druidic magical cosmology as the original Being, pre-existent, Son of the Great Mother. He is represented in myth and legend as both a prisoner and a liberator; many other heroic and divine figures are related to Mabon."**[80]

As the "pre-existent Son of the Great Mother," Mabon appears in the ascended master point of view as the Holy Christ Self. This Being, your own Higher Self, is portrayed as both a prisoner and a liberator because in His role as your personal Christ Self, through His "guilt by association," He might be thought of as limited, incarcerated right along with the soul (His feminine nature) in the "jail cells" of bad karma she creates by imputing bad vibes to the spectra of divine virtue.

Yet He is also the soul's liberator as He holds the balance of light and darkness for her while she masters her lessons on the homeward Path by fits and starts. Indeed, His unity with both the I AM Presence and the soul enables Him to supply the liberating forces that are available to soul every single moment, enabling her to break the bonds she foolishly forges by gluing her attention to illusion, to apparently separated false concepts.

In other words, the Holy Christ Self and Soul *are* One; and, particularly, One in and as the I AM Presence in evolutionary mode. The Holy Christ Self is the masculine aspect of the Presence in that mode, and the Soul the feminine. While in her human level of consciousness, lowercase "s" soul often finds herself acting as quite the scallywag. Such tugs upon the heartstrings of compassion always evoke looks from her Higher Self consort: not looks askance, but as the arrows of liberating compassion we experience as pangs of conscience.

Time-Space—A Closer Look

The temporal realm is called the time-space continuum because it comprises three dimensions of "time" and one of space. At any point of space-time, 3D space, a three dimensional "temporal" image flashes through our senses. This imagery originates as potential in the time-space realm.

Wilcock explains that these two realms are so delicately balanced that portions of the atoms composing the forms we perceive are constantly oscillating between the two realms. That is similar to figure-eight flow; but, with figure-eight flow, there is no oscillation of focus. Both inner and outer Self realization are present simultaneously. Such Self realized "flow" evidences divine consciousness as twofold intra-action:

- **Vertically**, between the I AM Presence in the state of pure Oneness and the Presence's agent, Christ/Soul, in evolutionary mode

- **Horizontally** nested within the Presence's evolutionary agency: the Holy Christ Self and the Soul

May the Force BE with You

The time-space parallel universe is the realm of spirit expressing the immaculate concepts God creates, driven by infinite mystery's unfathomable potential. This potential is what is referred to in the Star Wars movies as "the Force." The top-of-the-line potential produce it comprises is meant to be cooked up by soul as the supper of the Great Lord.

The naturally operative Force maintains consciousness in Peace. That is, the inherent, divine masculine-feminine balance of consciousness remains undisturbed in what Dowman calls the "natural dispensation." When a Star Wars character notes that there is a "disturbance in the Force," they are aware of an inharmonious adjunct attempting to modify consciousness with a less than divine potential.

Time-space is the inner realm where every configured possibility simply IS. Each of those possibilities is core perfection. Note well, though, that the Causal Body proposals there are just that: proposals. They, themselves, are not up for modification. They are part and parcel of consciousness whether soul chooses to express them or not, in whole or in part.

It is consciousness that changes as it brings those potential elements to life to produce Art, which then graces the Causal Body as what Dowman calls the *"maya* of primordially pure pristine awareness."[81] There, it becomes God's good karma. When soul associates impurities— out-of-synch resonances—with them, they end up on her bad karma ledger crying out for balance.

Sacred Astonishment

As we go about our daily lives, the events we encounter often seem haphazard, with little or no connecting linkage. Yet, our lives are actually being directed from behind the scenes. Jorge Luis Borjes fashions his fiction in just such a manner:

> **"Along with "vertical" superpositions of different and mutually qualifying levels, there are also "horizontal" progressions of qualitative leaps...Unexpected turns elude the predictable; hidden realities are revealed through their diverse effects and derivations. Borjes uses mystery and the surprise effect in literature to achieve that sacred astonishment at the universe which is the origin of all true religion and metaphysics."[82]**

I so love that phrase "sacred astonishment at the universe." It perfectly captures the wide-eyed, childlike approach to life that captivates those who have incorporated even a small measure of spirituality—that being infinite—into their Way of life.

Referring to Time-Space's Three Dimensions
As "Time" Is But a Humanly Worded Convenience

For a long time, I was completely befuddled by Wilcock's description of the time-space parallel universe. He says that form is experienced there in the same way as it is in space-time where we "normally" focus consciousness. I was futilely trying to imagine shapely form described as a measure of past-present-future in three dimensions. My brain just cannot grok such a conception. I cannot fathom past-present-future transpiring independently in three orthogonal dimensions together. That is because I'm stuck in the human conception of the arrow of time cascading space's three dimensions and producing records in *akasha*'s timeless realm.

The human experience of that cascade imparts our feeling of time's passing illusion here in our normal world. But time as we conceive of it does not exist as duration in what we are loosely referring to as time-space. That is, the realm of "time" there does not describe dimensions whose measure involves past-present-future. It is a realm of possibility, of spirit form that IS.

I relate to time-space's "time" as a timeless "flow," which is actually not a flow at all. It's a spectrum of channels that provides to consciousness its instantaneous access to the possibility engrams of the Causal Body, comprising the I AM Presence's divine personality: the patterns that render that individed Presence unique.

In other words, calling time-space's form "time" is just a worded convenience that allows us to relate to it as the converse of our use of the word "time" when we describe the ongoing events, and our feelings about their procession, in our everyday space-time.

This is a very important understanding. So let me emphasize this thought by saying it again. Space-time is our outer, everyday realm; time-space is its parallel-universe: an inner, timeless, arena wherein our immaculate, shapely divine plans reside.

Sadhguru Jaggi Vasudev differentiates the sort of time that passes by from the sort that IS:

> **"In eternal space, when there was no movement, when everything was still, there was Time, but nothing cyclical happening. That dimension of Time,**

into which everything dissolved, and from which everything sprang up, when certain energy touched it, took to cyclical movement. When cyclical movement happened, physical happened. When physical happened, we could measure time. Otherwise, Time was just space. So the [Sanskrit] word Kālá means both Time and space."[83]

So, happy me, Sadhguru ratifies my conception of time-space, where "time" is just as shapely as space in space-time. When everything (the potential engrams of basic immaculate *maya*) is still, "time's" reservoir of Causal Body potential lies in wait for soul to come around and put some of it in her shopping basket and subject it to the cyclic realm, i.e., render them subjects of activity.

This explanation also conforms to the Buddhist conception as feminine that which is totally beyond conception—what Kabbalists call *Ein Sof.* Buddhists call it the Great Mother. This is not to be understood in contradistinction to masculine as a polarity, but the ground, so to speak, out of which all manifestation arises. The beyond the beyond is simply considered to be feminine because humans relate to birth in that way. But it is truly genderless *that* about which naught can be said or conceived.

El Morya reveres the Great Mother so intimately that Her Presence unspeakably exalts Him. Here is His attempt to insinuate some of his devotion to Her with words:

"Ruleress, I Pronounce The great Co-worker of Cosmic Reason. Ruleress, Thou, beyond all cosmic powers, bearest within Thyself the sacred seed which provides radiant life. Ruleress, affirming all manifestations of the Great Reason, Thou art the Bestower of joy of cosmic creativeness. The Ruleress will adorn the aspiring realm with creative fire. Ruleress of Thought, Thou Who invokes life, to Thee We make manifest the radiance of Our Ray. Mother, venerated of the Lords, We carry in Our Heart the fire of Thy Love. In Thy Heart lives the ordaining Ray.

In Thy Heart life is conceived, and We shall affirm
the Ray of the Ruleress. Yes, yes, yes!

"Thus the Cosmos exists in the greatness of the Dual
Origins. Yes, yes, yes! Thus the Cosmos crowns the
Dual Origins. Thus the Mother of the World and
the Lords build life. Yes, yes, yes! And in boundless
striving the Cosmic Magnet welds its sacred parts.
Thus We venerate the Ruleress beyond all spheres."[84]

Microclusters: The Substance of The
Time-Space/Space-Time Interface
The Substratum of Figure-Eight Flowing Mater

Wilcock describes the Time-Space/Space-Time Interface as a little
known phase of matter composed of what are called microclusters.
These are neither solid, liquid nor gas. "Microclusters can be anywhere
between ten to a thousand atoms. The strangest thing about them
is that the electrons appear to orbit the center of the cluster, rather
than the center of each individual atom. Of course, this weird behavior
suggests there are no electrons. Instead, what scientists actually see is
geometrically arranged electron clouds, which appear to be where the
fluidlike flow of the Source Field enters into the atom."[85]

This softer interface-phase substance may specifically be the
substratum of figure-eight flowing mater, as opposed to hard and fast
secondary energy matter. Since it is situated right at the cusp of the
time-space portal, the material essentially partakes of three-dimensional
time's fluid nature even as it is also inserted into the more crystalline
three-dimensional geometry of space. I relate to this "stuff" of mater
more as a malleable pudding than as a set-in-stone persistence like
quartz.

Humans are able to contact this interface between the parallel worlds
and even to project its properties to matter. Wilcock quotes from Dr.
Claude Swanson's book *The Synchronized Universe* about "Peter Sugleris,
a young Greek boy in the 1980s who could move objects, bend spoons
and other metal utensils without even touching them—as witnessed by
many people. These spoon-bending feats can now be explained by the

atoms flipping over into time-space, so the material actually starts to be bendable."[86]

Of course, the more famous Uri Geller was probably doing the same thing. That is, if either of them can be believed at all, that they are using psychic powers to accomplish their manipulation of matter. Magicians have demonstrated how spoons, etc., can be appear to be bent using nothing but the illusions of magic sleight of hand and misdirection. This book is no place to indict either of these performers. I include them in my discussion only to indicate the parallel universes Wilcock discusses as an insightful basis for the possibility that their claims are valid.

Figure-Eight Flow in Detail

As described earlier in this book, figure-eight flow is consciousness sustaining full awareness of the One along with Individuality. The top of the figure-eight is considered to be the Presence of the One and the bottom the Presence of the One in evolutionary mode.

The following is my own interpretation. It helps me more imminently realize/feel the simultaneity of divine levels of Being operating in my momentary consciousness.

The center point of the top half of the figure-eight is the I AM Presence in its pure state of BEING; The circumference of the figure-eight up there is the Causal Body.

The center point of the bottom half of the figure-eight is the personal Christ/Soul. The circumference of the figure-eight down there is the time-space/space-time arena of the horizontal bar of the White Fire Cross.

The center nexus of the figure-eight positions the All-Seeing Eye of God as the Great Silent Watcher aligned with the activity of the Universal Christ/Oversoul All One; as well as the personal Christ/ personal Soul All One.

You can use this visualization to jump right into and through the flaming hoop of your divine out/inlook. By entertaining the feeling of Being all of these levels of consciousness at once, you can expand your conception of your here/now experience to a greatly expanded auric area, not just some nowheresville, nebulous point. This can pop you right out the confinement of a banal sleepiness into the a fiery, surging interplay spanning all space and time.

Here's Jon Rappoport's take on zoning like this:

> **"What I'm talking about here connects Zen, Tao, and other ancient practices that also ignore or give short shrift to creative force. When one is in the FLOW, he feels what is coming next, but at the same time he chooses what to create next. This paradox resolves by itself. He creates what he wants to, and he does it in such a way that it INSERTS into existing situations and realities, despite it being brand new.**
> **"FLOW. Creative flow. For the individual, this is a new world.**
>
> **"It replaces the world elites design for us, in which we fit in without the experience of FLOW..."**[87]

Free Energy Devices

Time-space/space-time-interface microclusters are also known to form quasi-crystals, which display a "gravity shielding effect and **may also be able to pull in energy directly from time-space.**"[88] In fact, scientists have used such substance to create free energy devices, but these have been suppressed by energy companies.

An Incident of "Lost Time"

Wilcock cites a remarkable real life example of how visiting the timeless realm is not only possible, but occasions of it are pretty much a certainty.[89] A National Airlines flight of a 727-passenger plane was on its approach to the Miami airport. At a certain time, its radar blip simply disappeared.

Big consternation!

All other planes and ground crew in the vicinity were directed to look for it. The plane was nowhere to be found. Then about ten minutes later, the plane reappeared and landed normally. The plane's passengers and crew were completely unaware that anything unusual had occurred! But all of the timepieces aboard the plane and passengers were ten minutes behind all of the others where they landed. In other words, the plane had hit a vortex which drew its focus out of the space-time realm into the time-space realm where "time" does not pass.

I find the most interesting part of this story to be that the passengers and crew were completely unaware of anything unusual happening. That, is, the temporal realm's shapes are composed not of spatially distributed waves, but of waves whose amplitudes, frequencies and phases were differentiated only "temporally," i.e., as the timeless/spaceless engrams of possibility. (Is your brain hurting yet?)

It is as if everyone on the plane went into a deep sleep, which they did not remember at all upon re-entering space-time. **In space-time, the plane never left the point at which it disappeared.** When it reappeared at that exact same place, only then did its space-time clocks continue onward through space's temporal flow, and amazingly, the watches of the passengers and the plane's clocks ended up ten minutes slow. Such time slips, or missing time, are usually blamed on UFO abductions. But it may well be that time-space vortices are sprinkled through space-time more densely than we have imagined.

Another interesting point this incident illustrates is that human consciousness as an agent of divinity carries on its processing of focused awareness independent of the realm in which that focus resides, be it space-time or time-space. For instance, we can remember time-space dreams in space-time and we can guide time-space meditation with space-time concentration. Yet, mechanical devices like clocks and watches cease to function in time-space. A way to conceive of this is that the passage of "time" in the time-space realm ceases because there is no space there to mechanically chalice its cascade.

Moreover, this incident illustrates that the parallel time-space/ space-time universes are truly parallel because time keeps marching on in space time, even when consciousness gets focused in time-space, where outer space-time matter focused there fails to operate as it does in space-time.

If the inner and outer universes were not independent/parallel, time would keep going in space-time when consciousness leaves it, as it did with this incident. But then when the plane rejoined space-time, the clocks in the plane would somehow jump forward to catch up to the then current space-time time. But they retained their time corresponding to when they left space-time with the ten-minute loss. So the two realms indeed function independently.

We have no problem understanding how a person's consciousness can go to sleep and wake at a later time. Such lost time happens every night for people. The big glitch in understanding in this case is how the plane and all of the time pieces seemed to have gone to sleep while space-time kept going along in time. It's as if those supposedly inanimate objects possess consciousness just like humans; and they could go to sleep, experience timelessness, and wake up later with lost time in space-time along with the human consciousness.

Maybe, if we could devise a way for us to sleep each night in time-space and also tuck our body in there, too, disappearing it from space-time, we could cancel the aging process for many hours a night. This plane incident seems to indicate that it is definitely possible. This may well be a good place for medical aging experts and partner quantum physicists to open up a whole new line of research.

Actually, pulling off events like this incident is old hat for high spiritual initiates. Remember, Jesus "disappeared from their midst" multiple times when the bad guys wanted to kill him. So all scientists would be doing if they could come up with a way to translate atoms and consciousness from space-time to time-space and back would be to accelerate an already extant process for people of lesser spiritual attainment. Maybe that would make it more available to more people, but there's probably a good reason that only high initiates are trained to do it. Only those who have proven that their only wish is to multiply divine Love should be endowed with the power to evade outer laws and interfere in other lives.

Another unanswered question is how did the physical bodies of the people fare in time-space? How is it that their physiology somehow kept going without damaging their space-time health while they were absent space-time? After all, the clocks stopped, so why shouldn't their bodies, too? How did all the people and the plane reconstruct upon reentry? I see this as confirmation of the point made earlier in this book that the entirety of the space-time universe flashes on and off as consciousness waves encounter the zer0-point cosmic mean twice every cycle—at zero and 180-degrees. We are coming and going between parallel universes all the time. We only seem to persist in our human imagery owing to the lagging nature of human consciousness. The flashing back and forth happens too fast for us to notice. So our outer dreamlike existence carries on without a flicker, like a movie film quickly projecting individual images.

We Live in a Consensus Time Line

Since many individual consciousnesses go in and out of the parallel time-space/space-time universes constantly, the space-time universe we visit is a consensus time line that all who share this life on Earth have agreed to. When members of other life wave consensuses exit and re-emerge into space-time, they share an entirely different time line and spatial blooming arena. For instance, the ascended masters relate to us that a very highly evolved civilization exists on Venus right now. We can't see it because it operates at a higher frequency than our perception can register. Thus, all is indeed consciousness based.

The Philadelphia Experiment

When I first read Wilcock's account of parallel universes enabling an inner type of outer expression that is invisible to our everyday perception, I thought of the so-called Philadelphia Experiment. This was supposed to have been conducted by the Navy in 1943. Its purpose was supposedly to cloak the space-time substance of a ship to render it invisible. Although this experiment has been proven to be a hoax,[90] some of its particulars relate well to archetypes Wilcock discusses wherein material substance can attempt to assume characteristics of the time/space-space/time interface or even to be translated between the parallel universes to jump time lines into the past or future.

I bring up this supposed experiment because one of the observations of its result is that some sailors were said to be stuck inside solid steel walls when the ship fully returned to space-time. That captured my interest in that it would be an example of the material experience world suddenly being forced into the softer micro-cluster realm of the parallel universe interface. I'm intrigued to contemplate such a possibility. (But I still don't try walking through walls without a door or window.)

Further Thoughts on the Nature of Space

No one knows, today, what really exists at a point in space. Think about that. It's the ultimate question for whose answer particle and quantum physicists are ever on the prowl.

For quite a while it was thought that space comprises points of substance called atoms. And these are said to consist of protons, neutrons, and electrons. But further scientific investigation and meditation has belied that conception, replacing it with a quantum realm in which nothing "exists" until an observer collapses a wave function comprising infinite possibility prior to its succumbing to a solid observation.

That is, God busies Him/Her Self in the time-space realm of infinite possibility, superimposing infinitely fine grained layers of consciousness sourced in a Being's Causal Body—and ultimately in the One Causal Body of the One I AM Presence. As discussed above, this mode of manifestation corresponds with the One experiencing Selfhood as Spirit form. Christ consciousness's point of decision is the time-space/space-time interface described above as the cloudy space of complex "atoms," called microclusters.

Across that plane of decision issues the Word, which is God as Christ proposing patterns of manifestation to soul. Soul, then can Artfully pronounce THAT Word, in the mode I AM THAT I AM. It is her perceptual posture that influences how closely she will follow the quality and texture guidelines Christ has wrought in time-space. Her decisions produce the nature of each point of consciousness/substance that tells His story (history) by configuring space-time *akasha.*

That is, soul alchemically "grasps" elements of infinite possibility as the building blocks of outer form consciousness. That their ultimate provenance is infinite means that seekers for them in space-time will remain infinitely baffled. There is no ultimate particle, no smallest space-time building block. The dream world we inhabit is entirely consciousness alchemically transforming itself.

Matter's Ultimate Building Block
Is a Moot Point

Since that last sentence may some day cost many materialists their jobs, I think some repetition is in order here. Physicists, quantum or otherwise, will never nail down the ultimate "building block" of spatial substance because none exists. "Existence" comprises the ongoing Self awareness of infinite possibility, which is driven by the Great Unknowing of infinite mystery. Its "building block" is all enfolding consciousness running in tandem literally with who-knows-what.

Free will observation is also an alchemical processing of consciousness. It collapses the probabilistic wave function of infinite possibility, but consciousness can perform the collapse in such a way that apparently separated entities composed of secondary energy are not formed. Collapsing the wave function I AM THAT I AM keeps it hooked up in tandem with infinite mystery. Such a collapse process produces forms that are absent but apparent.

Static, set-in-stone bad karma *maya* is formed when the wave function is collapsed and the question (infinite possibility) also disappears. Then this collapsed wave function object can only relate to others of the same ilk; others whose properties are fully knowable. And that defines death.

Life only exists when something remains to be hatched; when the Real object remains wrapped in a swaddling garment of Great Unknowing. That is, a Real, divine, image is formed when the wave function collapses but the Holy Ghost of its latent infinite-possibility-carrier remains. Thus anything Alive is a carrier of potential; it is not a *fait accompli*. So, a Real, living image is consciousness that builds its Art upon a substrate of basic immaculate *maya* that is focused both in time-space and space-time I AM THAT I AM. Performing this translation is what Christians call practicing the science of the immaculate concept. It involves planting basic immaculate *maya* in space-time so that consciousness can draw from the infinite potential of divinity there as a seed: a process that can **SEE D**ivinity.

In other words, the "substance" of a Real Image is Self awareness. It is not some "thing." It's the holographically arrayed magnetic attraction inherent in divine Love. Such magnetism attracts like a tuning fork stimulates resonant shapes at a distance. That is, mater form is ineffable magnanimity enfolding and mutually Self re-cognizing of its Spirit-form from the horizontal evolutionary realm I AM THAT I AM.

Evolving objects drawing Life from their corresponding spirit-form is the basis of what quantum physicists call nonlocality: simultaneously occurring action at a distance. Every so-called object IS its spirit form expression throughout all time and space. So nonlocality is not really "action" at a distance. It's resonant awakening at no-distance.

This also corresponds to consciousness that the Spiritual Hierarchy fractally comprises. That is, the shape of a state of consciousness is retained independent of the level of its inclusivity. "As above, so below" is an archetype that applies both vertically (to levels of the spiritual Hierarchy) and horizontally (to shapes within shapes).

Consciousness Is the Substance of Nothing

Many years ago, I often busied myself meditating upon living leaves. I wanted to know why/how substance appeared where the leaf displaced space while "empty" air filled space beyond its borders. What, precisely, is the difference between a manifest object and the space which contains it? Not to mention the empty space all around it.

I see now that there is no difference whatsoever. The leaf substance and its surrounding space are equally the pronouncement of God's choice of consciousness for THAT instant of time and THAT point in space—AS OUR INDIVIDUAL CONSCIOUSNESS HAS CHOSEN TO PERCEIVE IT. **The leaf substance and non-substance points are holographically equivalent. Each contains the fullness of the other.** The whole scope of our consciousness is present at every point of the *supposedly* variegated imagery. Visual "empty space" is not empty. Just as the Sanskrit word Kālá imputes oneness to time and space, their holographic nature imputes oneness to appearance and its lack.

I understand how hard this is to understand and assimilate—my own befuddled gray matter confirms this—so I will be trying explain it further in the next section below. But before that, I wish to look at the Art of living as it relates to that meditation which could never bring comfort to my mish-mashed mind those many years ago.

Inherent in consciousness is an awareness with the skill of perceiving some confection of time-space as an akashic personalized record in space-time. We, ourselves, are always creating the entirety of our consciousness, of our Self awareness, of our personalized Identity. Infinite time and infinite space are at our disposal. We ARE, in fact, God's alchemists.

Our perceived limitations arise out of the human habit patterns we have adopted as our personal realm of the possible.

Enlightened masters are humans who have extended their realm of the possible into the infinite Great Unknowing. These are they who have fully grokked "of myself, I can do nothing" and are blessed with the ability to always sustain that infinite stance.

Thus, the fine Art of living involves "acting" by allowing—allowing the One to disperse your sense of separation into Life's mysterious, infinite "core"—deconstructing the *maya* of false conception, by relaxing into the *maya* of primordially pure pristine awareness. In this way, golden inspiration will illumine to effervescence your perceptive realm wherever you ARE, including the dense human realm, which so many have polluted as the sodden depths of leaden mechanics.

Holographic Unity

The holographic nature of consciousness is the basis for the spiritual notion that all supposedly hard objects seemingly out there are illusions: not really "there." Niels Bohr, one of the original quantum physicists understood this well, as he explained, "Everything we call real is made of things that cannot be regarded as real." (Here, Bohr was using the word "real" to indicate outward, objectively hard matter.)

Every single solitary point of space radiates the fullness of the immaculate concept your Real Self expresses each moment of space-time. That is why, at core, every space-time Real Image is holographic. This comes about because *akasha* timelessly/spacelessly chalices All. Every piece of a Real Image contains all of the information needed to create the entire image.

Moreover, a*kasha*'s eternality and omnipresence characterize the configurations that compose the antahkarana's jeweled plenum of conscious Life as Spirit's *maya*. Composing spirit form's THAT, *akasha* brings about the spatial Web of Life's inherent holographic unity.

Likewise, the One's undergirding omnipresence subsumes the transient sense of mater form's spatial-temporal *maya* into its sensational mystery. We can imagine the One's nature as a vacuum cleaner that sucks all the separative walls out of a building, leaving a single room behind. It does the same to all of the items inside, removing their shapely borders, leaving only their essential nature behind.

Thus, Nothing ever displaces Anything.

That's Buddhist emptiness at its core. Do this as an exercise: hold a wad of nothing in your hand/mind and put it anywhere you wish. See it light up!

In consequence, fully realized Individuals wouldn't care to or dare to take the measure of any Being, for there is nothing Really there to measure them against. We're all graded on a sliding scale of greased lightning.

Each One portrays a uniquely flavorful plenum. Yes, we do well in our devotion to the Great Ones, such as Jesus, Maitreya, Gautama, Sanat Kumara...all the way up to our universe's twin flames Alpha and Omega and beyond. Yet, even though the spiritual Hierarchy and spiritual attainment do exist, in the final Truth, there is no such thing as a greater or lesser One. Only the One IS. **Surely, the greatness of the Great Ones is gauged by their humility.**

Coherence: Marching in Step

Each piece of a hologram is capable of reproducing its entire image. The bigger the piece, the higher its resolution, i.e., more detail that image expresses. That is, every point in a space-time image expresses the entirety of the moment's time-space conception, and that is why every element of the Real image coheres (hangs together) with all of the others. The coherence of the light enables every element of the Real Image to Truly reflect the entire nature of the One.

On the other hand, the light of maya's illusory secondary imagery is incoherent, like that of a regular lightbulb. Unlike the points composing the Real Image, whose coherence enables them to affirm I AM THAT

I AM, seemingly separated *maya*'s organizational construct is but that tale spoken of by Macbeth, told by an idiot, full of sound and fury, signifying nothing.

Horizontal Figure-Eight Flow
Translates Matter to Mater and Liberty to Freedom

Though spiritual freedom is available to space-time's tenants, we unavoidably navigate a terribly self-created sticky wicket down here. Tied to the wheel of birth and death by bad-karma glue, we stammer our forgotten lines in the Word's play and find ourselves subjected to the push-pull of seemingly uncontrollable perceptive habits. Until our vision in and as the One largely commands our awareness, we find ourselves alternating kicks against life's pricks with sowing seeds that sprout more and more sticker bush tangles upon our pathway. That misuse of her liberty lands soul in bad-karma jail cells. But this need not be. Figure-eight flow frees soul from that menagerie as its commanding Presence Agent simultaneously entertains viewpoints of the One and its diversity.

As soul conforms her consciousness to figure-eight flow, potentially deadly secondary-energy matter is translated to Life's sublime mater. When she victoriously accomplishes this, soul's liberty to choose Life is consummated and she enjoys her resulting freedom. Obviating bad-karma jail cells, she is thereby free to roam and explore light's illimitable precincts in joy.

Fun

Humans have conceived of the metadata they call time to describe the "ongoing" flicker of space's entirety on and off. That metadata is loosely thought of as a fourth dimension. But that is not rigorously so. Real Time *consciousness* is not ultimately measureable. Our measures of time only apply to the secondary energy space-time realm, and it doesn't apply to Real time even there.

Everyday time is nothing but a description of agreed upon physical effects. Even though we can measure a vibration we call time precisely, our experience of time is anything but consistent. *In consciousness*, the essence of all Life, "time" either plods or flies depending upon how much "fun" we are having.

"Fun" refers to the **fo**hat of **un**ion. That is, fun refers to an energy field caressing space into a zero-extension interface point. That is where space meets and KNOWS the parallel universe of inspirational potential's immaculate conceptions. At that point, time flies with infinite velocity.

We have been hoodwinked into thinking of time as a hard and fast measure of some sort. That's because we have arbitrarily chosen to correspond what we call seconds, hours, days, years, centuries as ranges of vibration of the electronic transitions between the two hyperfine ground states of caesium-133 atoms.[91] But that's not REAL. That simply caters to the human brain's need to place some semblance of order upon infinity's conceptions so that they appear to cascade. Yes, we wear watches, which more or less agree with one another about what time it is. But that only allows us to catch the bus when it appears at its stop. That notion of time is utterly incapable of capturing Time's provenance.

Making Time

I remember hearing one of the Beatles talking about how he was enjoying "chatting up a bird." That's Liverpool talk for making time with a woman. Sounds like naught but trivia; but think about that. When you are "making time," you are enjoying yourself—not just swaying a woman or man to your bent—but having any old kind of fun. And if you are involving your infinite provenance in that pursuit, your figure-eight flow is literally making time: manufacturing it along with its inner sense.

That infinitely flowing consciousness is producing instances of your space-time universe out of nothing. On the other hand, while you are not making time, i.e., inflicting Life with disdain, all you are doing is flopping around in space-time's illusionary, secondary energy jetsam. And it's a drag to be in drag. There, you are but lollygagging in outworn rubbish, when Really, you are sparklingly effervescent.

The singer Meatloaf knows all about the disappointments of trying to put together a loving relationship out of secondary energy building blocks. In his song "Two Out of Three Ain't Bad," he laments how he is wanted and needed but not loved. In another take on that secondary-energy predicament we are so prone to, Joni Mitchell's song "Woodstock" declares our unity with timeless origins yet we are "caught in the devil's bargain." You can free yourself from this sort of shillyshallying with illusion by relaxing into your Great Unknowing.

The flip side of Meatloaf's predicament is what Whitney Houston yearns for in her song "One Moment in Time."[92] She knows that her "fondest day is yet unknown," yet in the Great Unknowing she can find it every moment, independent of outer circumstance, in that entry point to the infinite, inspirational time-space realm (the Causal Body Garden). She longs to find her destiny there.

Remembering that "destiny" stands for "**D**eity **EST**ablished **IN You**," Houston is referring to her wish for soul in her outer life to inspirationally contact and dwell in her inner timeless perfection. She, like all of us, is meant to bring this about as she realizes divinity in her outer Artful Life imbued with free will.

As we now understand, the instantaneous Presence of your time-space, out-of-this-world perfection is imminently available. By meditatively practicing the Presence while going about your workaday business, you can feel eternity right in your space-time laboratory, where your destiny appears moment by moment.

As described above, an infinitude of spatial waves combines to produce the three dimensional shapes of the outer world. It's easy to visualize the forms appearing before you in space, captured at instants of time and progressing through time like a movie film. Not so easy to appreciate forms appearing before you in three dimensional "time," and delivered to outer consciousness through an infinite array of single points in space amounting to the Real Image overlaid with our personal versions of illusion.

Yet, wherever you find yourself, each point in space is arrayed with an infinitude of waves emanating from the time-space realm as engrams of the Causal Body inserted into space-time as soul's pallet with which, through her energetic Self realization, she "enacts" her Art to achieve victorious treasures in heaven. That is, the Causal body supplies the blueprints of individual identity through the Holy Christ Self; and, as soul expresses them as divine virtue the Causal Body radiates their Art as joy.

A Spiritual View of Building
In Three-dimensional Space

The masters characterize space in our ordinary outer realm of space-time as masculine and that realm's time as feminine. The arrow of time's one-dimensional Mother there acts like a birth canal channeling the blueprints of forms to be built in three-dimensional space. These completed forms would express the Father's Presence there.

Conversely, in time-space, time is masculine and space is feminine. The arrow of space's one-dimensional Father there acts like a birth canal channeling the forms built in three-dimensional "time," which expresses Mother's Presence. I confess that it is very difficult for my human brain to make any sense out of the previous sentence's reference to time as dimensions of form. I suspect that it may be throwing you for a loop, too. So let's demand some inspiration from our Higher Self.

First understand that Father stands for finality. Father IS; no ifs ands or buts. Every spatial image in three-dimensional space is a three-dimensional event catalogued in *akasha*. The Violet Flame can remove it from an individual's consciousness and from akasha's catalogue, cause, effect, record and memory. But in lieu of that, it is what it is—or was. Nothing finagles Father.

Mother force in three-dimensional space is the forcefully birthing urging which causes the feminine buildouts of Father's spatial image proposals to flip by like a movie. Mother's eternality sources the constancy of change in three-dimensional space. But it is important to understand that NOTHING is REALLY changing in three-dimensional space any more than it does in three-dimensional time. It is only the apparent flipping by of these images that infuses consciousness with the sensation of change.

Even when you are building something, and you think it is changing right up to its point of completion, nothing is really changing in 3D space. Each and every stage of the 3D "building" process is a point of completion, a point in one-dimensional time. The brainy sensation of treading a path to a greater goal is mere metadata, which our feelings partake of. The greater goal already exists in consciousness, which contains the Real situational reality. It is only the shortcomings of our addiction to the metadata of *maya* that requires certain outer accoutrements to be present for us to realize that goal. But I AM THAT I AM it is achieved NOW as an instance of infinite possibility.

The texture of Your Moments

Every space-time moment feels, say, serene and peaceful or bombastically intense or harmonious or jaggedly stressing, etc. When someone asks you how your day is going, they are requesting you to describe your impressions of the texture that your time-space forms have been realizing through your space-time alchemy. Each focal point of your consciousness brings together all of the vibrations you associate with your current point in space. These include the full spectrum of life qualities you have brought forward karmicly as well as the time-space Causal Body possibilities you script NOW in concert with your Higher Self. It also includes the qualities that God's angelic hosts carry about through you to bless and color your life; not to mention the slings and arrows of outrageous fortune you endure.

Your Experience Is Your Choice
Cleave to God-Control

The outer world matrix of space-time need not control your life. You need not be put upon by the unwholesome qualities of *maya*'s secondary energies. You can live primarily, by encouraging every divine virtue couched in your Higher Self to take its precedence in and through you. They are not somewhere else. They are here/now. Your life can assume the tenor of Archangels and Cosmic Beings, whose tones converge as the grace populating your chakras.

Your time-space realm of infinite possibility sources your power to run your everyday world as its CEO by drawing upon your imaginative power. Jon Rappoport describes this ever present boon:

> **"We re-learn to live through and by imagination, and then we enter and invent new space and time. But space and time aren't the superior forces. They operate and come into being at the tap of imagination."**

"I'm not breaking a system into parts. I'm not trying to teach a person how to tie his shoes. I'm talking about the proliferation of endless new worlds, not seen through a porthole, but imagined and invented."

"The EXPRESSION of imagination is the key. Instead of thoughts circling around aimlessly, you have projection out into the world. You make something that has never been made before."

"A metaphor for imagination might be warp drive. You skip ahead in space by huge leaps. It's not 1,2,3; it's 1,2, and then suddenly four thousand. You're not working by serial cause and effect."[93]

Courageously Take Your Stand
Upon the Precipice

Let me mention, in passing, the first story in his book *Labyrinths* "Tlön, Uqbar, Orbis Tertius," in which Jorge Luis Borges explores the sorts of nuclear explosions that occur in the finite mind when subjected to near direct contact with the time-space realm, which he labels Tlön. Read it to gain insight into the sort of precipice that consciousness stands upon when centered in the threefold flame.

The nature of this precipice and the mishmash that time-space makes of secondary-energy intellect is intimated in the following dust cover blurb on the Andrew Hurley translation of Borges' *Collected Fictions*:

"For some fifty years, in intriguing and ingenious fictions that reimaged the very form of the short story, Borges returned again and again to his celebrated themes: dreams, duels, labyrinths, mirrors, infinite libraries, the manipulations of chance, gauchos, knife fighters, tigers, and the elusive nature of identity itself. Playfully experimenting with ostensibly subliterary genres, Borges took the detective story and turned it

into metaphysics; he took fantasy writing and made it, with its questioning and reinventing of everyday reality, central to the craft of fiction; he took the literary essay and put it to use reviewing wholly imaginary books."[94]

Those themes of Borges are not just literary; they're literal. Ultimate divinity, infinite mystery, indeed, a great detective story, is not only the stuff of metaphysics but also the most intimate confluence of soul with the One.

The Causal Body, Your Divine Plan, *Maya,*
Your Treasures in Heaven: Your Eternal Victory
These Render the One Ever More Intimate
Right Here and Now

First, I wish to emphasize that you will derive a much deeper understanding of what I present in the following sections by reading two books The Summit Lighthouse publishes through Summit University Press: https://summituniversitypress.com.

- *Predict Your Future: Understand the Cycles of the Cosmic Clock*
- *Quietly Comes the Buddha: Awakening Your Inner Buddha Nature*

I mention these books only for completeness. Hopefully I will explain what I wish you to understand clearly enough here to obviate the need to read them to appreciate what I write. But they are foundational to the spiritual understanding your higher Mentors wish for you, so you would do well to avail yourself of them.

This section and the following five are like a play within a play. Take them as a very extended confidential aside to the audience. It comprises a mountain of grokking that will definitely not fit into the busybody intellect. I have needed lots of time to let it settle in; perhaps my whole lifetime and times before that. I hope you will make a similar investment; for, cashing in its chips will yield a deity's ransom of an expansively joyous return. Adopting the viewpoint imparted here can render the One ever more intimate.

My goal in this section is to impart an architectural vision of Life's masculine and feminine Agents/agencies acting to bring about evolution in and as the One: infinity transcending itself as your everyday life.

This is a more detailed approach to realizing how the basic immaculate *maya* and the *maya* of false conception are One.

The main point I will be making is presented at the end, but its supporting material is multifaceted. I hope you will find the gumption to fully assimilate it all to finally bathe in the conclusion's illumination.

The conclusion is something I have known about for decades. But the background material I have recently encountered has bonked me solidly enough to put some of my mental hangers-on to the guillotine.

So I'm sharing it all with you here so that our clouds of glory can unite in the magic.

It is important for you to know that some of the statements I will be making in this section arise from my own inner, meditative understanding. All of the concepts are based upon the teachings of the ascended masters, but some of the details and implications are my own. Also, be it known that I have not read most of the ascended masters' teachings released through Madame Blavatsky and the Theosophical Society nor those from the I AM Activity. So it may happen that the masters have given definitive teaching upon these subjects, and I am simply ignorant of them. So, having clarified that, let me begin.

"You" are an I AM Presence, configured as an in-divided facet of the One I AM Presence.

Surrounding the white fire core of your Presence, its centrosome, so to speak, are twelve spheres of light. These spheres, called the Causal Body, comprise two modes of Being. I am not aware of the masters telling us what a Causal Body looks like for a brand new individed I AM Presence. But, I suppose that it would likely consist of:

- A white fire core

- Five inner spheres of light, of a masculine/spiritual/yang polarity imbued with the Five Secret Rays. These Rays would carry the engrams (living shapes/forms) defining the I AM Presence's BEING, somewhat like the inner girders holding up a skyscraper.

- Seven outer spheres of light, of a feminine/expressive/yin polarity imbued with the Seven Rays. These Rays carry the latent engrams defining the divine intent expressed as that unique Presence's divine personality.

   I relate to the Causal Body engrams in this latent state like a script for a play or a film script. Every production of that script will be different, often radically so. The same lines may be spoken, and the same stage directions will be followed, but innumerable differences will characterize the result: location, stage props, facial expressions, tenor of the voices, etc., and, of course, the vision and skill of the director can make or break a play or film.

The same goes for the outer Artful free choice activities of soul.

Note well that the terms "spiritual" and "masculine" and "inner" and "yang" refer to the invisible, latent/unexpressed aspect of Life's state. The terms "matter/mater" and "feminine" and "outer" and "yin" refer to the visible/actively manifest, in the process of fulfilling or already fulfilled aspect of Life's expression. So the masculine polarity of the Secret Rays and the feminine polarity of the Seven Rays as described above apply only to the Causal Body, itself.

The I AM Presence along with its Causal Body are masculine spirit relative to its feminine, expressive nature in the Presence's evolutionary mode: its agents Christ/Soul. (I uppercase Soul when referring to Her ascended, immortal, or intrinsically pure state even when unascended. I lowercase soul in her unascended, almost always karmicly burdened, mortal state.)

Basic Immaculate *Maya*

Referring to the types of *maya* Keith Dowman describes, we can here view the latent engrams in the outer seven spheres of the Causal Body as the Tibetan Buddhist conception of the "basic immaculate *maya*." These are the possibilities of the divine plan made available to soul in the masculine time-space universe of the white fire cross's horizontal bar, where her Holy Christ Self presides. (I took some time to decide whether to say the Christ Self presides in His realm or simply resides there. I chose presides because your Higher Self is a commanding Presence, not just some joe-schmo hanging out there.)

Soul imbibes these patterns and Artfully expresses them in the feminine space-time universe of our everyday existence. As she dresses them in robes of divine virtue, they enfold themselves in the Causal Body to take their place as her treasures in heaven. (**I originally wrote here that the patterns rise back to the Causal Body, but the whole point of this section is that they never really leave the Causal Body. Outer and inner consciousness is One.**) In that form, they become what Tibetan Buddhists call the "*maya* of primordially pure pristine awareness." Thus Dowman writes:

> **"...the mother clear light (our natural dispensation)**
> **[also referred to as the basic immaculate *maya***
> **I've referred to as latent in the outer spheres of the**
> **Causal Body] and the son clear light (the individual's**
> **existential realization) [the Holy Christ Self] coalesce**
> **and the starting point is recognized as the goal."**[95]

Thus, as the masters say, we ascend daily (every cycle in which divine virtue is expressed). Having ascended daily so very often, the grand hurrah of the final ascension initiation is little more than a day in the Life for some high initiates.

Now I'm getting close to being able to make the point I have be shooting for in this section.

But first, realize that on the time-space side of the white fire cross's horizontal bar, the engrams of latent possibility that were considered to be feminine in the outer Causal Body spheres, here assume the masculine polarity and their form comprises three dimensions. That's because this is the unseen, night side of the manifesting universes: the Holy Christ Self's arena.

Then the space-time side of the white fire cross's horizontal bar, our workaday world, is feminine in relation to the time-space arena of the Holy Christ Self.

But...the Causal Body engrams of latent possibility assume the masculine polarity of the Cosmic Clock as soul activates them within the space-time realm of soul, while she alchemically traverses the cycles of outer precipitation in our everyday, walk-around arena.

Here, the engrams (the soul's projects) assume the energies of the Seven Rays as they first cycle through the masculine side of the Cosmic Clock on the 12-o'clock to the 5-o'clock lines. (Remember, I tried to incite you to read the book *Predict Your Future: Understand the Cycles of the Cosmic Clock* above, before starting this dissertation. This is largely where that would come in handy.)

This first half of the soul's work in the alchemical cycle of precipitation around the Cosmic Clock is masculine, since it is the invisible, inner activity of drawing upon etheric memory as divine intent followed by the production of a project's blueprints as thought forms. The last "masculine" line of the Clock (the six o'clock line) is actually a masculine/ feminine interface, in that on that line soul dips into the Divine Mother's coffers to draw out supplies, the building materials she will need to bring about the project's fully expressed feminine manifestation.

Then, in the feminine, emotional quadrant, soul engages the Secret Rays in the activity needed for Artfully building the project, guided by its masculine, mental blueprints. This is followed by the manifestation of the final physical form, which is also enervated by the Secret Rays.

The **amazing point** I wish to emphasize in this section is apparent here. The feminine energies that carry along the work on the 7-o'clock to the 11-o'clock lines of the Cosmic Clock are the five Secret Rays. In her book, *Quietly Comes the Buddha*, Elizabeth Clare Prophet delivers Gautama Buddha's teaching on the ten perfections, which characterize, two each, these lines of the Cosmic Clock.

Now, remember that these Secret Rays are precisely those comprising the innermost masculine arena of the Causal Body. Yet here, in the arena of manifestation, let me repeat: those Secret Rays carry the outermost feminine polarity. **Thus, full circle, Life's starting point and its ongoing outwardly, physically expressed goals are *in situ* carriers of the I AM Presence's identity.** That is:

INNER AND OUTER CONSCIOUSNESS ARE ONE

<u>THAT</u> Is the Whole Point of Consciousness

The big bad wolf of outer *maya* that spiritual seekers find so easy to denigrate just because it happens to be an illusory dream IS, in fact, just as Real as any other characterization of the One: only the One IS. It's up to "you" to realize that.

Don't Engage Illusion Collusion

It is only the training of our awareness, our habit patterns, which set apart the *maya* of false conception, that karmicly propounds us in illusion collusion wherein apparently separate entities are perceived and believed. The "original sin" of that habitual ignorance of the All's infinite, unitive provenance leads to all other criminality.

Do keep in mind ALWAYS the corollary to the One's imminence: What you do unto the least of these my brethren, you do unto Me.[96] No matter what you are up to, if it is not evincing infinite divine virtue, you will pay dearly for that divisive dirty doing at least tenfold as its karma gathers its whirlwind of like energy to return those multiplied dregs right to your doorstep.

It's important to repeat Dowman here:

> **[The]** *maya* **of our ordinary experience rests upon the structure that our intellect imposes. This is a diverse and complex system of concepts and beliefs that not only determines the quality and nature of our experience but also of the natural—seemingly external, world. This belief system and the** *maya* **of experience that it manifests, however, is never cloven from the vast expanse of compassionate clear light in which it arises. The '***maya* **of false conception' [reported by your outer everyday perceptions] and the 'basic immaculate** *maya***' of the natural dispensation [the Causal Body patterns] are one"** [97] **[My underline emphasis. If you still find that unacceptable, try writing down how much of the word "One" you don't understand.]**

Saying that the innermost Secret Ray identity of the I AM Presence and its Causal Body divine plan is one with the underlying energies of the outer *maya* you experience in your everyday, walk-around world are not just some nice sounding spiritual words.

The conception that "you" are far away from some high and mighty Presence up there in the high heavens is tripe.

> **"You" never leave your Causal Body to go off to do something. That "you" doesn't exist. It's pure fantasy. Only the One IS.**

The *maya* of false conception is…well…false, i.e., it's configured Truth, who's flashings never displace I AM. "They" ARE…I AM THAT I AM. If that's not what you seem to BE, it's only your perception that is off the mark, perception that will invoke your eventual return to the scene of the crime—or some vibrationally similar situation. Note that the word crime can be seen as: Covering Righteousness In Malignant Energy.

I love Keith Dowman's following description of the imminent paradox of nondual experience in everyday life:

> **The crucial point in this Dzogchen view is that**
> ***maya* is nondual experience. *Maya* is the starting**
> **point, which is our own circumstantial situation,**
> **our personal *samsara*, recognized as the ground of**
> **being out of which it arises. It is, therefore, also the**
> **path and the goal. *Maya* is the unitary container**
> **and the contents, the chalice and the elixir. This**
> **wholistic reality cannot be known by the intellect—**
> **only intuited or 'felt'. Unitary [figure-eight flowing]**
> ***maya* is aware of itself, intrinsically or spontaneously**
> **aware, and that awareness is intrinsic pure presence.**[98]

El Morya refers to unitary *maya* when he counsels us to attune to infinite mystery's most diaphanous efflorescence even in our everyday life:

> **"...it is necessary to feel how one should give oneself**
> **to the Highest Hierarch, in order that our being**
> **might be of benefit to the cosmic movement. Of**
> **course, motion may not be bodily at all, but spiritual,**
> **for you know that there are no boundaries between**
> **these domains."**[99]

Yes, indeed, the infinite IS right where you ARE: always. But your Self awareness of THAT is not on autopilot. You (soul) must kindle the fires of space and ride the lightning, all the while knowing that "you" are "doing" nothing. You ARE a meditative Life.

Anything less succumbs you to a case of somnambulism. Looking around with commonplace eyes denies the infinite vista I AM, and that definitely leaves you up *maya*'s creek sans paddle. El Morya would have you view your everyday ruminations like you would the Grand Canyon:

"You correctly recalled standing at the rim of the precipice, as if at an intensifying boundary. Only these crests of the waves will raise up the spirit and kindle it. But he who thinks of self, of self-affirmation, will never draw from the Eternal Fire. Thus, let us apply our striving toward spatial measures. I can hail you, mighty warriors, who are aware of the Phoenix rising from the ashes [reconfiguring consciousness to eschew <u>attachment to</u> the apparently differentiated entities of *maya* of false conception]."[100]

Indeed, drawing upon infinite, eternal fire even in its physical configuration casts you as a divine co-author, right there in league with God's laughing paradoxes. James Irby writes:

"The world is a book and a book is a world, and both are labyrinthine and enclose enigmas designed to be understood and participated in by man. We should note that this all-comprising intellectual unity is achieved precisely by the sharpest and most scandalous confrontation of opposites."[101]

Divine Love Resolves Paradox

A synonym for unitary *maya* is love. Sufi poet Hafiz puts it like this:

LAUGHING AT THE WORD TWO

Only

That Illumined
One

Who keeps
Seducing the formless into form

**Had the charm to win my
Heart**

Only a Perfect One

**Who is always
Laughing at the word
Two**

Can make you know

Of

Love.[102]

It takes but one touch of divine Love; One never to be forgotten. Yet, forget we do as we allow maelstroms of the commonplace to displace straight knowledge.

How to "Do" It
Sacred Labor Relaxation

The nonaction of a "you" acting somewhere seemingly out there **"allows cognitive relaxation into the primordial purity of the ground of being [the Great Unknowing] where primal awareness illuminates the delusory *maya* that is now immaculate *maya*."**[103]

ZZZZZZZZZZZIIINNNNNNNG

What becomes of that immaculate *maya* sings your Artful Soul. Your world glows within THAT Causal Body sphere of victory right here on Earth. Only the One IS!!!!!!! (If you see me jumping up and down, your eyes are not deceiving you.)

The spatial measures Morya refers to above are concentrations of the fiery One. It's commonplace for humans to mistake THAT consciousness for hard substance. Picture the gross materialist—maybe even yourself—pounding a table and screaming, "Ain't that there?" But Einstein has already put the lie to that with his $E = MC^2$. Thus that massive object is equivalently $M = E/C^2$. And the force pounding upon the object is written: $F = MA$. So that force is actually EA/C^2. Every term there is nothing but a descriptor for motion:

- E= energy. That is but motion; the hotter, the faster; the colder, the slower—unto zero motion at a temperature of absolute zero.
- A = acceleration. That is but the rate of change of motion.
- C = the speed of light, i.e., motion.

So all that hard stuff seemingly out there is just "something" moving. But what's moving? Can't be so-called atoms that seem to be so very hard. They have been proven to not only be almost entirely empty space, and the stuff of their supposed elementary particles has still not been found. All that's been found is more stuff we give names to, like quarks or strings or whatever the latest quantum theory may be presenting at the time. I suppose I can get an amen from the Holy Spirit about now.

Actually, what's moving is consciousness.

And consciousness is ultimately a focus of infinite mystery. Even the brain that you think enables you to think is but a collection of focused alchemical processes. So all that stuff you can stub your toe on "out there" is as empty as Buddhists claim it to be.

And the "you" who thinks it has a toe is just as empty as the one carrying on as that guy who admitted that of himself he could do nothing. Even so, both you and that guy host the Life everlasting.

If you really want to "get it," read Keith Dowman's take on the situation over and over and over until a wondrous "ah hah" hits you up-side the head:

> **"*Maya* is absent insofar as it lacks any substantiality as an ego, a soul or a 'Self.' It is non-existent, and likewise untrue and unreal. Yet it is still sensate, apparent, and visible. The force of contemplation upon absence is to nullify our inveterate propensity to conceive of substance in our perception of the external world and to 'feel' a separate individuality, a sense of self, in our inner lives and personality.**

Ego-loss is contingent upon recognition of this absence."[104]

That's a super "far out" (hippy talk) statement! To realize ego-loss, i.e., to transcend your humanly limited sense of who I AM, you need to not just ignore and all but vaporize the already nebulous "me" rummaging around in your body. But you need to do the same with all that stuff seemingly "out there," because it turns out that the "out there" is actually the "in here fantasy you" *maya*. That's right, Beatle Paul: Let it BE.

Dowman's advice exactly mimics the force of Sri Ramana Maharshi's technique for integrating consciousness with infinite mystery: simply asking "who am I?" And finding within the beyond-vibrational answer.

Perhaps the most far reaching implication of this is to rip away a commonly held belief of many, if not most, spiritually oriented people: that there is some Reality "out there" that is covered over with illusory substance, which must be stripped away so that Reality can shine unencumbered. But:

NOW HEAR THIS: NO PRISTINE REALITY IS SITTING AROUND "OUT THERE."

Reality is an inside job. Its mystery will foil Dick Tracy and any other gumshoe stuck in the *maya* of false conception's sense of separation.

I've Already Covered the Following
In This Book. But It's So Important That
I'm Going to Beat This Point to Death

Everything you perceive, everything you ARE, is not "there" until you put it there by establishing a resonant spectrum of standing waves in your consciousness/being.

Please stand aside and get this now: all that out there stuff is nothing but some perceptive standing waves you—li'l ol' you—have set up in your brainy consciousness.

Your free will and God's Will acting are One energy force field. If you set up a resonance that is foreign to God's will, it remains with you as an attachment—as bad karma. If you express divine virtue, it remains

144

with you as a radiant sphere of your Causal Body. In either case, it stays with "you." **It never left you in the first place**!

True: your bad karma must be balanced to "clean up your act." But that cleanup does not operate "upon" some "thing" out there called bad karma. Your bad karma and your consciousness is the same. That's why you are so indelibly responsible for it. As you realign your consciousness to conform to Your God intents, You, in and as God-Justice, alchemically convert/transmute your spiritual/material form to a mode of consciousness more capable of expressing Your living, breathing I AM THAT I AM as divine virtue.

The ascended masters teach, for the sake of normal everyday humans, that bad karma is substance that resides in what they call the "electronic belt." But, again, the bad karma is not a "thing" sitting somewhere out there away from you. Its overall effect is shielded from you out of mercy and out of God's own enlightened Self interest. He/She doesn't want to lose "parts" of selfhood any more than those apparent parts want to give up the Ghost.

The Mercy of the Great Karmic Board

The electronic belt is more like a bunch of accounting entries in a bookkeeping system that the ascended masters and Cosmic Beings known as the Keeper of the Scrolls and the Great Karmic Board maintain. This system enables the various modes of the sense of separation that you have invested your consciousness in to energetically become available *to your resonant awareness* a little at a time so that your human processing system can continue to function. You would be overcome with an avalanche of chaos if you had to deal with it all at once.

Again, your bad karma is not being returned to you from somewhere else. It is already associated with your being. Unascended masters who have already transmuted most of their bad karma can "thread the eye of the needle" and find themselves much less limited by the density of bad karmic energy debilitating them.

Some are so aligned with light that they can "walk through walls," i.e., penetrate dense substance with impunity. Remember how Jesus sometimes "disappeared from their midst"—poof! If you are not such a master, you painfully bump into density because your dense bad karma is right there, fully intertwined with your bloated consciousness.

ALWAYS. ALWAYS. ALWAYS. Only the One IS.

Just thinking of your bad karma as something that is not you that resides somewhere out there separate from you amounts to just so much more glue that ties you to the wheel of birth and death.

The Zen of it is that even though your bad karma must be balanced by invoking God's fires with the science of the spoken word or through direct service or meditational world service, the consciousness that was invested in the bad karma gets realigned within you as an alchemical process.

It is important to understand that your bad-karmic misaligned resonances are not energy that left you and will someday show up on your doorstep for redemption. You are NOT a convict on a chain gang pulverizing karmic rocks out there on the ground into nothingness so their substance can magically become light enough to float up to some receptacle. That jingle-jangling never left; **AND** it never really existed as *separated*, "out there" substance! Well, okay, yes, it's "out there" all right; but only in the sense that it is not permanently "in with Flynn": singing harmoniously in and as the entire Spirit of the Great White Brotherhood.

Bad-karmic patterns are, and never were, anything but illusion. Bad-karmic patterns are not divine virtue and will never occupy the Causal Body; period. The Real essence of bad-karmic energy *already IS in the Causal Body!* What *will* occupy the Causal Body, once its spectrum is alchemically realigned to divine virtue, is a radiant "treasure" having no resemblance to the illusory bad-karmic phantasms that once polluted the form of your lifestream as screwballs in your electronic belt.

Saint Germain clarifies this in His description of the spiritual Path:

> **"You cannot enter into and obtain your freedom...**
> **through placing your attention upon human discord**
> **and the patterns of imperfection...[or] through a mere**
> **state of surcease from outer distress....you must be**
> **able to enter into the heart of your eternal freedom...**
> **[to] place [the] attention upon the great light and...**

not direct [the] attention away from that to other things....By putting your attention upon your God Self, you are obtaining your identity; by putting it upon your human self, you are losing that identity.... in this process of the dying of the outer self (the old man with all of his corruptness and inequities), man comes to a state where there is a very dim coal-spark of the sacred fire remaining within him which itself seems almost to be extinguished. It is so tiny, so miniature! And yet it is real. Then gradually this tiny atom-spark of light begins its mighty power of Christ-expansion in the folds of man's being.... it moves into the temple of being, gilding all with a touch of God's golden radiance....[Eventually,]No longer confined to the mere eyes of earth, man possesses the dual faculty of seeing[, hearing, knowing] outwardly and within."[105]

That spark which Saint Germain refers to as the divine spark is never absent. As your threefold flame, it empowers what Dowman calls the "basic immaculate *maya*," which I refer to as engrams of your Causal Body, anchored in your time-space Christ Self. That flame of God is never displaced by misused attention. By sustaining your attention upon that inner light, and by God's grace accelerating its frequencies with Violet Flame, you reclaim/redirect the misdirected consciousness which is given the label bad karma.

As your attention shifts back to its I AM Selfhood, that karmic *misinterpretation* of your Real Self, which was Really never anything but your immaculate Identity, is glorified and it shines.

You can see and feel the light in the eyes of those who have, even in some small measure, accomplished this. These are they who are called light bearers, who have achieved some measure of balance in their threefold flame of love, wisdom and power.

Saint Germain goes on to encourage us to declare:

**"I will sustain the glory of life within my being
I will win my ascension
I will forsake all idols and**

I will forsake the idol of my outer self
I will have the glory of my immaculate divinely
conceived Self manifesting within me"[106]

Can you see then, how asking God to make you One with Him/Her is a tad silly? Your Real Self never, ever went on vacation. In whatever manner you may have mangled your consciousness by misdirecting your attention to a supposedly outer realm separate from yourself, your divine spark was and is always, infinitely One. And the jingling and jangling of bad karma never WAS.

Misusing the Law of Attraction as False Hope

Misdirecting your attention, creating bad karma, is like misusing the law-of-attraction/hope to affirm that there is something you do not have: that you want. That is, that there is something missing from you that you wish to attract to you. Again, and again, and again: The Real You *is* and never *was* and never *will be* anything but One inseparable from whatever notion you may have temporarily decided that "you" are.

You are not One *with* God. There is no "with" involved. Only the One IS.

The alchemy of soul ascension involves *resonating* soul spectra with Christ—I AM consciousness that already IS. Victorious alchemy involves right decisions to rivet your awareness to the divine plans you already are and allowing grace to embellish them as Art. Allowing your awareness to slip slide into illusory, static producing netherworlds doesn't "create" anything separate. The bad karmic "substance" that afflicts you is a magnetism which is associated with you, and which draws more of like vibrations to you. That is, you sow winds of magnetically attractive spectra and likewise reap their whirlwinds.

Think of karma like a troupe of a hundred dancers. Most of them may be getting the choreography right, but some may be dancing out of step. Nevertheless, the out-of-step ones are still up there, part of the troupe. They aren't shaved off and put somewhere in a heap. And when they do perform correctly, it will still be the same troupe up there performing.

More Science Regarding
There Is No "Out There" Out There

As you are well aware by now, I have lovingly beat to death the concept that there is anything which exists as a separated "out there" out there. This is so important that a whole library of books and scriptures have already been written about it. So now I wish to add a few dollars to the two cents I have already shared about that; this time getting a bit deeper into quantum mechanical thinking.

The following is inspired by chapter 6 of Ervin Laszlo's book, *Science and the Akashic Field*: "The Phenomenon of Coherence: A Deeper Look at the Scientific Evidence." I think I have already come close to exhausting my available "fair use" of that book, so I will be paraphrasing. I hope I don't mangle Laszlo's wonderful presentation too badly. (You would do well to buy his book; he deserves a few of your shekels for the illuminative service he has rendered us by writing it.)

Coherence is a scientific property of light and matter that decomposes the sense of separation. Saying light or supposedly separate entities or events are coherent imputes Oneness to the state of consciousness they embody and express. Coherence has been observed experimentally so often that, in my opinion and that of very well respected quantum physicists, it obviates the scientific need to pay obsequious homage to the supposedly real world "out there."

Amit Goswami describes how Niels Bohr completely discounted the need to know what a particle is "in-itself." Eugene Wigner asserts that quantum physics deals not with observables but with observations. Werner Heisenberg also threw out the notion of an atomic or micro-particular world structure.

Indeed, Heisenberg was so stunned by the implications of his own uncertainty principle that he publically concluded: **"The world is built as a mathematical, not as a material, structure. In consequence there is no use asking to what the equations of mathematical physics refer—they do not refer to anything beyond themselves."**[107] And I would add !!! to that.

Others, including David Bohm, have entertained the notion of a quantum potential, "Q," which influences how particles act and react. I have already referenced this potential as the time-space Presence of the Holy Christ Self. This "implicate order" expresses as a holofield, which has been referenced for thousands of years as the akashic field. This arena contains all possible states of the quantum arena, and the order arising there—along with the soul's free will—entirely removes the notion that matter is a random gadabout machine that just happens to bring about consciousness as an afterthought. I actually find it embarrassing that many well respected humans hold to that latter opinion.

Laszlo justifies introducing the akashic field into the scientific arena by documenting facts regarding the following areas of experimentation. I wish I could share more about these with you here, but "fair use" prohibits that. Thus I again strongly suggest that you obtain Laszlo's book. I attest that while it has not delivered any new spiritual insight to me, it has definitely deepened my grok of that which I have already known. Here are the areas Laszlo explicates:

- The fine tuning of various scientific constants necessary to bring about matter.
- Coherence in the quantum world.
- Coherence in the Universe.
- Coherence in the living world.
- The "horizon" problem.
- Microwave background radiation.
- The evolution of complex organisms. Laszlo shatters Darwinian notions to smithereens.
- Coherence in Consciousness.
- Transpersonal connections.
- Transcultural connections.
- Telesomatic connections. Consciousness in one person (such as a healer) affecting the body of another.

Regarding all of the above, Laszlo concludes that "A-field [akashic field] in-formation is the logical explanation of nonlocal coherence...this universe is so well tuned that in all essential respects it is both instantly and universally interconnected."[108]

As I said above, Laszlo's book has importantly deepened my

understanding of spirituality from a scientific perspective. So now I wish to summarize that:

Quantum physicists say that you cannot predict what something is until it actually comes to be. Everything, from a quark to our whole universe and beyond is an instant of consciousness. It did not "grow" to be what it is, based upon so-called laws of external, secondary energy growth. The entirety of the One IS what it IS moment by moment. Past, present, future do not exist. All consciousness is a momentous affair. That's why enlightened masters emphasize spontaneity in their approach to Life.

Only our viewpoints change and seem to "proceed," seem to "grow." But that "growth" is instantaneous Self transcendence. Each apparent moment focuses a timeless expression. Those moments seem to flow, to cascade, at the urging of infinite mystery, which is always asking "Who AM I NOW?" Consciousness IS the One, and only the One IS. Small "l" life is but a dream speculation re the One Real Image. The universal constants used to describe that image capture the nature of a universal Allness that expresses as quantum jumping transcendence.

The Certainty Principle

I relate to the Heisenberg Uncertainty Principle regarding consciousness as an understanding of what people mean when they say "it moves me." Performances like songs or films or dance or art engage the person's consciousness in a "chemical" reaction that changes their identity. They are "moving" from one Self reflecting state to another. Awareness focuses on the reaction's motion, the feeling of change. Settling upon any particular momentary state is out of the question.

Moreover, meditating upon a single concept or image produces a state of the One in consciousness, and that voids the possibility of conscious motion—for, as the One, awareness hosts no breakdown into component parts among which to move. So motion and positional state are mutually exclusive.

Where the Heisenberg Uncertainty Principle no longer applies is figure-eight flow in which infinite mystery IS both momentum and the whole moment's state of the One simultaneously. And no observer exists.

I call this the Certainty Principle, for in and as such divine awareness, infinite mystery is downright certain that I AM. Therein it eats paradox for breakfast, lunch, dinner, and snacks.

The Mighty Quinn

Time for some fun.

You can hang out in your hoodwinked soul creations for oh, so long. But eventually you must entertain the immanent Presence of your Real Self, your Holy Christ Self, right here in your space-time milieu. The figure-eight flow of soul acting in tandem with her consort is out-of-the-box, often awe inspiring activity that reminds all who witness it that Life is not mere dependency.

This is described most unexpectedly in the pop song "The Mighty Quinn," written by Bob Dylan and popularized by Manfred Mann. It is just about impossible that either Dylan or Mann see what I impute to its lyrics. Nevertheless, I think they entertained angels unawares. (Below, I will only comment on a few verses, but the song can be heard at https://www.youtube.com/watch?v=K13hH0pJx5s).

Also, I have not been able to get Bob Dylan's agent's permission to publish direct quotes from the song. So I will only refer to the verses and not include the actual quoted words. The verse being referred to will be obvious from what I am saying. The lyrics can be found here: http://www.metrolyrics.com/quinn-the-eskimo-lyrics-bob-dylan.html

I am still including my analysis of the song here without the lyrics because it amazes me how spiritual archetypes can appear in trite pop music. I find it fascinating how they hold together throughout all the verses in many Dylan songs.

I relate to the Mighty Quinn as the Holy Christ Self. I speculate that Quinn was chosen for His name because Quinn is a root that refers to the number five. Thus His energy relates to that of the five Secret Rays. The chorus invites consciousness to appreciate the Presence of those divine Rays both in their placement as the innermost Rays of the Causal Body and their activity as the outermost rays bringing about the manifest worlds. Indeed, the secondary energies of ordinary consciousness would never see anything like those Rays. That's why they're called secret.

Also, Quinn is said to be an Eskimo. Strange. Why would it be so significant for an Eskimo to be showing up all over the place? My take: Spirit is usually associated with the North, the night side of Life, inward and cold with respect to the outer friction-generating motion that characterizes the day side of life. So it makes sense that your inner Higher Self hails from the North and could be called an Eskimo. Otherwise, that reference is but insignificant pop nonsense.

The first verse talks about the random, hapless activity people so often engage. Verse two points to ordinary consciousness, caught in the *maya* of false conception's morass, which despairs until that energy is transmuted into joy by joining the **OM** to You.

Then part way through the next verse we're told how magnetically attractive infinity's engrams can be. And when those Christic engrams are focused in matter, the forces of nature and her agents, symbolized as pigeons, flock to mirror them, as above, so below.

Feeding pigeons on a limb symbolizes the secondary energy that soul pushes around in outer awareness, which feeds its forms by focusing attention upon them. Secondary-energy *maya* of false conception is like those pigeons on a limb snatching energy from whatever happens to be going by. But when Real contact with infinity appears, God's will strongly directs outer energy to leave off from its petty, matter concerns and conform to it.

In the outer realm, where everyone's into this and that, they're "stepping on" each other like CB operators not following chatter protocol. The energy's pretty much a chaotic mix up (that old tale told by an idiot). It takes effective spiritual practice to consciously get from the waking state to the inner Spiritual realm where we go during sleep. But when you skillfully invite your Christ Self to take over your com channels, then operating from Reality, even in broad daylight, can be a *fait accompli*.

Not being able to "get no sleep"—to go within to Reality—also harkens to astral *maya* capturing the attention like siren songs luring soul into its secondary-energy outer prison cells. Those alluring outer forms and activities grasp consciousness like super glue. It is so very hard to cut attention free from that involvement, says the song, because there's "someone on everybody's toes."

Granted, pop music usually talks trash or just sticks to surface miscellany. And without the above Spiritual insight, this song would remain but a bit of such fluff. But with writers like Dylan at the helm, spiritual Archetypes often have their say anyway.

Keep Your Sanity

Oft quoted is the anonymous saying, often falsely attributed to Euripides, "Those whom the gods wish to destroy they first make mad." The first step toward madness is to base your life upon the shifting sands of *maya*'s secondary energy, invested in meaningless tales told by an idiot.

Real Gods and Goddesses certainly don't want to make anyone mad. But if they were to desire to, all they would need to do for unenlightened mankind is to send an imp or two to hoodwink the victim through temptation, as C. S. Lewis so humorously describes in his book *The Screwtape Letters.* Resistance to temptation is not a strong suit for most of humanity. So we would all do well to eschew forthwith the real original sin: the disobedience to inner sense (innocence) producing the sense of separation from the One. Temptation has no power over such a unified Being. It cannot lure One so blinded by the light.

Remember, also, that we have already taken this line of thought further down the line. We have realized that you may let your attention set upon those illusory secondary forms that are the *maya* cackling about like a chicken looking for a nest to bring herself some comfort while she lays her eggs. Yes, you can take in the whole kaleidoscope. But still, that pile of feathers and motives and all the rest of the falderal is One. It IS You. BUT…it's up to you to interpret it correctly.

The problems, the sufferings only arise when you adopt false conceptions about them and irresponsibly claim they're not You because you don't like their shape or activity or some such. That's when the trap can swallow you up; when it can make you foreswear their manifestation. Such recognition of them, even to call them bad, sets them apart by entertaining the sense of separation. Don't do it. If it's there, it's you. Take responsibility for it and transmute it if you don't like it. Enfolding all in light is the only True Way. Name calling just seals your own Name in cahoots with the name being called out. It's similar to a diplomat recognizing another nation as sovereign. But the illusory separated-entity gaggle is no more sovereign than the sovereigns in Davy Jones' locker; deep dark down and destitute.

Obviously, the world's evils must be stopped and righted in the scales of God-Justice. Equally obviously, you cannot personally take them all on, yourself. But recognizing evil as an assault upon Your own body and consciousness, assuming the age of responsibility, empowers you to engage the light requisite to bringing about its healing. (Specific techniques for accomplishing this are beyond the scope of this book. By far the most potent tool for righting depravity is the science of the spoken Word: decrees, as taught in most recent times by The Summit Lighthouse.)

Now, I wish to depart for a bit from spiritually describing the composition of consciousness and take a more scientific approach. I was gratified to learn about what follows, myself, and have adopted this insight into my everyday outlook.

All Is Consciousness
The Higgs Field Signals That
The One Is Present and Accounted For

You may find this section a bit challenging because it may cause some of your brain cells to overheat if you are not of a scientific bent. But puhleez endure. The work will be rewarded with insight. And that will be physically grounded insight, not just woo-woo flights.

I know you probably sit around all day twiddling your thumbs, wondering how manifestation can ever come about in the space-time realm that Buddhists insist is naught but emptiness. After all spirit is massless; and its presence, which supposedly gives rise to everything, must somehow get transformed into energetic perceptions that can convince us to pound upon a table and claim that it is hard and that it is right "there" in front of us, completely devoid of balderdash.

It seems that physicists are such people. They won't stop their twiddling and fiddling until they can come up with explanations that satisfy their ingrown cravings. So, in 1964, a chap named Higgs came up with a couple of concepts that got the physics crowd to settle down a bit. These are the Higgs field and the Higgs boson. (I forbid you to come up with any Bozo jokes right here and now.)

Here is the only science jargon I intend to inflict upon you relating to how stuff appears out of nothing. Thanks to Simple Wikipedia, we can read:

"The Higgs field is a field of energy that is thought to exist in every region of the universe. The field

is accompanied by a fundamental particle known as the Higgs boson, which is used by the field to continuously interact with other particles, such as the electron. Particles that interact with the field are "given" mass and... will become slower as they pass through it. The result of a particle "gaining" mass from the field is the prevention of its ability to travel at the speed of light.

"Mass itself is not generated by the Higgs field; the act of creating matter or energy from nothing would violate the laws of conservation. Mass is, however, "given" to particles via the Higgs field's use of Higgs boson particles. Higgs bosons contain the relative mass in the form of energy and once the field has endowed a formally massless particle, the particle in question will slow down as it has now become "heavy".

"If the Higgs field did not exist, particles would not have the mass required to attract one another, and would float around freely at light speed. Also, gravity would not exist because mass would not be there to attract other mass."[109]

So, now let me encapsulate the above Higgs-field talk paraphrasing concepts taken from Ervin Laszlo's book *Science and the Akashic Field: An Integral Theory of Everything:*

- The Higgs field is omnipresent in the universe.

- Particles, which signal manifestation, must possess mass, but prior to Higgs' theory, it was far from clear how mass could come to exist out of nothing. Laszlo says that the mass a particle "acquires is proportionate to the strength of the Higgs field times the strength of their interaction...Without the different varieties of Higgs field there would be nothing for us to observe in the universe, nor would we be here to make the observation."[110]

- Thus, the mass of the particles in the universe is derived from them passing through the Higgs field and thereby having Higgs bosons somehow impregnated upon or in them. It is said that these bosons are only energy, and that they do not actually create mass. That implies that what we call mass is actually more woo-woo than what is usually considered hard and fast substance. Of course, Einstein's $E = MC^2$ implies the same thing. This lends substantial weight (pun intended) to the idea that *all* is consciousness. When you stub your toe or get hit by a 30-30 slug, you are merely participating in an illusory shadow show. (Of course, that doesn't help the pain at all; but at least your inner philosopher can offer you some comforting compensation.)

- There exists a specific value for the intensity of the Higgs field which signals the lowest energy level for that region of space. The amazing aspect of this is that one would naturally think of the lowest energy level somewhere to correspond to a field intensity level of zero. That the Higgs field's value is non-zero for the lowest energy/activity level carries spiritually profound implication.

Physicists are coming to understand that information, such as that carried by *akasha*, is a more fundamental aspect of the manifest universe even than energy. (And in space-time, nothing is more informationally fundamental than the plenum of white fire cores signaling infinity poking its nose into human matters.)

I conclude from the above that:

- The nonzero intensity Higgs field, corresponding to the lowest, quiescent energy level of a region of space, signals that **consciousness is present even where there is no external activity.**

- The information which that omnipresent consciousness conveys at the lowest energy level of **the Higgs field corresponds to the presence of basic immaculate *maya* waiting to be transformed into Art: into primordially pure pristine awareness.** That is, the nonzero level of the Higgs field at its lowest energy level corresponds to the presence of the white fire cores that are projected from the spiritual time-space realm into the material space-time realm of our everyday experience. These impart the divine potential invested in human free will.

- The all-pervading presence of the Higgs field signals the plenum known as the antahkarana. This holographic field connects everything to everything else. Physics terminology for this is that as the Higgs field increases its intensity, coherence increases. That is, more supposedly separate "things" become more strongly linked to each "other."

- The Higgs boson is a packet of energy that somehow adheres to massless particles, imparting "relative mass" to them, thereby slowing them to less than light speed. That enables them to crystalize into relationships of divine virtue. I interpret the Higgs boson to be a packet of Holy Spirit that imparts intelligent activity to consciousness. When a master blesses you, it's like giving you a pay-day loan of a Higgs boson or two. That blessing gets repaid in and as the One when that cycling consciousness becomes figure-eight flow, multiplying the light of the Individual Causal Body in both the giver and receiver of the blessing, both of which are intrinsic to that of the One.

Those are the neato cool insights I promised at the start of this section. Though they don't state it in these terms, some scientists now accept that **an all-pervading consciousness impels information (immaculate conceptions) into manifestation.** Most are not yet ready to dive in and experience the inner spiritual realm that proposes those informational building "blocks" of divine virtue to soul. Yet, some of today's more avant-garde scientists are at least willing to admit their presence into their musings as something more substantial than a Holy Ghost.

PART FOUR

Living the One's Viewpoints

Ours is a wondrous opportunity to access God in the Highest even while right here on Earth. The White Fire Cross symbolizes the living Presence of God right within you right here and now. That cross is associated with God's Eighth Ray, the ray of integration.

That is, the very structure of your Being IS the integration that produces heaven in earth. Spirit and mater are One. Basic immaculate *maya* and the *maya* of false conception are One. Only the One IS.

Nevertheless, the apparent activity of divine purpose abounds. If you don't believe that, just take a couple of citified golden retrievers to the ocean in the back of a van. Then open the door onto that great salty expanse. Then watch those canine rockets launch. No Marine ever ejaculated HOOWAHH any stronger than that. Or sit for some months watching a sprout push itself up through tar or even concrete. Or watch the Olympics or look at an author sitting in front of a blank page.

Quest IS; even as the One IS.

As we understand now, the time-space arm of the horizontal bar of the White Fire Cross opens upon an infinity of other worldly occasions, which can pop up into our consciousness, each a greater or lesser attractor wooing our free choice to a joyous tryst. As Werner Heisenberg put it: "[T]he atoms or elementary particles themselves are not real; they form a world of potentialities or possibilities rather than one of things or facts." When Jesus said that He was the open door which no man can shut, He was divulging how intimately available the time-space/space-time interface is to all of us.

Here, in this book's Part Four, I will offer insight into the sort of experience we can enjoy by consciously accessing our inner viewpoint and fulfilling it outwardly in our everyday life. In short, to practice Tibetan Dzogchen, by whatever name you wish to place upon it.

But before I explore the spiritual Path in greater detail, it will be useful to lay some foundations that are applicable to all spirituality. To illustrate how universal the Path is, I'll be drawing parallels between two highly divergent sources.

Spirituality 101
Basic Viewpoints of the Spiritual Path

Many ethnic so-called spiritual practices are found in Earth's cultures. Some of these are ultimately counterproductive. They misguidedly concentrate upon manipulating inner energies to control other people or forces of nature. Contacting lower invisible planes and employing their energies and inhabitants for human purposes is problematic in that it ties the practitioners to beings who have not earned their immortality, which is to say that they have not wholly centered themselves in divine Love.

In this book, I have shown how people adopt myriad points of view. To obviate spiritual detours, it is useful to point out a compendium of viewpoints known as the Higher Way, which is common to all true spiritual Paths. Thus I here discuss the basic spiritual teachings of the mahatmas and ascended masters, who began the Theosophical Society and continued their service through the publication of El Morya's Agni Yoga books, the I AM Activity and The Summit Lighthouse, even to the present.

I compare these with viewpoints that Celtic shamans have embraced to commune with higher spiritual Beings and forces in purity. This will provide a foundational view of spiritual life that succinctly describes viewpoints of the universal spiritual Path which remain free of specific religious dogma. Comparing this insight with El Morya's straight knowledge sets each of them off in a complementing, illuminative light. This can further understanding in a manner that many people may find more easily accessible.

I know that there may be some who would take issue with my comparing what I consider the highest spiritual teachings publicly available today (El Morya's Agni Yoga teachings) with any variety of shamanism, which is often associated with egoic manipulation of natural forces to bring about highly biased human effects—even the derogatory nature of witchcraft. To this, I simply say that any teaching can be misused. I have found much in the Celtic approach to spirituality that is worth embracing.

Shamanism is an umbrella term including a widely divergent class of spiritual practices. The major difference between it and the work of the ascended masters is that true shamans are largely concerned with living on Earth attuned with nature and alleviating human, earthly concerns and conditions. The ascended masters concentrate more upon helping individuals to graduate from their humanity—tied to the wheel of birth and death—to permanently realize their immortality.

That said, many correspondences bridge Middle-Age Celtic

shamanism with the teachings of the ascended masters. It's wrong to think that shamanism is uniquely applicable to long ago or just to forest or jungle dwellers or to far off ethnic folk. Its highest and purest precepts for contacting higher divine realms and drawing their energies into daily life are applicable to all today.

While shamanism is highly dedicated to attunement with nature, El Morya's teachings re spiritual Heart often run in parallel:

> **"How many of the ills of humanity are due to insufficient cooperation! The understanding of cooperation readily brings one to cooperation with the forces of nature. Where is the boundary between the forces of nature and spiritualization? The servant of the spirit must attain spiritual omnipresence."[111]**

In the comparisons below, I use **CS** to denote the precepts of Celtic Shamanism and **AM** for those of the ascended masters taken mainly from El Morya's Agni Yoga book *Heart* along with my own understanding.

- **CS**: It is so easy for people to take the hard and fast outer world they traverse as the only reality. But other realms do exist. And they are available for exploration to humans who embrace the spiritual quest.

  AM: Realms and dimensions that soul can travel to and experience include that of the I AM Presence, the Holy Christ Self, the retreats of the ascended masters in the etheric plane. As souls adopt the viewpoints of higher Beings in everyday life, they can draw upon the gracious blessings of Beings composing the entire Spirit of the Great White Brotherhood throughout the spiritual Hierarchy.

  As we have seen throughout this book, the cosmic cross of white fire is a metaphor for the two-way street of communication between the inner and outer manifest realms of consciousness. Saint Germain is said to have responded to a student who asked when He was going to step through the veil and appear to mankind. The master queried right back to that student, asking when *they* plan to step through the veil and appear fully clothed in light to *Him*? Be you a shaman or an ascended master student, the far off worlds that El Morya so often refers to are accessible NOW, right there in the secret chamber of your heart.

- **CS**: Your busybody self-awareness has no business in the higher realms of Spirit. Put off the old man before attempting to enter there. Bridging yourself into Spirit enables you to experience the consciousness of masters of light as well as that of the elementals who minister right here on Earth.

AM: The withdrawal from the outer sense of separation imposed by outer perceptions is central to all meditational practices. But deep meditation is not the only arena where such attunement can be realized. Practicing the Presence and awakening to radical Dzogchen in everyday life accomplishes the same result, so spiritual practitioners can realize the One while "up and doing" to bring about the divine plan imminently NOW. As El Morya observes,

> **"Verily, we are contacted by the gentle touches of the Subtle World, yet one must feel these not only during the stillness of night but in daylight as well. The error of mankind is that it notices all subtle sensations only at twilight. Now is the path to Light."**[112]

Soul must be centered in the threefold flame (the seat of the Holy Christ Self focused in the secret chamber of the heart) to contact and maximally serve her Higher Self: the immortal Beings of the spiritual Hierarchy. The threefold flame bridges the inner and outer worlds of awareness. It must be chaliced in consciousness to transmute the dark energies blocking direct communion with the masters.

When decreeing (using the science of the spoken word) to focus and direct higher spiritual energies in lower frequency realms, the practitioner is said to have "cut through" to the inner planes when this soul/threefold-flame bridge has been established. El Morya discloses:

> **"The Invisible World is, in reality, highly visible when the eye is not obstructed. Manifestations of mediumship are not needed in order to feel the Light of the Higher World, but one can ascend only to the Highest; therefore all forced artifices of the lowest magic are nought in comparison with the first light of the heart."**[113]

Did you catch that? Morya says that one can ascend "only to the highest." Meditate deeply upon that!

The only way to ascend to any higher "level" of the spiritual Hierarchy at all is to immanently recognize the One. THAT One is the only pathway to Reality. So it doesn't matter what rung of the infinite ladder of light you wish to lollygag on; you MUST first become the highest. Then you can focus your Being anywhere you wish.

- **CS:** Spiritual seekers are often perceived as madmen to those who populate only banal materialism. But such "madness" leads to the exaltation of heart the saints and sages have sought from earliest times.

AM: Soul centered in polarity with, in and as, her divine consort, her Holy Christ Self, assumes the posture of what El Morya calls "straight knowledge." In this way, she liberates her understanding from dependence upon the vicissitudes of *maya*'s idiotic tales told by its secondary energies. This is truly thinking out of the box. El Morya refers to the need for independence from the obstructions that block heart centered consciousness and keep soul tied to convention:

> **"...especially obstructive are the habits that impel the consciousness into conventional paths. They also deplete the abilities of the**

heart when it is prepared to re-echo to the Highest Guidance."[114]

- **CS**: Enter the Great Unknowing to center Truth in your heart before attempting to imbibe Spiritual Elixir. Introducing phantom energies will poison it. Allowing the lower human ego to seek power in this way will merely accrue the poisonous karma of witchcraft to you.

AM: The master of Purity's Ray, Serapis Bey, teaches his students to beware the dyes of the human consciousness. That is, even the most seemingly insignificant foci of dark energies will stain the entirety of consciousness. Any compartmentalization of soul consciousness is but metadata that enables us to refer to aspects of outer life. But soul consciousness is One and infinite. El Morya would add:

> **"...the man who has stored up a clear and benevolent consciousness on Earth will also be a good builder in the Subtle World. Instead of monstrosities, he will bring with him beautiful proportions and rhythm which correspond to the magnificence of the Infinite...Only the light-bearing consciousness of the heart will carry the subtle body into the higher realms."**[115]

- **CS**: Opening yourself to communication with masters of light on the inner planes of Being brings about healing to spirit as well as the four lower bodies: etheric, mental, emotional, physical.

AM: Being open to exploration of the inner realms simply means ceasing your concentration upon outer realms. That is the basis of all healing.

Surrendering one's *attachment* to outer form produces attunement with the Great Unknowing. Once in that state, the continuous Presence of light will bring you into concordance with Beings who espouse the light. Your communication with such Beings arises in your recognition of Oneness with those immortals dwelling in and comprising the higher octaves of light. Since only the One IS, healing your own breakages with higher spirits heals their own with you as well.

The big question, then, is of what does such healing communication consist? I assure you that immortal Gods and Goddesses don't just sit around bantering about who's wearing what style or any other such claptrap. Divine communication always concerns the expansion of consciousness, which is the healing of lower consciousness. The Maha Chohan, the ascended master representative of the Holy Spirit explains:

> **"The communication of the Word reinforces your identity as God here below. You receive communication, [whereupon you] return it to God, return it to each point of Light [time-space's single dimension of space] where there beats the heart of sacred fire."**[116]

That is, communication with the immortals is an empowerment to you for the increase of God consciousness in yourself and in all you contact—physically meeting or spiritually projecting that light. The Word: Be thou made whole, echoes both materially and spiritually.

Always keep in mind, though, that one may also encounter darker, manipulative beings while journeying in consciousness. You must always test the spirit of light through the heart.

• **CS:** Breaking the rules of established religions does not consign you to hell. Nor does following them lead to some sort of Paradise. Real spirituality lies in attuning to the living antahkarana whose entry point is the secret chamber of your heart.

AM: Yes, unending hell is a fiction, but the ascended masters disclose that thirty-three levels of the astral plane hold the hellish energies of karma as well as the discarnate beings and demons who are responsible for their creation.

When a soul of light passes from the screen of life, it is important for them and their loved ones to call for light's blessings as well as masterful escorts of light to help them navigate beyond those lower realms so that they may attend the universities of the spirit in the octaves of light between embodiments or in preparation for their ascension into their immortality.

A do-nothing paradise is a contradiction in terms. Divine paradise is the realm of light which comes about when consciousness entertains THAT of God's immanent Presence I AM THAT I AM. Whether in the higher octaves of "heaven" or in the lower realms of earth, identifying one's Self in all perceptions comes of an active sacred labor. The only possible do-nothing state is that of nirvana, the state of absolute rest that consciousness can assume as a sort of recharge for the ever active Life in and as the One's light.

- **CS:** First face the misqualified energies of bad karma that beset you. Then realize that you must find meditational surcease from these importunate burdens. Even Jesus needed to seek solitude at times. When you increase your sensitivity to higher spiritual realms, these times alone/within become more necessary. You can do this even in the environs of your workaday world. You need not trek into far off wilderness settings. Just find a quiet place to dust yourself off from the busyness of business from time to time.

AM: That "inner aloneness" can be found every single solitary moment. Figure-eight flow is soul realizing her all-One-ness right in the midst of even the most frantic of energies. Nevertheless, it is true, times of withdrawal into a peaceful environment are needed for respite. El Morya points out the need to recognize when such retreats are called for:

> **"The outflow of invisible energy during physical drowsiness is a true sign of participation in the repulsion of darkness.**

At any time We may sound the call to battle, therefore attention must be paid to an unexpected spell of drowsiness. Moreover, the expenditure of energy does not remain unnoticed. It will take away much of the heart energy, therefore it is only right to let this energy again accumulate. It is unwise to permit the exhaustion of this energy, therefore We remind about a respite in the form of a change of labor.119

Morya calls such change of labor "rest in motion."

- **CS:** You can always focus your attention upon the sacred spaces within you. There, the inner and outer realms intersect, and your eternally infinite Selfhood shines.

AM: Sacred space is the secret chamber of the heart and the centers of all 144 chakras of the human body. It is also the interface of the masculine and feminine sides of the White Fire Cross's horizontal bar, composed of those ethereal microclusters described in Part Three. The Third-Ray heart chakra centers soul in a fulcrum from which infinite leverage can be managed. Morya says:

> **"We insist so greatly upon the Teaching of the Heart. No other center can replace the essence of the heart. The accumulations of centuries in the Chalice [the secret chamber] are at the disposition of the heart. For the salvation of humanity does not consist in separate siddhis but in the central motive force—-the heart. Thus, beyond all divisions one must come to the root of motion.**[117]

- **CS:** Assuming a stance of consciousness outside of the vicissitudes of time, place and situational awareness introduces you to your inner sacred space. You can traverse the interface between inner and outer awareness at will. It is ever so pliable.

AM: Again, the "elastic walls" referred to are the microclusters of the time-space/space-time interface. That the timeless time-space realm is sacred is why the ascended masters refer to it specifically as your "Holy" Christ Self. It is the point of consciousness at which infinite mystery becomes alchemically Individualized and integrated with soul. Do your best to relax into it often.

• **CS:** The outer worlds are permeated by the inner. You cannot ever really leave your spirit behind. And you can always find that spirit focused in any outer thing or condition.

AM: The Beings of the spiritual Hierarchy can use any statue or picture or whatever item of matter to focus their consciousness as an outpouring of blessing to all of life in the outer space-time realm. Moreover, a shaman or spiritual initiate of any persuasion derives their Real Identity from the Heart. Thus where thou art, I AM. We know how much easier it is to find our inner wholeness in wilderness settings. But it is actually equally there in the lowest, rottenest slum. Flex your spiritual muscles and go find what I AM everywhere.

• **CS:** You can visualize your inner Selfhood using any focus of holiness or natural wonder. Repeated practice will allow you to bring about a spiritual mindset very quickly. The more tangible your spiritual focus becomes, the more power it can focus.

AM: This corresponds to the Tibetan Buddhist meditational practices of the first two schools of Dzogchen, Trekcho and Togal, as well as all other types of meditation, in which the practitioner develops concentrational skills to realize the One. Even so, as radical Dzogchen asserts, when sufficient clarity of the aura can be achieved—such as by invoking the Violet Flame and other Flames using the science of the spoken word—the arduous path can be considerably shortened by those who elect to do so; and the *instant* realization I AM THAT I AM can blossom out of nowhere.

- **CS:** It is important to become acquainted with the World Tree that stands at the center of the shaman's world. This Tree is a center post. It connects the upper worlds of higher light frequencies with the lower worlds of outer manifestation, as well as inner lower worlds. You can visualize ascending upwards through the upper branches of the Tree and downward through the roots. Or the image of a sacred mountain can also serve.

AM: That World Tree hosts the flame of Life: the threefold flame situated at the center of Being among the chakras. The upper chakras above the heart chakra are entry points to the Upperworld in humans, and the lower chakras below the heart chakra access the Underworld. When accessing these worlds, it is best to invoke the Presence of ascended masters and Cosmic Beings associated with those chakras to act as your guides.

- Crown: Gautama Buddha, Apollo and Lumina, Jophiel and Christine, Lord Lanto.
- Third Eye: Cyclopea and Virginia, Raphael and Mother Mary, Hilarian and Pallas Athena.
- Throat: Hercules and Amazonia, Michael and Faith, El Morya.
- Heart: Heros and Amora, Chamuel and Charity, Paul the Venetian and ascended lady master Ruth Hawkins, the Goddess of Beauty
- Solar Plexus: Peace and Aloha, Uriel and Aurora, Lady master Nada. Jesus.
- Seat of the Soul: Arcturus and Victoria, Zadkiel and Holy Amethyst, Saint German and Portia.
- Base of the Spine: Purity and Astrea, Gabriel and Hope, Serapis Bey. Goddess of Light. Queen of Light. Goddess of Purity.

- **CS:** The *axis Mundi* connects heaven and Earth. Also Mount Meru and Mount Arunachala in India are recognized as such connectors with spiritual realms. Haraberezaiti in Iran, Himingbjor to the Norse, the Mount of the Lands in Mesopotamia, and Mount Tabor in Palestine. These points in the Earth have been seen as sacred. They are taken to be origins where creation and expansion of spirit is highly focused. In some cultures, the symbol for this central point is a vine, cord, ladder, or thread of spider web.

AM: The ascended masters refer to the great pole that connects heaven and earth as the crystal cord. This can also be visualized as the pathway upon which can be realized the wings of the dove of the Holy Spirit as well as the passageway for the breath of Brahman. It especially energizes the human spine.

The Tibetan Rainbow Body

The inner, masculine time-space realm of the horizontal bar of the White Fire Cross is the spiritual foundation of the outer, feminine space-time world of our everyday experience. In his lecture on the Tibetan rainbow body,[118] David Wilcock describes the interaction of these realms as the successful culmination of the spiritual Path.

The rainbow body is produced when the soul of an initiate consciously ascends into their Higher Self at the end of an embodiment. While likely, it is unclear whether the attainment of the rainbow body signals the final ascension which frees the soul from the wheel of birth and death. Padmasambhava was the first to achieve the rainbow body in "modern" times (around 800 A.D.) About 160,000 rainbow-body occurrences have been documented since then.

The central practice of the school of Tibetan Buddhism that leads to the attainment of the rainbow body is called Dzogchen. It is also known as Ati Yoga or the "Great Perfection"

Dzogchen is the natural, primordial state of our being. [In space-time, it is also known as the Mother light.] Anent to this, the great devotee of the One, Ramakrishna, is well known for his consummate devotion to the Divine Mother.

Dzogchen teachings and meditations are aimed at achieving the Great Perfection: pure, all-encompassing primordial clarity that is the nature of all beings. The Great Perfection is timeless and has no form, and yet it is the nature of the universe, capable of perceiving, experiencing, reflecting or expressing all form. It does so without being affected by those forms in any ultimate, permanent way. It's like a mirror that reflects with complete openness, but is not affected by the reflections.

I conceive of the soul's evolutionary *modus operandi,* as a processor of the Causal Body's basic immaculate *maya,* precisely as this mirror-like wisdom. The soul's "creative" activity doesn't change the engrams; she just adds relational receptor cells to them so that the infinite elements of the One—in both quality and quantity—can access them.

It might be surmised that Causal Body engrams of basic immaculate *maya* just sit around latently. And then, sometime or other, soul acts to render them Art in consciousness. No way, José! Before and after do not apply to God's evolution. "Lesser evolved" simply means more of the One remains latent or hidden from a being's evolving consciousness. "More evolved" simply means more of the One is accessible. (I know, the human brain just can't get this. It thinks there just HAS to be some kind of before and after. Maybe it would help to relate the immense scope of a car driver's consciousness compared to the contained level confining the car's mechanical parts.)

The Way Carries Our Holographic Truth
Our Coherent Sense of Identity
Affirms Our Holographic Nature

Throughout our life, we traverse images that our own consciousness creates. Moving from one portion of our life's imagery to another, our sense of selfhood remains. In other words, it doesn't matter what portion or how much of our self-image is being illumined at any particular moment; the whole of our self is still present and available to our re-collection. That is the nature of a hologram. Every part contains information describing the whole.

This understanding is especially useful to keep near the forefront of our consciousness as we tread the spiritual Path. For it applies not only to our local self, but to the entire spiritual Hierarchy. No matter what portion of Life we are currently illumining, the Allness of the One I AM Presence and Its Causal Body is present and available to us through God's grace.

As we accustom ourselves to resonate with infinite mystery, our consciousness ever expands. This is literally true. The Christ I AM is the open door which no man can shut. Whatever you can conceive of is already occurring at some level of the One Dream I AM. "You" don't ever "create" anything; you simply choose to participate with it as an ordered relationship.

If you are not outwardly partaking of a portion of the Dream that you wish to, it is simply because you are choosing to focus awareness somewhere else. But, still, All THAT I AM resides in consciousness at some level. It is alchemically up to "you" to inspire your self-awareness to resonate with your Self-awareness, which can access the desired submatrix of ultimate possibility. In other words, to par (equalize with) take of it. Your alchemical mastery may be a far cry from such achievement, but it remains Life's opportunity for each of us.

Relating Directly to the I AM Presence
Is a Mighty Tall Order

How can you relate to "something" infinite? Obviously, you can't if you confine yourself to brain power. We already know that those who seriously pursue a spiritual life don't do that. Certainly formal meditation and decreeing work wonders, but what kind of approach can our everyday, busybody self shoot for to spiritually maximize our time on Earth? Practicing the Presence for sure. But what sort of outlook/ inlook is that, exactly?

Can't say for sure, but M. John Harrison's book *Light* is worth contemplating. In it, he refers to something he calls the "Shrander," which I take to refer ultimately to the I AM Presence. The protagonist, Kearney, remembers a time at a beach where he notices the fractal nature of all levels of consciousness. That paradoxical unique sameness, at whatever fractal level perceived; that hollow, absent shadow harkening to the Presence's infinite mystery, becomes a stark intimation, the incontrovertible permeation of awareness with the Great Unknowing.

Three Modes of Living upon the Horizontal Bar
Of the White Fire Cross

We change our focus of consciousness, from the outer space-time realm of doing, to the inner time-space realm of the potential of Being, while we sleep. Remember, as noted in Part Three, the inner time-space realm has nothing to do with the sense of cascading time. The three dimensions of so-called time there, capture the engrammatic forms available from our "own" I AM Presence's Causal Body, and the ultimate Causal Body of the One and only I AM Presence, which is to say, all of *akasha*.

Sleeping is like going on a shopping trip where we gather the raw materials of our divine plan for our next day. In both dreaming sleep and deep sleep, we are totally focused in what we would call a timeless realm from the space-time point of view. (That is, unless we are lucid dreaming, when we are consciously aware that we are dreaming right within the dream.)

When we dream, we approach nearer to the time-space/space-time interface. Our dreaming, indeed all of our time-space work, would seem outright wacky if it were to occur in our everyday space-time realm. In time-space, anything can happen anywhere. The everyday, outer "laws" of nature can be violated. It is there that the inconceivable is conceived. The space-time ordered cascade proceeding along the arrow of time is absent.

I suppose that during sleep, your Higher Self creates and programs microclusters, which are embedded through your chakras into your outer space-time vehicles. This is like tuning a musical instrument to some key. These microclusters nourish and guide your psyche during your waking life. They are "eaten up" as you convert those elements of your divine plan into your life's Art. That is, your chakras partake of the time-space/space-time interface where that softer, ethereal, microcluster state of matter inspires and emits your higher guidance. The table below depicts the horizontal bar of the white fire cross. It comprises three rows:

1. Consciousness comporting the normal everyday outlook
2. Consciousness oriented toward enlightenment
3. Consciousness oriented toward criminality

Time-Space/Space-Time
Interface

∧
|

Invisible Nightside Immersion Masculine-Masculine	Visible Nightside Immersion Masculine-Feminine	Invisible Dayside Work Feminine-Masculine	Visible Dayside Work Feminine-Feminine
1. Deep, dreamless Sleep. Gathering of Causal Body engrams of pure possibilities.	Rapid Eye Movement Sleep. Exploring possible relationships in dreams. These activities that can violate space-time laws. Equally weighted by personal karma and divine inspiration.	Project Conception and thought (blue-prints) about how to complete projects. "Inspiration" largely based upon secondary impacts.	Building activity and physical maturity. Subject to ongoing inspiration and mental guidance, personal karma and outrageous fortune. Highly subject to *maya*'s sirens, easily taken in by and attached to sticky illusory patterns that insinuate into a "me"- part that amounts to obsession.
2. Deep, dreamless sleep as well as conscious inner work on other higher frequency planes. Samadhi.	Same as above, but more intensely involved with divine inspiration. Conscious spiritual planning accessed through meditation.	Same as above, but much more fully inspired by divine direction.	Same as above, but much more fully inspired by divine direction and serendipitous events. Greater protection against outrageous fortune.

3. Seldom usefully accessed.	Same as 1 above, but strongly focused upon the astral plane.	Plans highly influenced by bad karma and mechanical mentality.	Almost total immersion in *maya*. Products devoid of true Beauty.

I further suppose that our work between embodiments is also like a more extended shopping trip in which the elements of our next life's divine plan are grouped together into some sort of holding area; and some of these are delivered little by little to the forming embryo. These influence the DNA and the character of the new child's psyche.

I think that it's likely that a relatively large percentage of the embryo's matter comprises those soft-state microclusters. Thus the substance of the developing embryo is likely much softer than that of adults. Some of these microclusters probably remain in young children, up to about age seven. This would account for the extraordinary memory and contact that young children retain with the inner time-space realm.

Self-erected Prison

Mode 1 of the above table refers to that which most of us assume most of the time: ignorant sleepy-eyed consciousness, only minimally in step with time-space direction. In this state, we encounter and identify with the *maya* of false conception's illusory phantom forms. Master Morya calls assigning reality to such activity "prejudice." It could also be called pre-conceived notions. He asserts that:

> "...prejudice—whether negative or positive—is wrong. It is opposed to every Yoga; it cuts off the phenomenal aspect of ascent. One often confuses prejudice with straight-knowledge, yet these qualities are directly opposed to each other. Prejudice is an offspring of the mind, whereas the abode of straight-knowledge is the heart. Thus, one cannot compare the offspring of the mind with those of the heart. The acceptance of such a thing is not only erroneous but also harmful, disparaging the activity of the heart. It can be observed

> **how strata of prejudice are accumulated until the
> entire life is turned into a self-erected prison. But
> straight-knowledge concerns cosmic truth, hence,
> in itself it does not contain anything disparaging.
> The self-development of straight-knowledge induces
> solemnity of feeling. Thus, through different gates
> we approach the Abode of Solemnity. He who has not
> experienced the sacred quiver of solemnity cannot
> understand the harm of prejudice"**[119]

It is easy to see, then, how difficult it is for normally upright "everyday" people to free themselves from the sea of Samsara, from the wheel of birth and death, and to attain higher consciousness and immortality. Yet, reassured, we can understand how our frequent visitations to the parallel time-space universe unfailingly delivers straight-knowledge to the heart. But *we* need to make the effort to fasten our attention there to partake of the unceasing communion of a sacramental life.

Yes, your life is an ongoing opportunity. Your time-space realm is always right there available to you as the molds awaiting soul to pour herself into them to forge her God Identity. In the book *Light*, Ed laments his neglect of these immense opportunities:

> **"He could only remember the fictional Ed, an assembly
> of diamond-clear events that never happened."**[120]

Your consciousness, awake to the diamond shining Mind of God, can assimilate Real Selfhood, your completeness, moment by moment and make every breath the fiery afflatus of Holy Spirit. But *you,* your soul, One with her consort Christ Self, must act as your God-Identity's catalyst in space-time to anchor your victories.

The Paradox Club

I reflect now upon our being told that Morya once turned to Mother Mary and said, "We must not fail." Thus even for ascended masters, the sensation of change is real. Moreover, if Paul the Venetian fashioned that chalice for the Maha Chohan, there must have been a "time" beforehand that it did not exist. There must have been a "time" beforehand that the Maha Chohan did not possess that gift from Paul.

On the other hand, the Cosmic Being Victory has told us that He has never met another man except Victory. Thus every single solitary event is eternally complete, and there is no such thing as some sort of progressive staging in "time." When Paul was fashioning the chalice, He did not have the sense that He, a separable self, was doing anything. He was simply acting as an agent of infinite Mystery. This is a paradox that the human brain and mind simply cannot fathom AT ALL.

Obviously, the ascended masters never contradict each other. They can't; they ARE One Being. So, no matter how contradictory two humanly directed statements from them may seem, there must be something behind the outer meaning which unites them and carries an inner significance.

For instance, Jesus said that he could do nothing; that it is the Father in Him who does the works. But the Father, ultimately the One I AM Presence, IS in fact ONE. No "work"—a worker acting upon an object— can ever be "done" by the Presence in ONENESS. There is no subject-object to do and to be acted upon. Thus, the Father must "act" through an agent: Christ/Soul, Son/Daughter of God.

Just take the whatever-color pill, and realize that the only thing you can in turn *do* as a human agent of Christ/soul is to try your best to identify with the Great Silent Watcher, who is as close as close can be with infinite mystery. And realize that there isn't anyone anywhere *doing* anything. All is realization, and choice as consciousness, in and as infinite mystery.

Then roll up your sleeves and get the heaven to work!!! Everything comes to those who wait so long as they work like heaven while they're waiting. Again, nothing is getting done, and nobody is doing it, but absent-but-apparent Individuals at ONE with infinite mystery will find themselves joyless unless they thrust themselves for a purpose with a mighty can-do spirit.

If this sounds like gobbledygook, welcome to the paradox club. ☺☺☺

The View from Three-dimensional Time

In three-dimensional time, Father, as always, is finality. As in three-dimensional space, the shapes in three-dimensional time are unchanging, as they are OF the Father. Apparent change in three-dimensional time is driven by the arraying points of view directed into space. It's like the views from a mountain trail. The shape of the mountain does not change. But as viewed from different places on the trail, your perception of the mountain is completely different. Thus in time-space, an entirely different infinitely based shape in time/possibility substance appears as consciousness is flipped through the one-dimensional points of space. Again, just as moments of time fly by in space-time, producing an apparent motion picture, points of space "fly" by in time-space to produce an apparent motion picture. I now see Alfred E. Newman smiling his "What, me worry?"

Moments

That brings us to the physics concept of "moments." Our everyday conception of a moment is that of a temporal standstill. Nothing happens in a moment. But in physics, a moment is a force applied at some distance from a point or axis. Webster's 10th calls a moment "a tendency or measure of tendency to produce motion." Hence each moment of supposed standstill is pregnant with motion.

A moment's force is said to be applied to a point or axis at ninety degrees to it to cause it to spin. The very presence of time in contact with three dimensional space is what produces the moments which impart spin, or apparent motion, in our everyday world.

Likewise, the very presence of space in contact with three dimensional time is what produces the forceful moments which impart spin or apparent motion to so-called "temporal" shapes. Time pushes space; and space pushes time.

Try to grok that "behind" all THAT, infinite mystery "pushes" the One. Good luck!

In other words, figure-eight flow is not confined within the individed I AM Presences. Each of them feasts upon the never ending paradox of infinite mystery's "identity" with ultimate Selfhood: the One I AM Presence.

So take a moment now to take a spin in the One.

It Only Takes One to Love
Soul Fire Blossoms In and As Divine Love

The substance of the time-space/space-time interface is THAT of divine Love. It is the very clasp of your Holy Christ Self with His dear Soul. The energies of THAT Love figure-eight flow with the I AM Presence within your Christ/Soul's heart. Through your attuned Christ/Soul union, Love anchors your soul as enveloping Presence. THAT Presence assumes its placement in space-time as the white fire core of every point of consciousness in your space, in each a petal of your fiery blossoming soul.

What's It Like to Consciously Traverse
The Time-Space/Space-Time Interface?

I had a lucid dream that was one of the weirdest ever. The following details are unimportant. The configuration of my dreamlike state is what's notable.

In the dream, I was riding a small motorbike to work in the morning, and that, in itself, was a very wild ride in which some impossible stuff was going on. So that tipped me off that I was lucid dreaming. I finally arrived at work, and I didn't recognize where I was at all. I only knew I worked there. I had pulled up to the loading dock of a big, very shabby looking warehouse. There were about five big, burly guys sitting around outside smoking. I didn't recognize any of them. Then, for some reason—maybe winter was coming on—I wanted to arrange to travel to and from work with someone in a car so I wouldn't need to continue riding my motorbike.

So I asked these guys if they knew anyone who lives in the SW area of the city. That was when the dream became weird because they asked me precisely what towns or areas I was talking about. Then I knew that was in Washington, D. C. because I started saying the names of various places I lived nearby those where I grew up.

The super strange disconnect that happened within my consciousness occurred because, since I was lucid dreaming, my identity knew that I really now lived in a city very distant from D. C. That is why I told them that I wanted a ride to the SW area, where I now live. But, when I was living in D. C., I only lived in SE and NE of the city and the NW suburbs. I never lived in SW D. C., and I knew almost nothing about it.

So, when in the dream, I realized this, I said one of the funniest things ever, "Hey, I'm in the wrong dream! Somebody get me outa here!" I felt completely out of place. I wanted to skedaddle badly.

Then I found myself moving very fast. Like I was in a car or train, but there was no visible vehicle. The only thing moving was my identity.

Then I quickly found myself in a white-out, like a heavy snow cloud or very dense fog, where you are driving along and all of a sudden visibility becomes zero. That's happened several times to me, driving about 70 mph in Montana. Every time like that, I felt significant fear, as I needn't tell you how fast things can go from bad to calamity driving blind doing 70. Road turns, oncoming traffic that also can't see you, ice on the road, not to mention the ever present deer and elk.

But this time, I was fearless. For about two to three seconds, all I saw was an infinitude of super bright points of white light. Each point could be distinguished, but they were so close together as to effectively be a spiritual cloud.

Since I have now learned about the time-space/space-time interface, composed of microclusters, I believe that that was what I was traversing.

The Ritual of the Cloud

This cloud is a direct reference to Saint Germain's ritual of the cloud. Therein, He has the participating alchemist use visualization to invoke a cloud comprising an infinity of steely white-fire points of light. This cloud is then to be seen to envelop whatever location where dark energies are to be raised into higher frequencies of divinity.

Directing the intensity of this white-fire cloud through your inner awareness integrates its target with your unique service of infinite mystery. This authorizes God's will to act to alchemically bring about the Presence of divine virtue. The longer this cloud can be sustained with ever greater intensity, the greater is the darkness that can be consumed. The cloud can be used to turn around devilish activities, lift overlays of dense energy and transform consciousness to greater light wherever it encounters misqualified energy.

Right after that dream white-out, I found myself coming-to in my bed. So I knew that I had just concluded a dream, which I remembered well enough to write down.

But, then I wanted to see if I could consciously go back to the dream state and continue where I left off. That is when I clearly experienced the difference between dreaming and imagination. I tried to get back to the dream by imagining the same scene at that warehouse with those guys. But I was not able to reproduce the white-out, which I took to be the white fire cores of my 3D space. In other words, I was not able to consciously leave space-time and reenter time-space. So I was then experiencing the "dream" scene with my identity firmly anchored in space-time simply as a memory.

Traversing the Time-Space/Space-Time Interface
The Quantum Level View

Even though I, at my macro level of consciousness, was unable to jump the time-space/space-time interface, it happens continuously at the quantum level. Ervin Laszlo writes:

> **"Every particle, every atom, and every molecule possesses not only the state that it occupies when it is observed, but also states that are empty and hence are said to be 'virtual.' Virtual states are described by probability functions and bits of information. They become real when a particle, and atom, or a molecule 'jumps' into them...Every system that emerges in the manifest world represents a selection from among the set of virtual states that is available to it [through the Holy Christ Self]. There is a constant transformation from virtual into real states and also from real into virtual states. Quantum physical-chemist Lothar Schäfer describes this as "an 'incessant restless dance' where the occupied states are constantly abandoned and become virtual, while the empty states become occupied and real. [This is figure-eight flow] And he writes, "at the foundation of things transcendent (that is, virtual) order and real order are interlocked in an uninterrupted frantic embrace."[121]**

Of course, we now know that the set of virtual states available to your consciousness, your system, is the basic immaculate *maya* (the engrams of your Causal Body) portending manifestation in your outer awareness. Moreover, this cosmic dance, this uninterrupted frantic embrace, imputes to you the all-consuming twin flame union realized as divine Love.

This continuous entry and reentry of consciousness between the virtual and real (outer) states of awareness is also related to its succumbing to the zero-point cosmic mean twice in every wave's cycling. This happens many times per second. Thus, to human awareness, it is truly continuous. This continuity is eerily significant in that it enables you as a normal, everyday human, to experience infinite divine Love right out front in your outer walk-around world.

Consensus Reality

The probability functions Laszlo mentions, which determine when a virtual possibility becomes a real element of your outer awareness, are highly dependent upon the intensity of the mass consciousness, the shared consensus, upon them.

A consensus is the result of an election. Participating parties cast their ballots and the overwhelm stands out. In consciousness, the consensus you create receives votes from your active senses (all 144 of your chakras), from karmic waves returning to your doorstep, as well as from the radiation of neighbors amplifying and jangling your vibes in a milieu hosting everything from loving consideration to outrageous fortune. The multidimensional image you elect assumes office as your identity moment by moment.

Since yours and everyone else's identity is so up for grabs, how on earth do us humans ever agree so much on what our commonly experienced, hard matter, world appears to be? Moreover, how can we avoid the traps that can so easily spring upon those merely basing their awareness, even their identity, upon consensus.

The problem is, binding up your identity in consensus places limits on your sense of identity in and as the One. It collapses infinite potential's shining crystal clarity into a blurry, shimmering gel. That gel's mold of the moment is empty, moldy decay just as soon you cast it in your play as a separate entity prancing around or sitting about "here" or "over there."

Here is a further explanation from Laszlo that explains consensus reality from the quantum perspective:

> "...in 1935 Erwin Schrodinger suggested that particles do not have individually defined quantum states but occupy collective states. The collective superposition of quantum states applies not only to two or more properties of a single particle, but also to a set of particles. In each case it is not the property of a single particle that carries information, but the state of the ensemble in which the particle is embedded. As the particles are intrinsically "entangled: with each other, the superposed wave function of the entire quantum system describes the state of each particle within it.

> "The mutual entanglement of quanta indicates that information is subtly but effectively transmitted throughout the quantum world. As this informational linking is both instant and enduring, it appears to be independent of space as well as of time."[122]

For instance, you can carry a table from one place to another, and view it from one century to another.

Suffering arises from Suffrage

Buddha described outer, apparently separated activity as *dukkha/* pain, which arises from voting for which "other" you choose as your identity each moment. Such outer phantom entities, their likes and dislikes, fears and suffering, stem directly from its suffrage. By voting, picking favorites, while ignoring the One sun, the only power that IS, you produce some apparent "other." This simultaneously creates a "me," an ego add-on with the supposed power/right to install that element of duality as an active agent of your little identity's menagerie. This is how your ego is created, formed, reformed and multiplied.

Adopting consensus reality as your own reality is tantamount to configuring the *dukkha* that you suffer the One to endure. Your suffrage is an attempt to install the One into a rickety office in which your ego is enthroned not as Your Highness, but as "your emptiness."

Consensus reality is not necessarily "bad." It is simply a sharing of consciousness. It only becomes "bad" when consciousness segregates the shared elements into apparently separate entities. The sharing, itself, is actually enabled by the Universal Christ.

The forms that the Mind of God produces are available to be shared by everyone. It's the personal Christ that enables individuals to *independently, freely,* modify consensus imagery. Indeed, the Rashamon effect describes how this is always occurring. Thus, because, independent of ego, I AM THAT I AM, we all agree that a specific table or chair is "there" and that it more or less looks the same to each of us. But the spectrum of our current moment's personality—our personal-eye-tie— modifies that viewpoint, and can render it eternal Art or rubbish.

The Path of spiritual initiation governs how soul ascends eternally as she attunes her personal options to divine virtue. In this way she assumes the ever expanding inclusivity of the spiritual Hierarchy. The Key to personal soul accelerating her Path is to concentrate upon the Universal Christ/Oversoul, knowing always that "of myself I can do nothing."

Awareness Is Not Firmly
Tied Down to Consciousness

I now have a clear feeling for the manner in which imagination works. Awareness somehow gets to traverse the time-space/space-time interface while leaving your identity/consciousness behind in space-time. That is, awareness is not firmly tied to consciousness. It can roam around in any realm while consciousness remains tied to whatever version of identity you currently entertain. It's like a butterfly net hauling in forms you'd like to harness into service.

That's a lead-in to the next section, in which I will explore the nature of the viewpoints that consciousness assumes and the folly of thinking that any one of those false conceptions is You. (Of course, they're all the "Big-Y" You, but tsk-tsk if you fall into their sticky nest of apparently separate attachment receptors.)

The Rashamon Syndrome

"Rashamon" is a film directed by Akira Kurosawa. A woodcutter and a priest are keeping dry under the Rashamon city gate in a driving rainstorm. The woodcutter and a newly arrived commoner tell the priest the story of a very disturbing event they witnessed. The very same event is said to have also been experienced by a bandit, a samurai and his wife. As the film proceeds, each of their stories is acted as if it is happening in real time. They end up being completely different mini-plays. As any cop on the beat will tell you, eyewitness testimony is all but worthless. And these stories are no exceptions, so divergent are their plots.

Each narrator creates a version of the single series of events they all claim to have witnessed. Thus the film illustrates how we all create our worlds out of the whole cloth, highly modified by the filters our consciousness runs them through. This is the Rashamon syndrome. It shoots to pieces the supposition that there is some fixed reality seemingly out there, which any sane person can easily and factually report.

There's nothing actually out there. All awareness happens *inside* you; and you; and you. That's why quantum physicists now know that nothing exists until an observer puts it "there." And, again, "there" is *inside* the observer.

Materialists Pounding on a Table
Are Hoodwinked
By Consensus Hardening Consciousness

It's easy to understand how frustrated a materialist person might become when confronted with some "w00-woo" spiritually oriented person telling them that a hard table they are pounding upon is not there. Yet even such totally science oriented personages like Max Plank, father of quantum physics, admits:

"I regard consciousness as fundamental. I regard matter as derivative from consciousness. We cannot get behind consciousness. Everything that we talk about, everything that we regard as existing, postulates consciousness"[123]

Thus "out there" is a myth. Quantum physics describes how the supposedly hard and fast sensations that materialists covet become so convincing to them. Consensus at the quantum level of consciousness is the answer.

Laszlo explains how this works as quantum "teleportation," which is an extension of quantum entanglement. (Please don't go all blank faced on me now. This is really not complicated at all.)

Quantum entanglement describes how two particles that once shared an identical state in outer manifestation become related to each other and change their states in unison no matter how separated they may be in space or time. This violates Einstein's assertion that the speed of light is tops. Instantaneous state changes in separated particles is called nonlocality. The famous "EPR" (Einstein/Podolski/Rosen) thought experiment proved nonlocality to be factual and that quantum mechanics must be an incomplete theory. The "new" concept that the EPR experiment hatched is called quantum entanglement.

Laszlo refers to "sharing an identical state" as sharing the same coordinate system. I understand a "coordinate system" to refer to the individual Christ/Soul. In other words, you "make sense" out of your perceptions, rather than seeing them as utter chaos, because your consciousness, itself, is a coordinate system that allows for hosting an ordered awareness.

Now here comes the "woo-woo" part that throws materialists for a loop: Only the One IS.

No one has yet come up with an adjective that can aptly describe how important that is for launching your consciousness rocket out of materialistic attachments to hard and fast *maya*. So here's a proposal for such an adjective that Polish people will love: "swytmkmwjtgi." Okay, you can stop laughing now so we can get back to cases.

Since only the One IS, we **all** effectually share the same coordinate system!!!

That is precisely how quantum entanglement enables us to agree that the table your material hand is pounding upon is "there." It's there all right. Right inside the noggins of every observer: observers who all ultimately share the same coordinate system and who happen to have voted for the same consensus reality.

Then add to that, quantum teleportation, which states that quantum entanglement extends to entire atoms, not just quanta. Laszlo writes:

"...current teleportation experiments show that when a pair of correlated atoms is further correlated with a third atom, the

quantum state of the third is instantly transferred ("beamed") to the other of the initially connected pair—no matter how far away that atom may be."[124]

Did you get that? Just as transferring correlation to a third atom is possible, transferring it to an infinitude of atoms IS. That says that we are One. No impenetrable walls separate us.

And...the more elements of that One who place their attention upon an outer manifestation, the stronger grows its consensus reality; the easier it is for others to host it in their own consciousness; the more common that manifestation becomes. Thus, when that materialist is pounding on the table, the echo that is heard by all observers—through the teleportation of the pounding's outer state—convinces them to vote for that consensus and magnify its supposed solidity.

Fourteenth century mystical Tibetan poet Longchenpa relates to such echoes:

> **"Like a clear echoing voice**
> **returning words spoken at a rock face,**
> **all situations are without substance or ego;**
> **we recognize them as unequivocally devoid of truth.**
> **...**
> **due to a loss of presence entailing mental structuring**
> **the fictive mundane world looms absent yet**
> **perceptible, like an echo.**
> —
> **Here, wandering as one of the six mythic modes of being,**
> **inexorably envisioned by karmically induced propensity,**
> **troubled mind is captured by the fictions that pervade it.**
> **...**
> **Craving truth, the unwise see this all as solid matter;**
> **for the yogin who sees the lie, it is unitary space.**
> **Believers who take 'fleeting' as 'lasting' see an eternity;**
> **for those whose belief in eternity implodes, it is**
> **empty form,**
> **and free of confining conceptual parameters, we are**
> **happy!"**[125]

In passing, note: "Believers who take 'fleeting' as 'lasting' see an eternity" is similar to Morya saying "one can ascend only to the Highest." When you are functioning consciously in and as the One, even the smallest notion of duration is seen as eternity. Every cognized fleeting moment ascends only to the highest: eternity.

In Reality, every event is happening inside each observer's uniquely personal coordinate system. So there is really no way to know what they are *actually* agreeing upon. For example, when you say you see the color blue, what are you actually seeing? Who knows? Nobody can know. We just have an agreement that whatever it is that each of us is experiencing will henceforth be called "blue." So Longchenpa encourages us:

> **"Smile lovingly now at these delusive appearances,
> at pure evanescence with nothing to hold on to, airy,
> elusive, dissociated wisps and billows, flickering make-believe,
> a glittering phantasmagoria.**[126]

Who Am I?

So what will happen if you understand the wispy nature of your self-conceptions. What happens when your wisdom allows you to apply the Rashamon Syndrome to your own identity?

Who you think you are is largely based upon the "flickering make-believe" of what you have experienced and reacted to throughout your life. So, tell me, how many eyeball witnesses do you have neatly tucked up and tied with a bow in the precincts of your consciousness? How many identities do you have to choose from in your "Whitman's Sampler" box? The answer, of course, is myriad, even though you are not officially afflicted with multiple personality disorder.

It's safe to say that the Rashamon syndrome creates all of the misunderstandings between people; indeed, all of the suffering within oneself. That's because everyone and every figment of a person living in our own consciousness can disappear. When THAT happens, even in the outer realm of manifestation, you move a step closer to realizing/Being only the One IS.

In my Self, doing nothing, as an afflatus of infinite mystery, no disagreement, no suffering can be recognized. Sri Ramana Maharshi describes this "no mind" state:

> **"By the inquiry 'Who am I?' [thought becomes quiescent]...When other thoughts arise, one should not pursue them, but should inquire: 'To whom do they arise?' It does not matter how many thoughts arise. As each thought arises, one should inquire with diligence, 'To whom has this thought arisen?' The answer that would emerge would be 'to me.' Thereupon, if one inquires 'Who am I?' the mind will go back to its source; and the thought that arose will become quiescent. With repeated practice in this manner, the mind will develop the skill to stay in its source. When the mind that is subtle goes out through brain and the sense-organs, the gross names and form appear; when it stays in the heart, the names and forms disappear...When the mind stays in the Heart, the 'I' which is the source of all thoughts will go, and the Self which ever exists will shine. Whatever one does, one should do without the egoity 'I'. If one acts in that way, all will appear as of the nature of Siva (God)."[127]**

So simple, yet so powerful. Placing yourself in the framework of asking (Who am I?) brings you into a "resonant" state with infinite mystery. It dispels your ego's affirmation of being this, that or the other personage or outer thing after the manner of the Rashamon syndrome. Being answerless, allowing yourself to emerge as a mysterious stranger, implodes the scaffolding that upholds the *maya* of false conception. Then God-Reality stands strong in and as the basic immaculate *maya*, one with the *maya* of false conception and radiating as the primordially pure pristine awareness.

I find it useful to notice that Sri Maharshi chose Siva as the aspect of God you become when asking "Who am I?" Siva is known as the destroyer. So the God you notice that you ARE when asking "Who am I?" arises in your awareness by destroying all extraneous imagery, leaving only the One.

"Your" Free Will

Advaita Vedanta explains that ultimately all is One, and so free will cannot exist. For life **as** the One allows neither a separate "me" to do the willing nor anything out there to exert will upon. Sentience, according to Advaita, is naught but spontaneous awareness of Self—one Self—ALL I AM. Only the One's mystery is alive and free—per Advaita—no more need be said.

The foregoing illustrates that Advaita's purpose is to **enable** Individuality: Real activity sans the sense of separation.

Advaita says nothing about what's to be done after such unity is achieved. But, developing Individuals just sitting around as inert bumps on logs, or even on multiverses, is hardly worth the passionate effort required to birth soul and train her to BE Life everlasting.

(Considering humanity's current state, training souls to liberated Life seems to be so tremendously distant a goal that I can see why Advaita considers that just achieving Oneness is quite enough for our plate right now. El Morya's book *Hierarchy*, however, goes far, far, far beyond that, elucidating Life's purposes.)

Having achieved what is loosely called "enlightenment," freely acting, liberated masters of light express the One's infinitely beautiful Art. Enjoying that state of Being, Advaita has served its purpose, and masters blooming the One leave its raft behind to concentrate upon their readiness to undertake higher initiations endlessly as the unfurling consciousness of the spiritual Hierarchy.

The Phantom Me Will Never Surrender

Marrying suffrage to suffering persists 'till death/entropy do them part, or 'till Life's lightning grace consumes the phantom "me."

People embracing spirituality often point to surrender as the way to Self realize the One. They often think that their lower ego must surrender unto the higher Son of God, their Christ Self. I used to find myself saying the same thing.

But that will never happen.

It can't happen.

The phantom ego and all of its constituents—the madding crowd that it has voted for it up to now—cannot surrender because true surrender involves threading the eye of the needle of consciousness with infinite streaming light. The phantom ego has zero access to light's provenance, and, besides, that chicken hearted groveler would never delve there, where its own death resides. Ego will never invite the sickle bearing man into its home ground, for self-preservation is that impostor's primary concern.

Thus, Grace—blessing from humbler precincts—is the *sine qua non* of surrender. This is a corollary to "of myself, I can do nothing." While surrender is, indeed, a requisite spiritual concept, the only way that "you" can act as its catalyst is by directing the sword of your attention to embrace the One Great Unknowing, rather than to concentrate upon cutting away rubble.

In the absence of a "me" to enter into something called surrender, no gain, no loss transpires: only radiant stillness shines in the aplomb I AM. Of course, "radiant stillness" is a paradox. Understand that what is "still" is the sense of separation; what is radiant is Individual Selfhood in and as the One.

Seeing Is Not Believing

Placing your attention on rubble empowers it. So, even though this planet currently offers your attention a great deal of occasion to fall upon rubble, your job is to strike it from your ballot; to discount its candidacy for a place in your identity.

This is a very subtle Zen skill for you to develop.

For instance, while decreeing, while directing light into specific areas of darkness, clearly identifying specifics greatly accelerates light's action there. That is like applying antiseptic directly to a cut, rather than applying it very thinly over the whole body. The spiritual key to this alchemy is to STAY centered in and as the One while your recognition of the rubble is taken as naught but trembling phantom shadows begging for balance.

Don't Traverse Life
Merely Forming Consensuses

You build your sense of "me" out of perceptions and memories which strongly condition each moment. For example, to a policeman or Secret Service agent, most everything out there is a potential threat. To a painter or photographer, most everything out there is an opportunity to express a vision. To a comedian, it's all one big joke.

Moreover, whatever your consensus has elected you to is shared by others who operate similarly. In the same community you may find an underworld of criminals and a cadre of cops who resonate with them as their opponents. A community may support an artist colony or a clubbing set who give and take entertainment, whose residents focus mainly on amusement or partying. It is so easy to go through life doing little more than classifying and activating perceptions, joining categories. Identifying with a particular consensus becomes the passion that your suffrage uses to dress the One in disguise and you cling to it like a drag queen.

Your Categories Are Your Style
Only Misplaced Identity
Can Restrict You To Them

Amidst all of life's hoopla, that old black shadow, Life's night-side Spirit, never lets you "settle." Infinite mystery is omnipresent, always nipping at your heels like the hound of heaven, of Francis Thompson's poem of that name:

> **"The name is strange. It startles one at first. It is so bold, so new, so fearless. It does not attract, rather the reverse. But when one reads the poem this strangeness disappears. The meaning is understood. As the hound follows the hare, never ceasing in its running, ever drawing nearer in the chase, with unhurrying and unperturbed pace, so does God follow the fleeing soul by His Divine grace. And though in sin or in human love, away from God it seeks to hide itself, Divine grace follows after, unwearyingly follows ever**

**after, till the soul feels its pressure forcing it to turn
to Him alone in that never ending pursuit."**[128]

Aretha Franklin was no stranger to that race. She has been called "a lady of mysterious sorrow because that sadness seems to be her underlying conviction. You might say it's mysterious because you can't identify what may be causing it. Any given day is probably an accumulation of a lifetime of bad breaks, disappointments and just plain unpleasant experiences. And only when she sings can Aretha explain all of the pain and share all of the passion."[129]

Indeed, losing yourself in your passion, the consensus silt settles out, and you can radiate the selfless One I AM. Oh, but that every moment could be such a passion play. Radical Dzogchen says all of your consensuses can resolve to the bright shiny daylight right now. Do you believe it? I hear Aretha asking, "Can I get a yeeeaaahhh?"

The Name of God's Like an Easter Egg Hunt
Resurrecting You
Every Which Way, Every Which Where

All walks of life express the One. So the apostle Paul recognized the value in becoming all things to all people. Though it is obviously impractical for anyone to be conversant with all of life's specialties, your Real identity comprises them all. So the skillful grace that blooms in anyone is really your own. Adhering them to your own Self awareness as your divine personality involves flicking the switch in your consciousness that assumes the One's name: I AM THAT I AM.

Consider the first "I AM" of your Name to be your male suffrage cognizing a possibility in the One, such as the play of art, music, accounting, sports: whatever walk of life you engage.

Then the second "I AM" is the Divine Mother's enfolding female suffrage re-cognizing your own individuality. She can respond to you fully because She has already implanted the potential for Self realization throughout *maya's* precincts.

As time flies, you experience consciousness beholding an apparent subset of the One, and simultaneously that subset beholds you holographically. The Mother is holographic because however closely you focus your attention, anytime, anywhere, the unfathomable One coherently/resonantly takes the stage as your Selfhood.

I AM the Consensus of Joy
Focus Infinity's Fulcrum as Your Awareness

Can you see how the Divine Mother transfers your identity out of *maya*'s constricted consensus reality into the One's open ended consensus of joy?

The Mother's magic mysteriously translates apparent subsets into infinite radiating breath by enlivening your cover story. The gaggles of objects your elections would install as protagonists turn out to be the One's polarities, which timelessly assume your office. The fiery One magnetically draws "them" into service as your agents, your own I AM availing joy in all Hierarchies and universes at once.

This magnetic love affair—I AM THAT I AM—activating infinity's fulcrum as your awareness, is echoed in the preamble to The Summit Lighthouse's decree 70.18: "...by the magnetic power of the Presence of God which I AM and by the magnetic power of the sacred fire vested in me...."

In this state, everything you observe is your Self. Your *own* light radiates in and through all you contact, all you perceive, as an informing, consuming activity I AM THAT I AM; wherein polarity maintains infinity's homeostasis.

The *maya* still exists when you partake of this perspective. You still observe the particulars of your world. Yet, in your consensus of joy, the OM is joined to you. Subject and object lose their vote. *Dukkha*'s suffrage is whittled down to a ghostly, zero extent, zero duration point: infinity's tickly, prickly, electric touch.

Practice the Presence
Seek No Otherworldly Bliss

Consuming apparent separation like this is what is popularly known as the "The Practice of the Presence of God," which Brother Lawrence, a seventeenth century Carmelite lay brother, illuminated not only in his book of that title but through the exaltation he brought to his most menial tasks. Like the Advaita masters who preceded and followed his earthly sojourn, he sought no otherworldly bliss. His common sight was down-to-earth supernatural clarity. He exalted not in rigging his elections to bring about a consensus through suffrage. Instead, he beautified the mundane by gerrymandering his precinct to include only the One. Thus every "election" was a joyous *fait accompli*.

Do thou likewise, okay?

Liberty Enables God

Assuming victimhood, some may question, "Why does God have it in for us? Why is this crap fest willed or allowed at all?" The answer: space-time is a laboratory of liberty, a realm of opportunity. Lacking the liberty to pursue opportunity, the One would be stifled. The infinite mystery enlivening the Word would become a mechanistic menagerie whose denizens could spell every illusory word and be lulled along by that spell.

That is, every concept would be encased in *maya*'s charm. The Word, then, would be a beginningless-endless book with no Real readers, for only mindless phantoms would be skittering about in its pages. Indeed, lacking deep-delving liberty, the One's omniscience would render its mystery moot. Taking away liberty and opportunity stalls Life. The One I AM would be but a haply dispossessed, stick-in-the-mud codger with Alzheimer's.

Mystery's Great Unknowing
Is the Midwife of Life's Inexorable Drive.

Although Life's short term memory ranges eons of eons backward and forward, cradled in its Great Unknowing, force fields of tangible mystery flourish in and cherish their space-time midwife. Yes, space-time enables the One to be eaten, digested, assimilated and assembled ever anew into *akasha*'s titillating delights. Such Light beacons Beauty and frees the All from omnijail like a sailor on liberty.

Space-time translated as horizontal-bar mater enables consciousness to electrify simple purity with the incandescent hope of a starry mother pregnant with nebulae of universes without end. Settled within Her visage is a vastness to which even a big-banged universe is but bling. Right here and now, both time-space and space-time and all "levels" of the spiritual Hierarchy partake of Her ongoingness. This is the Divine Mother's essence fertilizing Her mysterious smiling regard for the smallest of her minions, even as Her incipient omnipresent breast nourishes the variegated fields of Her greatest dominions.

I AM Awake

Humans tend to misuse space-time by falling asleep at the wheel. On the other hand, Gautama's great feat of enlightenment was a waking up from his humanly somnolent romp.

We can all do that, but our habits sucker us in. I think it's possible that inertia is recognized as a law because we have come to accept human passivity while ignoring the awakening alchemical surrender that involves infinity in the space-time milieu. That passivity configures our perception, lending time its seeming duration and space its seeming extent.

If we would eschew our passive framework and live spontaneously I AM, the apparent separation of space-time's *maya* of false conception would not control and contort us. We would live both in and beyond it, in and as our Presence using our Christ/Soul agency to sow creative freedom through our Words and works. Our Life would enshrine Beauty: the **B**right **E**nergy of **A**lpha **U**nited **T**o **Y**ou. Our awareness would encompass Father God, Alpha, unceasingly enjoying relations with Mother Omega, right within us; for, as in gestalt psychology, space-time components would not be perceived as separable particles but as tonalities of the unbreakable One. Only the One IS.

Right Decision
The Decisive Moment

Saint Germain says he earned his ascension by making two million right decisions. So I'd say it is very worthwhile to meditatively examine the moment of choice. Where is it in your consciousness? What is it? How can it be proactively used to further spirituality?

A central character in the novel *Light* was intrigued by these questions. He decided to try to encounter the precise moment that consciousness changes from one image to another, to attempt a head-on collision with that spookily diaphanous point of intent. He tried to locate it by making a video of himself changing channels on a TV, and then examining it frame by frame. That was a very klugey, mechanical approach and, of course, he was unsuccessful.

As we now understand, the point of consciousness this character was attempting to capture is the time-space/space-time interface realm from which "right decision" can guide outer activity and whose outer substance is the semi-solid microclusters we have described in Part Three. This spongy material is the ground between out-of-body dreaming and outer memory/thought in which decisive willpower is nourished and impelled into manifestation.

That "unknown station" the above character sought to examine is precisely the Great Unknowing, the entry point to infinite mystery. It is the point of surrender that you can locate within yourself, which you can repeatedly attend and find there the inspiring, imaginative shopping cartful of engrams you've gathered on your time-space shopping trip during sleep or in deep meditation.

The "rightness" of such decisive moments carries you along like a surfer gliding in, through and over space-time's waves. Then your resonance with infinite mystery seizes upon liberty and clasps victory to your heart. Your Great Unknowing caress of the moment renders you a catalyst for Being's graceful Presence. Your disappearance into the decisive moment leaves trailing clouds of glory in your wake.

What Lies in Wait at the Core?

So, once you've located that Great Unknowing position in your consciousness, what do you find there? For sure, it is not some particular "thing." No, not at all. What you find is an inner alchemical processing akin to surrender, which enables the freeing of consciousness from attachment to the *maya* of false conception. It is the engine that introduces you to the only Real choice possible: the choice to sing along with Paul McCartney's anthem, "Let It Be." Therein you permit your Higher Self to BE: timelessly, spacelessly in league with Father-Mother God's cheerfully expectant progeny. Jesus disclosed this ongoingness as the essence of His Sonship, saying "I can of mine own self do nothing." [130] "...the Father that dwelleth in me, he doeth the works." [131]

That means that even though the outer, lower, ego thinks it is the actor, that it does this and that, Really it is only a receptor, an executive processor of perception. And, so long as you identify with that human ego, all you are "doing" is pushing illusory space-time dust around, flashing phantom firefly pictures all about.

Our inability to locate the precise frame/moment our images change derives from the empty, secondary, relative nature of outer perception. There is IN FACT nothing there to find. It's all flashing lights (plural) rather than light's eternality as ever transcendently, infinitely fine, points of view.

The only Real accomplishment is THAT, which involves infinity in consciousness; THAT, which figure-eight flows your individual Art; THAT, which produces your treasures in heaven (your Causal Body spheres of light, the radiant BEING surrounding your I AM Presence.).

Assuming the Catalytic Point of View
Of Motion Picture Producer

Think of yourself as a movie producer. In the motion picture industry, the producer is the person who handles how a film is made. The producer is the one selecting the script, coordinating writing, directing and editing, and arranging financing. They hire a screen writer and oversee the script's development. They supervise pre-production, production and post production. They hire the director and other key crew members. They try to deliver the film on time and within budget. [132]

The producer is not the one who manufactures the film or acts in it. Thus the producer is neither the film itself nor the "takes" nor the scenery nor the actors playing their roles. Nevertheless, the producer configures the secondary energy *maya* of the film's supporting outer environment, which does contribute to the film's success. In other words, when the film is watched, the producer is absent, yet apparent.

As the producer of your own life story, the closest you come to actually "doing" anything to bring about its imminence is to also assume the role of director. In that capacity, your role only becomes effectively Real when your consciousness assumes that of Great Divine Director. In that capacity, you occupy and configure the set and declare "roll 'em" (the cameras of perception) to initiate the spiral of each scene's awareness and "cut" to arrest the spiral of a completed scene or even one moving as darkness in lieu of divine intent.

The Gender Point of View
Viva La Difference

Re the creative imagery that consciousness entertains:

- **Masculine** consciousness is realized unity.
- **Feminine** consciousness is distributed expression: instances of THAT unity.

Thus, in our everyday realm of the soul, in the feminine pole of the white fire cross's horizontal bar:

- Space is masculine, since each moment it is a unity perceived all at once as a single image.
- Time is feminine, since it is a distributed (one by one) cascade of single masculine spatial instances, each an image of the One.

Moreover, we can conceive of the soul's feminine space-time realm as a womb where the sustained immaculate concepts of her masculine counterpart, drawn from time-space, are Artistically gestated and developed into fire blossoms of the One.

Then, in the inner realm of the masculine pole of the white fire cross's horizontal bar, the gender functionality is conversely switched.

- "Time" is masculine from that point of view, since it comprises the unity of all Causal Body possibilities at once.
- Space there is feminine, since it is a distributed pointillistic array of the masculine instances of time's unified mandala of the One's Causal Body possibilities.

It is interesting to note that, alchemically, masculine unity comes first. Then that is femininely developed as its distributed expression. Hence the biblical metaphor of Eve being created from one of Adam's ribs. Adam's ribs are like a latent feminine array of the One nested within his masculinity.

This is similar to the petals of a single flower bud. The flower's whole expression requires both the feminine petals and the masculine central stem from which the petals emerge. That is, the intelligent Life force, whose self-preservation goal is to create the flower, must develop the requisite mastery to create and sustain both the functions of the masculine stem and the feminine petals.

But notice that masculine functionality of the stem is replicated many times on a single rose bush. Thus, the Life force also encapsulates some lesser measure of distribution—of femininity—in each one. Similarly, for the petals. Although the many petals in a single flower are a feminine expression, they always produce the same sort of flower. This is because they masculinely all draw upon the same engrammatic source that is the species "rose" as well as that of their particular variety.

In other words, life is like a university of the One in which students adopt a major and a minor field of study. Healthy, upright instances of "rose being" exhibit the properties of both genders, wherein the masculine remains far and away mostly masculine, and likewise the feminine, whilst each also sustains a minor, balancing amount of its opposite pole.

Astute readers already know where I am going with this. Nature and beings (or parts of "beings" like those of rose bushes) that are aligned with the divine consciousness governing Life know and act upon the functions associated with their natal physical gender. For instance, no healthy rose bush would sport stems that swing too loosely about and even fray apart like a fan. They couldn't support their buds and flowering petals that way. Likewise, the petals don't remain compressed, refusing to femininely express their inherent beauty.

This Section Is for Education Alone
It's Neither a Call for Governance
Nor an Attempt to Incite a Riot

My very first word on this subject must be that in Truth I have nothing at all against people who have chosen to adopt a same-sex lifestyle. And I am not speaking from a vacuum on this. I have had plenty of interaction with those of this stripe, and have always come away in admiration of their talents.

In fact, I find it pretty much impossible to imagine that anyone who has read this far in this book, and understood/assimilated even a pittance of it could think that I would engage name calling or wish any sort of harm upon anyone at any level of consciousness. We are One. My only desire is to encourage spiritual growth. So now, please do hear me out. Only benefit can result.

Extending the above conformance requirement for goal fitted health and wholeness as alluded to in the above description of rose bushes, humans are meant to concentrate upon developing their masculine consciousness when born as a man and their feminine consciousness when born as a woman.

Okay, I know I've probably gotten some dander up in some readers with that. So now that I'm on a roll, I might as well get some dander up in people on the other side of the fence. Maybe this way, we can all get together and rip up the fence.

Life is, *your* life is, amazingly complex. So much so that shrinks and therapists get to make a profession out of that. So, even though some readers may find themselves taking me to task for what I say below, know well that I understand that where they are in life, the attitudes and lifestyle they have engaged, may have been a necessary stepping stone needed to move them closer to where they need to eventually BE; and maybe not. Maybe adopting same-sex proclivities and/or activities was a sort of therapeutic addition to life they needed in order to sort themselves out amidst a Gordian knot of perplexities; *and maybe not.*

Nevertheless, HERE is the One NOW: every moment ushering in the New Day. As master Morya says, the past is prologue. No one is so bound to self-definitions adopted in the past that they must ignore the liberty now at hand and its ability to illumine fulfillment's pathway.

I'm certainly aware of the spiritual motto "never a backward step."

But if you are hiking along a mountain trail and find that it leads to a high cliff with no way around it (as I have done) a backward step becomes unavoidable. Maybe such readers will consider me to be but a finger pointing condemner of the same-sex lifestyle in that I have the audacity to label it a backward step. Not so. My intent here is not finger pointing condemnation, but an invitation to consider what I present as a viewpoint that leads to the unlimited realms that we are all destined to become.

I'll Not Press the Political Hot Button

In this discussion of sexuality, I will use the term LGBTQ only once. There, you just saw it. I will not use that term again because it has become one of many that have come to be inflicted upon us to divide, rather than to unite us. It has assumed the tenor of a politically charged hot button; and I want no part with such inharmony.

Every person is a unique individual, and should be honored as such.

Plopping people into categories and then expecting them to identify with those categories confounds each one's True, infinite nature. It also sets up warring factions whose warfare profits only those who benefit by keeping people at odds with each other. Please let me assume that my readers left that kind of stuff in the dust long, long ago.

It's foolish to judge an individual. One cannot know the entirety of their lifestream; what they have done over many embodiments and what their dreams are now. What each of us *can* assess for ourselves is how present activity aligns with the cosmic, universal harmony needed to progress along the homeward spiritual Path.

Energetic Flow

Let me begin by explaining something that seems to me to be so obviously simplistic that it actually embarrasses me, as a member of the human species, to find it necessary to elucidate.

So here it is: nothing exists without energy. Everything that does exist in the manifested universe IS energy.

Simple, right? I thought you'd agree.

Even Einstein kept it super simple. He showed us that $E = MC^{133}$.

That is, energy is mass times the square of the speed of light. That implies that some form of flow is involved in conveying the property of energy/existence. Flow can take the form of many types of energy, such as heat, light, sound and electrical. Here, I'll symbolize all types of energetic processes by using an electrical example.

Stuff is brought into manifestation and can appear to our senses by pushing out something (electrons, for electrical energy) and then the energy is applied to a load to perform some activity, and then balance is maintained when that energy returns to the source in its opposite polarity. For instance, the positive pole of a car battery supplies electrons to a circuit that shines headlights, and then the electrons return to the battery's negative pole to complete the circuit and keep everything in balance.

My point here is that nothing happens, nothing exists, without the presence of a positive pole and a negative pole. And the word "pole" refers to something that is purely what it is. A positive pole is not maybe-kinda-positive. It is nothing but positive. Same with negative. Consciousness works the same way. Positive/masculine/yang/Father polarity impels, and the receptivity of negative/feminine/yin/Mother polarity brings about its balance. In this way, conscious existence comes to be. The big trick of living a spiritual Life is to keep that balance in unity to live consciously awake in and as the One.

And again, I need to emphasize here that living in unity has nothing whatever to do with adulterating the pure masculine and feminine polarities of Being that produce Real imagery: the manifest One. Your outer awareness identifying in purity with your natal gender electrifies your world; it attracts the pure power of your opposite to let light flow in you concurrently and consummately.

Utilizing two elements of the same polarity will not produce flow/energy/Real existence. For instance, two like poles of a magnet repel each other, and hooking an electrical system up with one pole of a battery as the input of a circuit and also hooking up the output wire to the same pole will produce nothing.

Such a non-circuit could be termed "electrically unsuitable." I would add to that, regarding its spiritual implications "for infinite expression." Thus, to steer clear of the politically divisive term mentioned at the top of this section, that is how I will refer to the same-sex/same-pole approach to life. I will refer to consciousness that is "electrically unsuitable for infinite expression" as EUFIE.

Keep Government Out of This
People Must Make Their Own Choices

Know for sure that I am not about to suggest that government should outlaw or support EUFIE activity. That would just be one more instance of people possessing the force to back up their will requiring others to live according to their edicts.

I'm not of that ilk. I stand for liberty and the right use of it, which produces freedom. My wish here is to inform, and have people make their own choices.

My purpose is to draw out of each person's inner knowing the viewpoint that will resonate with their divine victory, to spur them to their graduation from the human level of evolution to their immortality as an ascended master. That can't be accomplished by rescinding free will.

I also want to repeat something from El Morya already quoted above. Anyone who thinks I'm out to pick a fight must read this and then reevaluate. If you entertain a EUFIE situation and you read the following sections and then choose to renounce that persuasion, I predict that you will thank your lucky stars that you got this book into your hands. Here's Morya:

> **"Thus the Cosmos exists in the greatness of the Dual Origins. Yes, yes, yes! Thus the Cosmos crowns the Dual Origins. Thus the Mother of the World and the Lords build life. Yes, yes, yes! And in boundless striving the Cosmic Magnet welds its sacred parts. Thus We venerate the Ruleress beyond all spheres."**[134]

The "Dual Origins" are masculine Father-God and feminine Mother-God. These live as Your twin-flame I AM Presence. The **purity** of these Origins enables all manifestation. That purity crowns them when their *maya* is interpreted to have arisen from basic immaculate *maya* and morphed into the *maya* of primordially pure pristine awareness. Then your creative purity evinces your royal identity as an instance of **ChRist's OWN** consciousness.

That purity is muddled up by denying either the fullness of your inherent masculine polarity or feminine polarity in each embodiment. That purity vividly extends your multicolored aura as a beacon of hope. Its vibrancy literally magnetizes and raises up like vibrations all around you to remind others who bear them that they, too, portray the living power of the Almighty One.

Morya's reference to the "welding of sacred parts" does not attribute to creation a process of setting out objects and joining them together. Instead such inner consciousness is an alchemical recognition of relationship *completely inseparable* from the One.

Again, again, and again: this involution of infinity with consciousness demands that the poles of the Cosmic Magnet be absolutely pure; especially in the consciousness of mortal, growing souls newly acquainting themselves with infinite consciousness. Same-sex ignorance of the One's pure polarities might be likened to cheating on a test, only to find out that your neighbor's answers were wrong.

Thus, below, I emphasize to the utmost the importance of embracing in gratitude the opportunity for male humans to put on the pure consciousness of the divine masculine and to develop everlasting male momenta and females to don and develop pure femininity. Attuning to such purity requires keen insight and discrimination. While the pure in heart will see God, there's definitely no telling what will be seen when the purity of the heart's twin flames are ignored.

It Is Way Beyond Foolishness
To Believe That Your Natal Genitals
Have Mistakenly Grown upon You

I have often heard EUFIEs say how sure they are that their physical gender is mistaken. Nevertheless, all of us come to Earth embodying a predesignated gender which we—our Higher Self, along with the Lords of Karma and all who will be embodying with us to complement a group karma—have chosen in order to fulfill the plans of the current embodiment. Thus, your natal gender IS your own choice. It was not foisted upon you.

So it's downright foolish to renege on all of that masterful inner wisdom and planning that was put into designing a life that maximizes your opportunity to bring about heartily hopeful spiritual progress.

Every embodiment is like a scholarship to a top university of the spirit. Your present equipment has been chosen to maximize your opportunity to graduate from your present embodiment, completing all the required courses, as a valedictorian.

Getting Pulled Off Track

Imagine you and your friends get together for a smash-up-bang Super Bowl party each year. And this year, it's your turn to bring home the pizza. So you go out to get it; it's all been ordered in advance and it's piping hot ready now. But on your way, you get it into your head that you ought to go into a 7-11 store first. You meet some other people there and get into a heated discussion about the game. And your pizza goes down those hatches. You look at your watch, and you are now very late. So off you go, taking a shortcut home. You walk through the door to a roomful of expectant faces and hungry bellies. And all you can do is to put a little Gatorade you got at the 7-11 on the coffee table.

☹Not so good.☹

Likewise, a big part of your reason for being in a particular embodiment is to bring Home gender oriented mastery. Your twin flames are counting on that. So gender detours can only disappoint.

Sexual Balance

However obviously true it may be that each of us must develop both masculine and feminine mastery to attain wholeness, that mastery is attained and honed, embodiment by embodiment, one gender at a time. That is not to say that men should be cruelly forceful or women limpidly acquiescent. True yang gentlemen bow to their gentler side, and true ladies assert their commanding presence whilst never losing sight of their essential tender, yin nature. Be neither light nor heavy in your loafers, but walk the middle way while honoring your divine plan's gender emphasis.

Some might think that saying sexual balance is to be applauded means that we should all be bi-sexual AC/DC types. No siree, not at all! True sexual balance can only be achieved by purely attuning to one's natal gender, for that purity is precisely what brings about the ability to merge twin flame magnetics.

People with a EUFIE Viewpoint
May Just Be Impelled By
Past-Embodiment Momenta

People who choose to be EUFIE either do not understand their own Higher Self's intent to honor their natal gender or are so emotionally caught up in energies of past embodiments that they choose to ignore it.

The gender opposite the current one was appropriate for other embodiments, for other life plans. But, gender identity and sexual orientation are metadata that, relating to the universal architecture of consciousness, are non-negotiable while in embodiment.

Emotional Niagaras

That is intellectually simple to comprehend. But people choosing a EUFIE viewpoint encounter emotional Niagaras countermanding their obvious gender. These river falls do not appear to be illusory to the outer self who identifies with them. They arise from real, deep memories.

A male may find himself beset with memories, intimations and proclivities of maybe the past ten embodiments when their life plans sent them to Earth as a female. And maybe as those ladies, that lifestream mastered the feminine viewpoint, with or without hubby after hubby. Those women assumed the role of the divine Mother, each one more or less enrobing herself in Her nourishing, prudent solicitude for all life.

So now "she" has been born as a man. Now it's a whole new ballgame. Now he must man up or others will chow down on him in a dog-eat-dog world. Such a man, being pushed this way and that by female momenta of past embodiments, may say, "What planet did you say this is? WhadamI doin' here, anyway? Ya know what? I think I'll just stick to my girlie momenta. Don't let this physique and those obvious genitalia fool you. I

208

know what I really am inside. I'm a loving, caring individual just looking for someone to recognize my real needs." Maybe this gay guy is actually the butch half of his item. Nevertheless, this nearly machoesque gay still feels that he prefers to not truly uphold the masculine pole of a relationship with a female counterpart.

Or if a person is bi-sexual, he may be subject to some combination of psychological detours, such as excessive lust or simple resentment against natal-gender limiting sexual liberty. Human egos can complicate immensely. But unless the solution proffered honors the natal gender, the drumbeat of conscience will never depart.

It's Cosmic Law; Not Manmade Imposition
Life's Magnetic Nature
Cannot Be Violated with Impunity

I see a EUFIE viewpoint as an attitude seeking to preserve one's distance from the *inherent* sexual tenor of Life, itself. The symbol of the Tao renders that polar sexuality slap-in-the-face obvious. Yang/yin wholeness applies equally to the vertical flow of an individual's I AM Presence with its evolutionary agent Christ/Soul, as well as the intimate horizontal flow of human man/woman relationship—not to mention the appearance of the entire manifest universes.

The key word here is "intimate." Men can be deeply close friends with other men and women with women. But the wholeness of sexual union and the ongoing consonance with Life's higher octaves must involve interlocking Life's polar archetypes—indeed, uniting them magnetically. That's not so complicated, eh? Life focuses its major masculine polarity in men; feminine in women. Messing with that is like pouring water on an operating circuit board. No gonna work no mo.

Misaligning one's outlook at odds with the Great Central Sun Magnet by adopting a EUFIE viewpoint automatically short circuits the inner electronics of consciousness. It may take many embodiments of ignoring Life's whole magnetic style, but eventually Life *will* take care of itself karmicly.

Human Love Is Not to Be Gainsaid; But....

If you are currently engaging a EUFIE viewpoint, you may truthfully point out that your love for your partner is a wonderful, fulfilling thing. And, yes, the love, itself, is! Nevertheless, the spiritual architecture of consciousness cannot be changed by outer human proclivities, however intense they may be.

EUFIE "Rights" Is a Misnomer

Some who have adopted a EUFIE viewpoint may not possess wholeness as a life goal. They may simply wave that off and assert their "right" to any lifestyle they choose. And, truly, that choice is theirs to assert. The right of free choice cannot be gainsaid. Never would I wish to curtail that liberty.

But conscientious—spiritually successful—living includes the understanding that misused liberty produces bad karma, which *curtails* freedom. Asserting such "rights" is counterproductive to the max.

Little by little are the prison chains forged and donned. Yes, foregoing immortality is allowed, but it can't go in forever. Only those who consistently choose Life will survive throughout the ages.

Straight or EUFIE
Is Not Just a Question of Morals

While I do morally oppose the EUFIE viewpoint and political agenda, I do not oppose it only on those grounds. While morals are not merely a minor detail of life, they are culture driven, and moral absolutes are hard to come by. What is considered morally approved in one culture may be eschewed in another. The only moral absolute is the golden rule.

As important as morals are, the purport of this book decries same-sex intimacy not on moralistic grounds but because such consciousness flies in the face of divine universal architecture. It is a denigration of its light generating intent, for only unified plus-minus polarity can produce and support spiritual light and its catalytic effect as infinity's transcendent agency.

That is not to say that those who engage a EUFIE lifestyle never carry spiritual light. Obviously, many successful, well-known artists and performers are out of the closet. Nevertheless, independent of their talents, their spiritual journey is stunted. (And this is not just Lloyd judging them. The fact is that whatever their spirituality may evince, it would bloom much more if they were to get straight with their Real Self.)

Well has it been said that we seek no continuing city down here in the soul's incubator. We need to fearlessly approach Life and demonstrate our mastery of light's alchemy. We would do well to maximize light's indelible inclusion in our consciousness as divine Love. Only thus will we enable our soul to ever leave our human condition behind permanently and set forth upon our immortal destiny.

A EUFIE Viewpoint
Doesn't Make You a Bad Person

Though it is morally wrong, overlaying your soul's purity with a EUFIE viewpoint doesn't make you a bad person. The core of your soul's purity always remains intact. It's how you use energy—perceptively and actively—that positions you on the spiritual Path. Most all of us still here on earth have for many centuries walked more or less out of step with Life's evolutionary proceedings. We've all got quite a load of karma to transmute to render our Path a thoroughfare.

So it's incumbent upon anyone discovering that they are set upon with EUFIE proclivities to boot them out forthwith. For I'd say that veering so far afield from the operational architecture of divine consciousness steadily and quickly buries one under so much karma that they would need beat a fox in a hole digging contest to get out from under it.

Humans Cannot Redefine Life

The world is now so topsy-turvy with the demand for so-called EUFIE "rights" that so-called leaders of our youth, with the power to direct their mindset, have begun to be overtaken by this misguided dead end. This news item shows the unbelievable length to which this can be taken:

"The board in the Fairfax County, Virginia, school district has decided to ban the fact that there is a 'biological sex,' and instead teach all students that sex is a 'fluid spectrum.'"[135]

That is so outlandish as to render even me speechless.

Fundamental to possessing a human body at all is the innate relation of its evolutionary microcosm (feminine divinity) to the macrocosmic state (masculine divinity) to our Reality. So denying of basic human sexuality extends its damage to evolving consciousness from its human focus right up to the collapse of one's respect for Father-Mother God as the poles of all manifest BEING.

We are compelled by our salient human features—not just our genitals, but all of our chakras (energy centers)—to realize an ascent from our microcosmic viewpoint to our macrocosmic identification with our twin flame provenance: the very seat of our conscious awareness as Father/Mother God. That is never written or to be understood as "Kinda Father/Kinda Mother" God. Even lifelong celibate monks and nuns, having no contact with the opposite sex, are intended to realize, through their attunement to masculine and feminine purity, their inner polar unity. El Morya explains:

"...the microcosm resembles the Macrocosm. I affirm that the fire of the heart purifies the densest darkness. But along with purification the fire of the heart is impregnated with the qualities of a magnet, and thus it becomes the natural link with the Macrocosm."[136]

That is, just as same magnetic poles repel, you need only adopt a same-sex viewpoint to repel your own Spiritual Self. Sustaining a EUFIE viewpoint, embracing sexuality as a "fluid spectrum," effectively disassembles in consciousness an awareness of and tie-in to the pure divine magnetism required to realize your intended ascent to immortality.

BOTTOM LINE:

- Masculine God IS: Father God empowers All possibility and its expression as the Son and Daughter of God (See the section "The Daughter of God" above for an explanation of how cap "D" Daughter of God can be seen as masculine).

- Feminine God IS: Mother God and Soul bring about joy, balancing pure masculine polarity with pure feminine polarity.

Soul takes human form to achieve such Great-Central-Sun magnetic mastery. A EUFIE viewpoint puts blinders on soul. It leaves awareness stuck in a rut, encapsulated and unable to fully achieve the wholeness that liberates soul from such ruts. This is not name calling or morals or anything but Self-obvious Truth. 'Nuff said.

The Spiritual Hierarchy
The Beginningless Endless Compendium
Of All Points of View

A spiritually childish person is self-centered, mostly concentrating upon their human ego in the beginnings and endings of things.

A spiritual adult identifies I AM THAT I AM with the unmitigated All in ALL.

Similarly, unascended souls, still stuck in human form, are more or less like children, and they are fully occupied in the task of identifying with "their own" I AM Presence.

Ascended Souls and those who are close to their ascension, along with those who have earned their ascension yet remain unascended to better serve mankind have achieved consonance with "their own" I AM Presence. Consequently, holographically, they realize their identity with all instances of the One I AM Presence.

Did you get that?

Did you REALLY get that?

Huh?

Okay, let's put this another way.

Spiritual initiations, the signals of spiritual growth, continue endlessly beyond the ascension of a human. The One's Self-realization expands, expands and ever expands. So now, let's say, you passed a milestone initiation and expanded your consciousness as an ascended master. Now you are, say, a Lord of a World. Your heart flame nourishes all the lifestreams on a planet, just like your human heart does right now in the universe of your physical body.

Now do you get it?

What happened to "your" I AM Presence?

Did it just go poof? Utterly disappear because it now identifies with and catalyzes, nourishes, the evolution of many "other" Presences?

Remember, now "your" I AM Presence has expanded. That is, its Causal Body now realizes it comprises all of the I AM Presence/Causal Bodies assigned to the planet for which you are the Lord of the World.

So what happened to the one out of the billions of I AM Presences assigned to Earth that "you" used to be?

Was it ever "there"?

Now let's say you evolve and evolve and evolve and now you are galactic. "Your" I AM Presence is a point of awareness whose Causal Body personality comprises galactic arms of billions of stars and planets and all of the lifestreams thereon.

And, by now "you" realize that "you" are actually the I AM Presence and Causal Body of the galactic supercluster above you in the Spiritual Hierarchy. But you haven't "yet" passed the initiation to BE that super cluster.

So who are you now? Are you the supercluster or the single galaxy you've been for oh, so many cycles?

And when "you" do become that supercluster, what about all those lifestreams in your old galaxy that still need to be nourished? Will some other Being come along to take up your old office in Hierarchy? What if they get there before you leave and you jointly serve? Just like you getting to your new supercluster before its current Hierarch leaves and you jointly serve there.

Whose I AM Presence are "You" then?

Ever onward it goes.

"You" can focus your awareness at any level of the spiritual Hierarchy you have in humility goal fitted yourself to nourish.

Is Saint Germain *only* Saint Germain? Is Morya *only* Morya?

Is there an I AM Presence, a facet of the One I AM Presence, who wholly contains the consciousness of both Saint Germain and Morya, both of whom masters know themselves to be One with? The Elohim

Hercules is El Morya's guru. The Cosmic Being The Great Divine Director is Saint Germain's guru. So what do you think Hercules and the Great Divine Director have in common? Don't ask me! I'm the one asking the questions around here.

Does an I AM Presence receive a new name as it passes ongoing initiations in its ascent through the spiritual Hierarchy? A new name that can act as the keynote for that Being's new, higher vibrational abode? If So, what happens to the name left behind? When lower beings call upon that name for blessings, does some force field of that lower name respond? Or does the greater You act from the height at which you now abide?

Don't answer until you meditate upon my nonstop rant: Only the One IS.

Remember, the One and Only I AM Presence in-divides to facet itself into innumerable I AM Presences. **So how big is a facet?** Does each facet stay precisely that big for more than a moment?

Who/what are you, anyway? Right NOW.

Do "you" own "your" I AM Presence?

<u>When it comes right down to it, the One focuses consciousness through innumerable points of awareness: each One simply a point of view, an office in the spiritual Hierarchy, shared in concert with all "others."</u>

Tooling Around as the Whole Shebang

Now let's take a quantum leap from our galactic super cluster, and identify with Alpha and Omega, the twin flames whose outpictured Selfhood is our entire universe. Now we ARE Alpha and Omega, the Father/Mother God who nourishes a cosmos at least fifteen billion light years across (and probably much more than that, given that the fifteen billion figure says more about the limitations of our current technology than the actual extent of our universe).

We can say, "I AM Alpha and Omega in the white fire core of being." And we can understand that Alpha and Omega are not just friends from "over there" who are visiting the salons of every cell, atom, electron, quark and all the microcosmic levels "below" those. Alpha and Omega are all of those points of view. **And so are "you."**

You Are a Fractally Resonant Agent of the One

If you think Alpha and Omega are some bigshots out there draped in ermine on some Great Central Sun Magnet throne, who dwarf "you," take it from me: "you" dwarf them.

That's right. "You" are also the multiverse in which they are merely a cell. You need not pass all of the initiations required for achieving full consonance and consciousness with all "levels" of the spiritual Hierarchy to realize I AM; to BE, to live in and as the One. You can *always* identify with the One and realize your concordance therein as a fractally resonant agent. To assume anything else is to squish your Self esteem down to that of a pipsqueak—not recommended. The fractal nature of your resonance NEVER goes away. "You're" always somewhere in the middle of the spiritual Hierarchy.

Getting Down to Cases

"You" ARE already, eternally all that the One IS. Your True Identity traverses worlds without end or beginning. Yet, you are also a unique personality of God. Your task at hand is to realize your intimate identity with the I AM Presence, "yours" first and foremost as a soul, but also, identically, ALL that the One and only I AM Presence comprises: an infinity of infinities of infinities with that phrase "of infinities" going on forever and ever, Amen and Ahhladies.

As an unascended soul, you accomplish that by surrendering the human ego and holding meditatively fast to the Great Unknowing, not to mention all the true grit of karma balancing. Using the science of the spoken word (decrees, fiats, prayer, mantras, etc.) greatly accelerates that. And consciously decreeing God's Rays into action will also assist your laboring to fulfill your divine plan: All that divinity in your Causal Body intends for your full blossoming.

Offices of the Spiritual Hierarchy
Who Is Planet Earth?

I was recently meditating on ascended higher service, imagining that I had become one with Planet Earth. But then I realized that even though the ascended masters have released the names of a great many of our elder brothers and sisters, I don't know the name of the Cosmic Being/Twin Flames whose body is the Earth. The ascended masters have released the names associated with very few large bodies. For instance:

- The hierarchs of the earth element managing Earth's physical body: Virgo and Pelleur.
- Lord of the World of Earth: Gautama Buddha
- Our sun: Helios and Vesta
- Hierarch of Venus: Sanat Kumara and Lady Master Venus
- Omri Tas, ruler of the Violet Planet (We don't know where that is.)
- Mercury: God Mercury

There may be others that don't come to mind now, but that's enough to illustrate the point I wish to make.

I have long considered the sun to be the heart chakra of Helios and Vesta; and all of the planets in our solar system to focus the energies of their other main chakras. But, in addition, I have been sleepily considering the sun the BE Helios and Vesta. Now I understand that all of the above Beings have chosen to hold an *office* in the spiritual Hierarchy. For instance, when Helios and Vesta gain the mastery/humility needed to nourish a larger star or star system than this, our own, They will move on and another Being will take over their office.

This dovetails perfectly with the message of this book and especially with the previous few sections above. Your identity—indeed, Your entire God Identity—is but a viewpoint of the One. Indeed, even li'l old you hold an office in the spiritual Hierarchy.

You are not set in stone as an iconic, static viewpoint. No lifestream can be said to be confined to "being" any planet or star or system of worlds or the domain over which you, yourself, rule right now. It's all in flux all the time and not time. Each One evolves their viewpoint endlessly. You—the One—are ever evolving; evolving every moment of

"Your" Life. So "You" are not just what you identify with right now. Only the One IS! arraying consciousness through a plenum of spiritual offices.

Your Microcosm Is Also Infinite
You Are the God of a Universe Right Now

As a busybody soul down here, you may find it difficult to look up to your Self as a masterful Presence rubbing elbows with Cosmic Beings. But consider this: you are already the God of a vast universe known to you as your physical body. Just take a physiology course if you need some help in blowing your Self-limiting mind. Such a course will open your eyes to an amazing physical cosmos appearing fully integrated with your willing supervision effected through your body's CEO, your body elemental. (We need not even mention the goings on of your thoughts, feelings and memories in those other bodies of yours. Just considering the mastery it takes to stick around here physically in space-time is impressive enough.)

You are essentially an Alpha and Omega of your physical body. Just being a human shows that you have already achieved so much proficiency that you can delegate your physical body's maintenance to the being mentioned above, your "body elemental," so that you can concentrate upon higher levels of mastery.

You can also partake of one heck of a lot of "independently" living points of view that Alpha and Omega have activated and delegated in their own physical body (our physical universe). Here are but a smattering of them: seraphim, cherubim, angels, archangels, Elohim, Chohans (Lords) of the Rays of God, cosmic councils, Lords of the Worlds, courts of the sacred fire, great karmic boards, humans, ascended masters, and all those other things that Hamlet informed Horatio he knew not of. There are correspondences to all of those points of view right there in what you may have been relating to as your puny little River City.

So what say you to surrendering? Giving that measly, apparently separate "me" a mighty heave ho! Grokking the following will help.

Assume you are now a cell in "your" kidney. When it extracts a toxin molecule from your bloodstream, what/who is acting? Is it just that cell? Or your whole kidney? Or your whole self? Whatever you answer, it's just a point of view, right? In fact, all are equally acting. In fact, all spiritual growth/initiation involves realizing as a living flame a greater Selfhood that is acting through "you".

Yes, indeed, you have already accomplished a mighty measure of Godhood, just being human. Just put on your subatomic divining helmet and peruse one cell in your physical body. You will see so many functions occurring in there that you will likely come away realizing that you have just visited a whole specialized universe whose larger function depends upon the physical body site where it is found.

Then come up a bit from there, and take a look at your kidneys, spleen, heart, etc. Pretty galactic, huh? Then visit your big ol' liver. Looks something like our old friend the galactic super cluster, doesn't it? Still think you're a pipsqueak? How about changing that point of view to assume your real role of Being as a direct agent of the Blesser. Maybe even radiate your blessings from the white fire core of every conscious entity within and without you. You know what's coming next, right?

Only the One IS.

How Long, O Lord?
Don't Look Around, That Lord Is You!

Suppose your Godly body gets a pimple on its skin. Ouch! You can just let it go, and suck up the pain. Or you can decide to bless that segment of your cosmos with faster healing. So you actuate your power to shorten the days of suffering for the elect cells there who crave homeostasis with the One—You. So you lance the pimply protrusion, purge the pus, pop in some drops of tea tree oil every few hours, and voila, "your" blessing will have returned that skin to its normal joyous song in just a day or so. That pimply skin's pain was its prayer to you, its God above, for intercession. It was totally dependent upon you exercising grace to intercede on its behalf. Otherwise it would just be stuck with its choruses of "how long, O Lord?"

It's easy, then, to appreciate the fractal nature of "as above, so below;" how beginningless and endless it is. How your Godhood is functional RIGHT HERE NOW as you adjust your viewpoints in and as the One.

Don't get me wrong. I know full well how hard that is to do, given the thousands of years of karmic mangling of our own consciousness and the muddy waters of outrageous fortune we have had to deal with... and, dare I come right out and say it...even embraced. But getting our points of view aimed right is a big boon to our freedom. So saddle up and sing along, "OM, OM on the range; let the fear and the I-can't-cope fray; where never is heard *maya*'s deadly reverb; and the light poofs the phantoms away."

Two Meditational Approaches

Ramakrishna was known to approach life using two meditational approaches. The first is "not this, not this" and the second is "this, this."

Practicing "not this, not this" involves rejecting from consciousness all forms of any kind, which your perceptions, thoughts and feelings deliver to your seat of consciousness. In their stead, "you" joyously succumb to the clear, pure light of infinite mystery, yet remain wholly conscious of the elements that perception presents to you as "wide-open doorways to serendipitous integration."[137]

Practicing "this, this" involves concentrating upon detailed elements of perception as a mandala of the One. Unique in its own right, each solicitous member of that rendezvous of consciousness proclaims with overwhelming pizzazz the same serendipitous integration *in* the One which "not this, not this" imparts *as* the One. THAT teeming Beauty exhibits a granularity so fine as to render all separating borderlines invisible.

These two meditational approaches can be seen to correspond to two of the last (higher) stages of the path for the Nyingma School of Tibetan Buddhism. After the eighteenth century, says Keith Dowman, gradualists had come to dominate, and Trekcho—"the phase or aspect of the resolution of duality where the luminous mind shines through as alpha-purity"—("not this, not this") came to be presented prior to Togal—"the phase or aspect of the same resolution where that same luminous mind is perceived in a unitary experience of spontaneously arising phenomena"—(this, this).

Thus the two assumed a fallacious sequencing that led to their being taught as inherently different. This ordering and consequent separation remains a stumbling block to true liberation for those who adhere to this view. Dowman counsels:

> **"In order to reach the plane where there is no ladder of spirituality to climb and no pyramid of meditational**

accomplishment to hold us in awe, we need to be free of the notion that we can fall to a lower level of existential cognizance or rise to any higher state. Only then can we relax into the all-embracing matrix of the now."[138]

Certainly, consciousness as an observer, can change and it can focus very limiting conceptions of being. But, as the "we/us" that Dowman referred to above, cap "W" and cap "U" are in order, as our Reality; as the One we ARE, which simply IS ultimately unlimited Self realization.

Is Ascension/Liberation a Goal?

In other words, this counsel from Keith Dowman does not negate the evolutionary nature of Life, of the Spiritual Hierarchy. Rather it simply restates that only the One IS. Every element of consciousness is inherently only the One, and relative, confining so-called higher and lower levels are moot. Every so-called "level" of the Spiritual Hierarchy is You! "You" are already there, at every "level." Spiritual progress only involves your continually transcending Self **realization** of the One you already ARE. Indeed, as I love to remind myself: you live in eternity NOW. THAT is no far off goal.

Another important point of radical Dzogchen's pathless path confounds the intellectualism that enthralls those who misunderstand the Togal praxis of experiencing God in every "thing" (this, this). Developing intellectual, analytic skill may be useful for navigating space-time, but it is much less useful to spirituality. Humans must overcome the fantastically heavy handed inclination to intellectually create phantom goals and then revel in accomplishing them. To spiritual Reality, that amounts to no more than your body's "automatic" process of digesting a cup of soup so you can get on with your real work of surrendering the ego and living the One: As the guys and gals used to love saying in the '60s: BE HERE NOW.

Hence, Dowman is not merely name calling when he says:

"If intellectual arrogance raises its ugly head, it is the demonic head of ego assuming that there is a

goal, near or far, that needs to be accomplished and that there is a technique, the prerogative of superior intellect, that can accomplish it."[139]

This shoots to pieces the notion that most everyone on the spiritual path possesses that "they" have bad karma, which must be balanced in order to achieve the goal of liberation or ascension.

From the viewpoint of karmic accounting, that may very well be true—each soul is responsible for reestablishing harmony to the sore thumbs they have left sticking out.

But holding onto a separate "you" who has bad karma feeds right into the original sin: the sense of separation.

Holding the sense of a limited "you" in the forefront of consciousness is a counterproductive viewpoint that unnecessarily burdens the purity of your soul.

From the viewpoint of radical Dzogchen, surrendering to the resolution of karmic dissonance in the NOW is not goal achievement, but pure living I AM. As Dowman writes:

"The crux is the place where dualities are resolved, where mind is never distracted or drawn out; it has no motivation and remains in its natural disposition, transcending all goal orientation."[140]

I of my supposedly separate self, can do nothing, right? You got that a long time ago. So why would you now adopt the mindset of a "you" who "has" karma? That just affirms and recreates the illusionary sense of separation that is THE stumbling block on the homeward Path.

Better to ever realize you live in eternity NOW.

The Keeper of the Scrolls and the Lords of Karma must have to bend over backward to bring themselves to somehow associate magnetics that are dissociated from the One with a personal element of the One. But that's Their job, not yours. Let them do it as you keep on keeping on in and as the One.

Another way of looking at that silliness of separation is to know that, of course, you have bills to pay each month. But you don't go around intensely focusing on that process all month long, every month. When bills come up, you just pay them when you have enough money as a matter of course. Your attention is free to concentrate on other stuff all the rest of the time. So let your bad karma balancing just ride along as a minor detail of your life and keep your solid gold concentration upon your high flying greased lightning.

The Liberation of Zen and Radical Dzogchen
Is *Sine qua non*
As Is Fully Realizing Advaita Vedanta's One

Until you realize the One, liberated largely from *samsara*, the wheel of birth and death, your major task is first to center consciousness, to live in Reality. For that will empower every moment's contribution to infinity's transcendence.

William Wordsworth describes what life would be like, having attained the ability to maintain such centeredness. He says he owes to the beauteous forms that such divine posture brings about all of his joyous Self realization; "the burthen of the mystery":

> **"...sensations sweet,**
> **Felt in the blood, and felt along the heart;**
> **And passing even into my purer mind,**
> **With tranquil restoration: –feelings too**
> **Of unremembered pleasure: such, perhaps,**
> **As have no slight or trivial influence**
> **On that best portion of a good man's life,**
> **His little, nameless, unremembered, acts**
> **Of kindness and of love. Nor less, I trust,**
> **To them may I have owed another gift,**
> **Of aspect more sublime; that blessed mood,**
> **In which the burthen of the mystery,**
> **In which the heavy and the weary weight**
> **Of all this intelligible world,**
> **Is lightened:–that serene and blessed mood,**
> **In which the affections gently lead us on,–**
> **Until, the breath of this corporeal frame**
> **And even the motion of our human blood**
> **Almost suspended, we are laid asleep**

In body, and become a living soul:
While with an eye made quiet by the power
Of harmony, and the deep power of joy,
We see into the life of things."[141]

Indeed, having surrendered soul's love affair with your own half created phantoms and having for a time retained this Way, Truth and Life, your outlook and Being become more and more immune to the screeching, worldly-sweet grasping of illusion's phantoms:

"That time is past,
And all its aching joys are now no more,
And all its dizzy raptures. Not for this
Faint I, nor mourn nor murmur; other gifts
Have followed; for such loss, I would believe,
Abundant recompense. For I have learned
To look on nature, not as in the hour
Of thoughtless youth; but hearing oftentimes
The still, sad music of humanity,
Nor harsh nor grating, though of ample power
To chasten and subdue. And I have felt
A presence that disturbs me with the joy
Of elevated thought; a sense sublime
Of something far more deeply interfused,
Whose dwelling is the light of setting suns...
"Knowing that Nature never did betray
The heart that loved her; 'Tis her privilege,
Through all the years of this our life, to lead
From joy to joy: for she can so inform
The mind that is within us, so impress
With quietness and beauty, and so feed
With lofty thoughts, that neither evil tongues,
Rash judgments, nor the sneers of selfish men,
Nor greetings where no kindness is, nor all
The dreary intercourse of daily life,
Shall e'er prevail against us, or disturb
Our cheerful faith that all which we behold
Is full of blessings."[142]

I interpret this as Wordsworth entering into the solemnity that El Morya so reveres as the safe harbor of climbers upon the upward Way.

Having Realized Some Measure
Of Your Primal Disposition,
You Are Enlisted in the Army of the Lord

Okay, so let's say "you've" entered into radical Dzogchen's great satisfaction. Pretty blissy, huh?

Now what?

Now "what?" is that it is incumbent upon those who have a ticket to ride with God's bands to travel in league with the Great Teams of Conquerors; to play your part in the army of the Lord.

This is because the bestowal of free will upon souls dictates that God allows them to fail, to choose to activate evil in their world. And so very many of us do just that! Surely I need not inform you that diabolically intense levels of evil now exist on planet Earth. And all of that evil, most of it not aimed directly at you, still assails your Own body and those of your loved ones: the One body of God.

Feeling the weight of such abominations, many people are left crying "How long, O Lord?" OF COURSE, the divine will ultimately be All that is left after the vast outplaying of the manvantaras. But in the meantime, the space-time incubator in which tender souls evolve, preparing for their immortality, must remain relatively free of obstacles to victoriously achieving their lesson plans.

Light bearers are not meant to be doormats to evil forces! Allowing the Divine Mother's womb to be overtaken by totalitarian, demonic entities is not to be sanctioned. **Achieving the perfect rest that is radical Dzogchen is only the very first step on the infinite Path of the ever evolving Spiritual Hierarchy of light.**

Earth's Cleanup Is a Do-It-Yourself Project

People pray to God to intercede to clean up planet Earth of its criminals. And God is ever so willing to do so. But that can only be brought about through divine agents on Earth, acting in the vibrational range in which the evil takes place.

Don't look around. That's you.

It's "you" who needs to get down to cases not by becoming some self-styled vigilante, but by assuming the consciousness mode of nonaction. Keith Dowman beautifully describes the state of nonaction (acting from a state beyond the human ego) that must be assumed to become a full-fledged warrior/actor on the divine stage:

"No matter what situation arises, we do not engage it in order to improve it or try to suppress it, for the key to pure presence is freely resting in our natural disposition. Thus nonaction is the key and the crux. In the Dzogchen view nonaction is recognized as noncausality, nonduality, unitary sameness, indivisibility and immediacy."[143]

Reading this, one may be tempted to conclude that the goal of Life is to sit around watching a nice, automatic, spontaneous movie show.
NOT SO!!!

NOT SO!!!!!!!

NOT SO!!!!!!!!!!!!
(This neon sign is flashing!)

Indeed, Dowman clarifies:

> **"Non-action...does not necessarily imply inaction, passivity or stasis; it entails neither a loss or diminution of efflorescence nor any particular manner of being."**[144]

True: it is necessary to be able to step back from the zinging-around-here-and-there-busybody-space-time-realm—through radical Dzogchen or any other spiritual practices you find effective. Whatever methods you use to catalyze your Peace commanding Presence, your soul must realize your primal disposition in light and only light, divine Love and only THAT.

Realizing the nonaction of the Dzogchen view buys your passage upon Maitreya's clipper ship; upon your *Merkabah* chariot to timelessly, eternally "travel" along the "Via Victoria" that is the One's infinite transcendence. (In Ezekiel Chapter one, the prophet describes a vision of a chariot of the Gods. I understand that vison to describe the format of consciousness which soul can assume to navigate *maya* without being caught in its snares. Thereby, even unascended soul can identify with

God's ongoing, infinite transcendence, contributing to it as the feminine aspect of the I AM Presence in evolutionary mode.)

Never—NO, **NEVER**—take Life for but an irrelevant game of tiddlywinks. Given *maya*'s insubstantiality, *maya* could rightly be viewed as a cosmic joke; yet, even when appreciated in that way, God is concomitantly imagined as the joke's inwardly solemn standup comic, so that *maya*'s jokes are what puts bread on the table for the whole cosmic family.

Serious spiritual aspirants are familiar with the paradoxical nature of their consciousness, in that they KNOW themselves to be All One and simultaneously Individual. So it will not be surprising to them that radical Dzogchen's nonaction paradoxically brings about the figure-eight flow of divine Individuation. This in turn enables world service by involving the infinite One in what would otherwise merely activate the *maya* of false concepts. Such service in and as the One turns up Gaia's rheostat, intensifying the light here, paying Her electric bill. That brings about a greater divine judgment and removal of personal and planetary evil. For wherever light IS, darkness is not.

Sluggards? BAH! OM-AH-HUMbug

Some points are so important that I feel it incumbent to repeat them in several different ways. This is one of them.

Gautama Buddha is no sluggard. Nor is the great Master Morya. The "nonaction" Dowman references corresponds to the realization "of myself I can do nothing; it is the Father in me who doeth the works." That is, it is your divine Self, holographically in league with all other agents of infinity, who acts through you—all One. It is the hubris of your human ego and that of the mass consciousness that is nullified when achieving some measure of liberation. Then it's time—yes, it's always the right time—to work the works of the Lord.

I'm reminded of a friend who once told me, "Everything comes to he who waits; as long as he works like heck while he is waiting." Radical Dzogchen's nonaction is the viewpoint that must be assumed while following Master Morya's motto: "Let us be up and doing." Corollary to this is His injunction to identify with God's will in a "thrust for a purpose" to enable the Cosmic Being Mighty Victory to live and move and have His Being in you.

It would be safe to say that El Morya has written voluminously about the need for striving on the spiritual path. Here He counsels:

"You are right in asserting that the Lord Buddha had to give the concept of Nirvana to the world because there are few who are willing to labor eternally for the creation of new forms. Nirvana is only a step in the endless cosmic periods. Our disciples, accumulating the earthly inheritance, can rejoice, transporting themselves with striving consciousness toward the higher worlds. Is it not better to serve the manifestation of the great eternal reworking and transformation from the lower to the higher than to be slave to stagnation?"[145]

I'm reminded here of the disciple who asked his master what he needed to do to achieve enlightenment. One would think that a master would counsel non-attachment and the denial of desire. But this master took his disciple out into a body of water and held him under for so long a time that he was super close to drowning.

The master then told the disciple that he must want enlightenment as much as he wanted his next breath just then.

It's sure paradoxical how much nonaction it takes to allow the One to inhabit your consciousness fully. Gautama Buddha was no blissed out sluggard. Sluggards fail. So cry out with Morya: Let us be up and doing! Indeed, says El Morya:

"It is a festival for Us each time a pure direction of the thought is projected into the sphere of invisible existence. One must lead into the abode of the Elohim with complete perseverance, as though danger pursued the entering one."[146]

Note Morya's phrase "pure direction of the thought." Such directed thought does not arise from wishy-washy blissed out people. Cosmic festivals arise from the penetration of higher spheres by mighty vanguards of an aspirant's concentrated awareness.

Spirituality Is No Walk in the Park

So horrendous is the pall of evil that must be erased from the space-time grounds where the One's tender shoots dwell that a group of the heavenly hosts who counter that evil is called the wrathful deities. These are divine warriors of light who are so fearful to fallen angels and all who defame consciousness that no amount of the latter's darkness can stand in their presence.

The Wikipedia article on the wrathful deities is well worth reading in its entirety. Here is an introductory part of it:

> **"In non-Tantric traditions of Mahayana Buddhism, these beings are protector deities who destroy obstacles to the Buddhas and the Dharma, act as guardians against demons and gather together sentient beings to listen to the teachings of the Buddhas. In Tantric Buddhism, they are considered to be fierce and terrifying forms of Buddhas and Bodhisattvas themselves. Enlightened beings may take on these forms in order to protect and aid confused sentient beings. They also represent the energy and power that is needed in order to transform negative mental factors into wisdom and compassion. They represent the power and compassion of enlightened activity which uses multiple skillful means (upaya) to guide sentient beings as well as the transformative element of tantra which uses negative emotions as part of the path. According to Chogyam Trungpa, 'wrathful yidams work more directly and forcefully with passion, aggression, and delusion - conquering and trampling them on the spot.'"**[147]

Higher Initiations

Details re the higher initiations immortals undergo are beyond the scope of anything I can convey. But one thing is clear. Immortals, too, must overcome supposed limitation circumscribing attunement with infinite mystery. They accomplish that through the mastery of alchemical skills of such fine grained discrimination that it is impossible and plain silly for such as us still-aborning-ones to attempt to understand such exacting realization.

But my intimations tell me that the main difference between unascended and ascended spiritual growth lies in the number of I AM Presences the aspirant is working to include in Self Identity. We, down here, have all we can do to fully realize the scope of our one, supposedly "own" I AM Presence.

But it seems to me that after the ascension our opportunities for greater humility abound unto consonance with universes and beyond. After our ascension, in our immortal state, our viewpoint, our appreciation for the scope of consciousness will veritably explode. We will be given a magical mystery tour to beat All. The Cosmic Being Mighty Cosmos has offered to take newly ascended masters on a grand tour of our universe. And maybe He will throw in a tidbit or two about the multiverse. I can just hear Mr. Rogers' Higher Self up there offering a big smile and a "Welcome to the neighborhood."

The Two-Way Street of Service Above and Below

Never ending spiritual initiation is a process that proceeds in two directions at once, throughout the spiritual Hierarchy:

- From below, from which aspirants realize that they are capable of expressing more by intensifying humility as they expand their understanding and skill.

- From above, from which Beings develop receptors which enable them to assimilate I AM Presences of lesser attainment as emanations of "their own" I AM Presence. For instance, Avalokiteśvara needed to prepare a place in His consciousness that could nourish and express all of the divine virtue that is known as Kwan Yin. Thereby, He/She could "Individually" emanate that consciousness as Her "own" I AM Presence as a concentration of compassion and mercy.

We, as humans do the same. For example, consider a think tank dedicated to furthering and improving education. The organization as a whole would have to prepare offices and means of communication for each of its emanations in the areas of teaching, curriculum, testing, etc. Adding new areas of concern to be helped requires that activity to develop receptors and disseminators to handle the development of the new levels of that activity.

Those whom such an organization serves would be rising in their own mastery and service simultaneously with the organization expanding its ability to serve from above. How useful it is, then to develop those viewpoints of simultaneous service from above and below in your own consciousness.

The Tai Chi Symbol and Your Caduceus Energy Signal the Time-Space/Space-Time Balance That Truly Expands Consciousness

The Tai Chi symbol expresses the balance your consciousness assumes between your inner, time-space immaculate conceptions and your outer, space-time Art. If you ignore this *Tai Chi* balance or simply find your microclusters in short supply due to stress or lack of sleep, *maya*'s secondary energies will find it easier to overcome your divine diligence. You will then more likely to become a sleepy eyed wanderer through space-time's "dime stores and bus stations" as Dylan puts it. That is, enlightened wakefulness will be harder to come by.

Living the time-space/space-time *Tai Chi* balance energizes both your inner and outer expression of consciousness through the caduceus enfolding your spinal column. It focuses universal energies as *prana*, also known as the life force, which energizes the microcosm of the human body and the macrocosm of the entire universe. According to a

Wikipedia article, prana, "...creates a fine biochemical substance which works in the whole organism and is the main agent of activity in the nervous system and in the brain."[148] I would not be surprised if that fine biochemical substance is composed of the time-space/space-time microclusters Wilcock describes in Part three, above.

In Indian medicine and spiritual science, *nadis* are subtle energy channels, which carry prana throughout the human body. The three most important of these are the *ida*, which runs vertically along the left of the spine, the *pingala* along the right, and the *sushumna*, which runs along the center, the spinal cord.

"When awakened, kundalini travels upward within *sushumna*. The *ida* and *pingala nadis* are often seen as referring to the two hemispheres of the brain. *Pingala* is the extroverted (Active), solar *nadi*, and corresponds to the right hand side of the body and the left hand side of the brain. *Ida* is the introverted, lunar nadi, and corresponds to the left hand side of the body and the right hand side of the brain (there is a contra lateralization). These *nadis* are also said to have an extrasensory function, playing a part in empathic and instinctive responses."[149] Thus, it would appear that the *pingala* is more heavily related to the space-time realm, and the *ida* to the time-space realm.

Conscious Contact with Inner Planes
It's Important to Practice Discrimination

Earth's peoples practice a wide variety of means for contacting inner (higher than physical frequency ranges) planes of consciousness. Some of these produce insight, healing, general wellbeing, psychological problem solving, as well as establishing a reverence for the infinite One whom practitioners show to be imminently available.

But not all of these practices bring about the true spirituality of pure Self realization. Some draw upon the astral plane, which the ascended masters describe as the sewer of the human consciousness. Just being invisible doesn't make such energy good.

The key to discriminating between karmicly divine, liberating practices and those which karmicly imprison lies in the attitude and the intent as well as the self-image of the practitioner. Righteous transmission of higher plane energies and knowledge involves the unremitting assumption: Of myself I can do nothing.

The Difference Between
Black Magic and Witchcraft

To the extent that the human ego is involved in bringing about change in ignorance of the infinite flaming Presence of God in the heart, the result is more or less black magic and/or witchcraft.

Black magic thwarts God's will by obstructing divine energy, inhibiting its entrance into the space-time realm. Black magicians divert divine energy to empower illusory self-aggrandizement. This is like the Wizard of Oz lording himself over his subjects from behind his cloaking curtain.

Witchcraft manipulates already extant space-time energies to inflict the *maya* of false conception upon the lives of others. Being the antithesis of divine love, a witch's ego casts spells and incantations to bring about pain and suffering, as well as to reinforce the sense of separation from the One. Remember the weird sisters of Shakespeare's Macbeth and their bubble, bubble, toil and trouble.

I know; many people consider witchcraft to often be the work of nature lovers in harmony with the outer world to bring about useful human results. But, again, to the extent that the practitioner identifies with an ego manipulating energy, it degrades divine opportunity and can even invoke loathsome, demonic spirits.

A Higgs-Field Interpretation of Black Magic

In Part Three, I discussed the Higgs field as the presence of divine potential anchored in the outer space-time milieu. There, it was pointed out that the lowest energy of outer activity—where the divine Presence remains completely in potential—corresponds to a positive, non-zero Higgs field. So it occurs to me that a way to characterize black magic may be that it is signaled by a Higgs field that is less than that zero-energy amount. Such a depressed Higgs field would indicate energetic processing intended to inhibit divine potential from being activated. That is what black magicians do. They impose force fields upon matter that are intended to degrade divine virtue's potential or to deform its patterns so that activating that potential will produce off kilter results.

Psychedelic Drugs: Bah, Humbug!

Another negative indicator that a practice used to contact and draw forth inner energies is to be shunned is the use of chemical substances to bring about an altered state. LSD "trips" may, in some cases, be useful in opening up consciousness to an awareness of inner planes beyond the hard-and-fast physical. But they are certainly not needed, and real spiritual teachers would strongly countermand LSD's use. Dependence upon any drug or natural substance for such inner spiritual experience is ultimately counterproductive. Human spiritual energy centers (chakras) can contact and channel pure, higher frequency consciousness without such substance dependence. Spiritual progress for the soul is countered rather than augmented through the use of LSD, marijuana, magic mushrooms, DMT, peyote (mescaline), psilocybin, ayahuasca or any other substance.

I know that many spiritually oriented people think that ritual use of ayahuasca is okay to do; even to be encouraged because they think that it can enhance spirituality. But my two cents on the matter is that such substance should ONLY be used if a person is so utterly dumbfounded—riveted to matter—that only cannon fire can deliver the push needed for them to realize that there is indeed more out there/in there than the hard and fast workaday world of relativity, of apparently separate entities. But for people who are already spiritually oriented, all chemical interventions upon consciousness for so-called spiritual enhancement is to be avoided.

Conclusion

Dustin Hoffman's character Bernie gets it all wrong when he says to his son in his movie "Hero":

"What you learn when you get older is there ain't no truth. All there is is BS—pardon my vulgarity. Layers of it; one layer of BS on top of another. And what you

do in life when you get older is: you pick the layer of BS you prefer, and that's your BS, so to speak. You got that?"

"No."

"Well, it's complicated. Maybe when you go to college."

Your BS is the bits and pieces of *maya* you mix and match and piece together into the mess of pottage your senses consume to push and pull you through the rushing cameos you take as your unlawful wedded life. It's that beloved push-pull ego you wake up to each morning hoping for a sunny outlook, even while decrying the stupid crud it, itself, clogs you with.

Bernie would have done better to tell his son that when ego is surrendered enough to let love's mystery singe the senses, the BS fades into the wind beneath *maya*'s wings and crystalline consciousness shines.

Here is another warning against choosing a way of life that is little more than choosing your self-styled form of BS:

When you call yourself an Indian or a Muslim or a Christian or a European, or anything else, you are being violent. Do you see why it is violent? Because you are separating yourself from the rest of mankind. When you separate yourself by belief, by nationality, by tradition, it breeds violence. So a man who is seeking to understand violence does not belong to any country, to any religion, to any political party or partial system; he is concerned with the total understanding of mankind.[150]

Yes, attaching yourself to any concept or "thing" does violence to all that is left out. There's really only one lawful "category" to cleave to: THAT of the One afire with God's willing infinite mystery.

Even so, saying that all *maya* needs to be accepted as all the One, definitely doesn't mean that all of the warring faction content of *maya* must also be condoned. As previously said, *maya* that is not expressing divine virtue is to be eschewed, for spiritual discrimination is also a *sine qua non* of the spiritual Path.

Revisiting Who Am I? What Am I?

I recently had a lucid dream that was so amazing that my writing about it can't put a finger upon the vivid awe it struck me with. I will only give a general description here of some of its scenes. The dream took place in realms that are not of this world. Where they happened is irrelevant, as I was traveling around cosmos instantaneously among "places" or states of consciousness.

David Wilcock and Corey Goode describe a race of beings they call the blue Avians, who look pretty much like humans, except that they are very tall, have a birdlike head, and they are colored blue. Weird, right? Well, for what it's worth, Goode says he has met with these beings often. He says they are "of the light" and are here to help humanity evolve beyond its current slave state. So the beginning of my dream did not seem completely fantastic to me.

I was contacted by a blue colored being (I don't remember at all what its head looked like,) and was taken to a large convocation of mostly blue beings but also several other types. I do not remember what was said there; only that I was supposed to help with something, which I don't remember now. They indicated that they would be providing powerful backing for that mission. That is all I remember from that part of the dream.

Then I went to various places in cosmos, the details of which I do not remember. But the important part that I do remember is that I always, upon arrival, took the form of whatever kind of beings were there. That happened automatically. Also I could speak to them and they could understand me. Obviously, though, their language was not English. And when I heard them, I heard English. Neato cool.

Then I remember getting trapped in some force field that I just could not free myself from. I was actually becoming quite a claustrophobic scaredy-cat. Then, before I actually started freaking out, a blue being walked through the wall of that force field and led me out of it. He took me back to the original place where I was in the beginning of the dream.

That's all I need to relate about the dream, itself. My take away from it has a lot to do with it happening during the time I am writing this book. I think my Higher Self wanted me to experience and feel deeply the concepts I am writing about here. I do not know or care whether the events of the dream were "real" or totally imagined. Whatever happened in the dream, I believe, has nothing to do with me, personally. That is, I do NOT have or want conscious contact with unascended aliens. (Ascended "aliens" ARE the spiritual Hierarchy and are not alien at all. They are One with All Life.)

What I experienced and have now much more deeply assimilated, is how very true it is that "you" are but a viewpoint of the One. Our Higher consciousness can easily assume any form it wishes, and even have that on instantaneous autopilot, fitting you in as the needs of the hour dictate. Same with language. So the dream has imparted to me a profound sense of freedom from attachments I had re being a person called Lloyd who looks like I physically do and who hosts my desires. More deeply centered in a consciousness beyond space-time, and even beyond time-space, I more consciously now experience most all of my life as rapidly changing viewpoints, while my Reality sustains I AM THAT—best as my karma allows it to, that is. I'm still quite a forgetful fellow, and must continually remind myself of who/What I AM. But having written this book, and you having now read it, we have plenty of ammo to use against weirdo slings and arrows.

I think that the real strength and usefulness of what I have conveyed in this book is that I certainly am not worthy of any claim to any degree of spiritual attainment whatever. I'm still the same old Lloyd with the same old limitations, making the same old mistakes over and over. That's precisely why even a whit of a greater feeling of freedom is so appreciated in this precinct. That is the whole point of the mater: spiritual progress is utterly available to all who are willing to persistently avail themselves of their peace commanding Presence.

A Final Four

I wish to leave you with my version of answers to four questions spiritual seekers entertain:

- **Who Am I?**

  Only the One IS. Individuated, the One comes to realize its infinite mystery immanently as God's name I AM THAT I AM. You are that Name's agent and its viewpoints, from ultimate quiescence in nirvana to worlds without end.

- **Why am I Here?**

  Your Individuality—"Your" I AM Presence in its state of Oneness coupled with its evolutionary mode Christ/Soul enable infinity to transcend itself as joy.

- **Where Am I Going?**

  Infinite mystery comprises the spiritual Hierarchy, which is the journey therein. You already ARE multiverses of sentience. Yet infinite mystery marks its guideposts of Self realization with "levels" of the spiritual Hierarchy such as You.

- **How Do I Get There?**

  By realizing "You" are already "there."

I AM beginningless endless joy.

The spiritual practice known as the science of the spoken word (decrees) combined with the practice of the Presence are the most effective catalysts of which I am aware.

A TRILOGY IN MAYA
BIBLIOGRAPHY

First, I wish to alert anyone who doesn't know about the free online availability of all of El Morya's Agni Yoga books from the Agni Yoga Society. They have given me permission to use any content from those books, which can be downloaded from:

http://agniyoga.org/index.php

Next, let me put in a plug for M. John Harrison's novel *Light.* That book is a real treat for those who wish to have a peek at what it's like to oscillate back and forth through Life at the macro and quantum levels as soul goes through her growing pains.

Dr. Amit Goswami is a quantum physicist who has definitely beat me to the punch. If you found my book useful, you will definitely <u>not</u> want to neglect his book: *The Self-Aware Universe: How Consciousness Creates the Material World.* There, he finely details the quantum physics approach to consciousness.

I would also, in passing, suggest that you watch the film "Peaceful Warrior" with Nick Nolte and Scott Mechlowicz. It does a great job of portraying many of the concepts in this book.

Now, here are the sources used for this book:

- Amit Goswami, *The Self-Aware Universe: how consciousness creates the material world* (New York: Jeremy P. Tarcher/ Putnam, 1993)
- Bhagavan Sri Ramana Maharshi, *Who Am I?* (Tamil Nadu, India: Sri Ramanasramam, 2010)
- D. J. Conway, *By Oak, Ash & Thorn* (St. Paul, Minn.: Llewellyn Publications, 1999)
- Dr. Eban Alexander III, *Proof of Heaven* (New York: Simon & Schuster Paperbacks, 2012)

- El Morya, *Heart* (New York: Agni Yoga Society, 1932, 1975)
- El Morya, *Hierarchy* (New York: Agni Yoga Society, 1933, 1975)
- Elizabeth Clare Prophet with Patricia R. Spadaro and Murray Steinman, *Kabbalah: Key to Your Inner Power* (Livingston, Mont.: Summit University Press, 1997)
- Ervin Laszlo, *Science and the Akashic Field: An Integral Theory of Everything* (Rochester, VT: Inner Traditions, 2004, 2007)
- Jorge Luis Borges, *Collected Fictions*, trans. Andrew Hurley (London: Penguin Books Ltd., 1998)
- Jorge Luis Borjes, *Labyrinths,* (New York: New Directions Publishing Corporation, 1962, 1964, 2007)
- Longchenpa, *Finding Rest in the Nature of Mind: The Trilogy of Rest, Volume 1,* trans. The Padmakara Translation Group (Boulder, Colorado: Shambala Publications, Inc., 2017)
- Longchenpa, *Maya Yoga: Finding Comfort and Ease in Enchantment,* trans. Keith Dowman (Kathmandu, Nepal: Vajra Publications, 2010 and 2014)
- Longchenpa, *Spaciousness: Longchenpa's Precious Treasury of the Dharmadhatu,* trans. Keith Dowman (KeithDowman@gmail.com: DzogchenNow! Books, 2012, 2014)
- M. John Harrison, *Light* (New York: Bantam Dell, 2004)
- *Pearls of Wisdom* (Gardiner, Mont.: The Summit Lighthouse)
- R. J. Stewart, *Celtic Gods Celtic Goddesses* (London: Blanford; Cassell Illustrated, 1990; 2006)
- Rainer Maria Rilke, *Letters to a Young Poet* (Novato, Calif.: New World Library, 2000)
- Ramesh S. Balsekar, *The Final Truth: A Guide to Ultimate Understanding* (Redondo Beach, Calif.: Advaita Press, 1989)
- Shams-ud-din Muhammad Hafiz, *The Gift,* trans. Daniel Ladinsky (New York: Penguin Group, 1999)
- Swami Venkatesananda, *Vasistha's Yoga* (Albany, State University of New York: 1993).
- Thomas Moore, *Thomas Moore's Complete Poetical Works* (New York: Thomas Crowell & Company, 1895)

ENDNOTES

1   Swami Venkatesananda, *Vasiṣṭha's Yoga* (Albany, State University of New York: 1993), p. 31.
2   James Altucher newsletter, "What is The Truth? The Real Science of Inquiry", 10/10/18.
3   Swami Muktananda, front piece, "Blessing," in Swami Venkatesananda, *Vasistha's Yoga* (Albany, State University of New York: 1993).
4   American President Ronald Reagan is famous for demanding in Berlin of former Soviet Premier Gorbachev that he tear down the Berlin Wall.
5   Ramesh S. Balsekar, *The Final Truth: A Guide to Ultimate Understanding* (Redondo Beach, Calif.: Advaita Press, 1989), p. 39.
6   Ervin Laszlo, *Science and the Akashic Field* (Rochester, VT: Inner Traditions, 2004, 2007), p. 122.
7   Longchenpa, *Maya Yoga: Finding Comfort and Ease in Enchantment*, trans. Keith Dowman (Kathmandu, Nepal: Vajra Publications, 2010 and 2014)
8   Level is in quote marks because in Truth, the beginningless endless spiritual Hierarchy has no "levels."
9   Keith Dowman, Introduction to Longchenpa, *Maya* Yoga, op. cit., p. 20.
10 Charles Wyzanski, Radio broadcast in the 1950s, "No Mortal Answer."
11 Bob Dylan song, "Visions of Johanna."
12 Focusing the night, Spirit, side if Life.
13 https://en.wikipedia.org/wiki/Indra%27s_net
14 Ibid.
15 The spiritually astute know so-called waking reality to be as much of a dream as the sleeping type.
16 Carlos Ruiz Zafón, *The Shadow of the Wind*, Lucia Grave, trans., New York: The Penguin Group, 2004), pp. 5, 6.
17 Ruiz, op. cit., p. 7.
18 Every six o'clock and twelve o'clock lines of the Cosmic Clock.
19 Ibid.
20 https://en.wikipedia.org/wiki/M%C3%B6bius_strip
21 Judy Garland and Fred Astaire, in "Easter Parade," illustrate this to a tee. https://www.youtube.com/watch?v=-xxfm5-zRHo

22 Bob Dylan song, "Is Your Love in Vain?" If your love is in vain, it's vanity ego based; ugh!

23 Bob Dylan song, "Love Minus Zero, No Limit."

24 That's the name of a Rolling Stones song.

25 Rainer Maria Rilke, *Letters to a Young Poet* (Novato, Calif.: New World Library, 2000), pp. 79-9.

26 William Wordsworth, "Ode: Intimations of Immortality from Recollections of Early Childhood"

27 Rumi, Masnavi i Man'avi, the spiritual couplets of Maula.

28 El Morya, *Heart* (New York: Agni Yoga Society, 1932, 1975), p. 239.

29 https://www.youtube.com/watch?v=aiRgq08-lgw Atheist and Yogi about belief, Bill Maher and Sadhguru jaggi vasudev.

30 William Wordsworth, "Ode: Intimations of Immortality from Recollections of Early Childhood"

31 Rainer Maria Rilke, *Letters to a Young Poet, op. cit.,* pp. 76-7.

32 Ervin Laszlo, *Science and the Akashic Field,* op. cit., pp. 26-7.

33 http://www.buddhanature.com/buddha/aval.html

34 Dordogne, of the Padmakara Translation Group, Translator's Introduction to Longchenpa, *Finding Rest in the Nature of Mind: The Trilogy of Rest, Volume 1,* trans. The Padmakara Translation Group (Boulder, Colorado: Shambala Publications, Inc., 2017), p. xx.

35 *Mother Mary, Pearls of Wisdom: A Trilogy of the Mother: The Mother Flame and the Incarnation of God I,* Vol. 17 No. 50 December 15, 1974.

36 Elizabeth Clare Prophet with Patricia R. Spadaro and Murray Steinman, *Kabbalah: Key to Your Inner Power* (Livingston, Mont.: Summit University Press, 1997), p. 85.

37 Scholem, *Kabballah* (New York: New American Library, Meridian, 1978), p. 156.

38 Note that different passages in the Zohar equate the soul with different trinities of *sefirot.* See note 5 for chapter 5 in Elizabeth Clare Prophet, *Kabbalah.* Tishby, Isaiah, and Fischel Lachower, comps. *The Wisdom of the Zohar: An Anthology of Texts.* 3 vols. Translated by David Goldstein, 1989. Reprint. New York: Oxford University Press for the Littman Library of Jewish Civilization, 1991.

39 Elizabeth Clare Prophet, *et. al., Kabbalah,* op. cit., p. 98.

40 M. John Harrison, *Light* (New York: Bantam Dell, 2004), pp. 91-92.

41 James Irby, Introduction to Jorge Luis Borjes, *Labyrinths* (New York: New Directions Publishing Corporation, 1962, 1964, 2007), p. xvii.

42 Dr. Eban Alexander III, *Proof of Heaven* (New York: Simon & Schuster Paperbacks, 2012), p. 83.

43   Rainer Maria Rilke, *Letters to a Young Poet, op. cit.*, p. 77.

44   El Morya, *Hierarchy* (New York: Agni Yoga Society, 1933, 1975), #69, p. 44.

45   https://www.youtube.com/watch?v=kSzBl5Oyoec

46   Amit Goswami, *The Self-Aware Universe: how consciousness creates the material world* (New York: Jeremy P. Tarcher/Putnam, 1993), pp. 105-112.

47   Ibid.

48   Ibid., p. 112.

49   Beloved Arcturus, *Pearls of Wisdom*, vol. 50 No. 13 (Gardiner, Mont.: The Summit Lighthouse, 2007), p. 92.

50   El Morya, *Heart*, op. cit., p. 127.

51   James Irby, Introduction to Jorge Luis Borjes, *Labyrinths*, op. cit., pp. xv-xvi.

52   Keith Dowman, Introduction to Longchenpa, *Maya Yoga: Finding Comfort and Ease in Enchantment*, trans. Keith Dowman, op. cit., p. 17.

53   Ibid., p. 42.

54   William Wordsworth, "Ode: Intimations of Immortality from Recollections of Early Childhood"

55   Ibid.

56   Ibid., p. 18, 19.

57   Swami Venkatesananda, *Vasiṣṭha's Yoga*, op. cit., p. 49.

58   Ervin Laszlo, *Science and the Akashic Field*, op. cit., p. 43.

59   Jiddu Krishnamurti.

60   M. John Harrison, *Light*, op. cit., p. 89.

61   Ibid., pp. 89-90.

62   Go to The Summit Lighthouse site to get started: https://www.summitlighthouse.org/

63   Dowman, *Maya* Yoga, op. cit., p. 20.

64   The Duino Elegies.

65   http://www.writing.upenn.edu/library/Tzara_Dada-Manifesto_1918.pdf

66   Ibid., #71, p. 46.

67   Steven Weinberg, quoted in Ervin Laszlo, *Science and the Akashic Field*, op. cit., p. 2.

68   El Morya, *Heart*, op. cit., p. 10.

69   Ibid., pp. 41-2.

70   El Morya, *Hierarchy*, op. cit., #238, p. 127.

71   Much of these preceding paragraphs is transcribed from the script of a video called, "The Simulation Theory—Hacking Reality." Written, directed and edited by David Jakubovic. Hosted by Marion Kerr. https://www.youtube.com/watch?v=eRmZ_sNf2mE&t=13s

72   El Morya, *Hierarchy*, op. cit., pp. 43-4.

73   Ibid., p. 43.

74 El Morya, *Heart* (New York: Agni Yoga Society, 1932, 1975), pp. 40-1.

75 David Wilcock, *The Source Field Investigations* (New York: Penguin Group, 2011).

76 Keith Dowman, Introduction to Longchenpa, *Maya Yoga*, op. cit., p. 53.

77 Amit Goswami, op. cit., pp. 59-60.

78 Saint Germain, "The Way of Love," Decree 30.10 in The Summit Lighthouse, *Prayers Meditations and Dynamic Decrees for Personal and World Transformation* (Gardiner, Mont., The Summit Lighthouse, 1984, 2010).

79 https://www.youtube.com/watch?v=DR5aYgcch8Q

80 R. J. Stewart, *Celtic Gods Celtic Goddesses* (London: Blanford; Cassell Illustrated, 1990; 2006), p. 70.

81 Keith Dowman, Introduction to Longchenpa, *Maya Yoga*, op. cit., p. 20.

82 James Irby, Introduction *to Labyrinths*, op. cit., p. xvi.

83 https://www.youtube.com/watch?v=gxs0tgwXHV0 "Time & Space Explained | what is the space time continuum?"

84 El Morya, *Hierarchy*, op. cit., p. 14.

85 Wilcock, op. cit., pp. 330-1.

86 Ibid., p. 309.

87 Jon Rappoport, Email Newsletter: "Exit From The Matrix: Getting in the creative flow," 11/2/18.

88 Ibid., p. 333.

89 Ibid., p. 273.

90 https://en.wikipedia.org/wiki/Philadelphia_Experiment

91 9,192,631,770 cycles per second.

92 Sung by Whitney Houston and written by Albert Hammond and John Bettis. https://www.youtube.com/watch?v=c84ogrNEds0.

93 Jon Rappoport, Excerpts from "Exit from the Matrix," in email from 5/2/18 "The Positive Power of Imagination".

94 Dust cover blurb on Jorge Luis Borges, *Collected Fictions*, trans. Andrew Hurley (London: Penguin Books Ltd., 1998).

95 Keith Dowman, Introduction to Longchenpa, *Maya Yoga*, op. cit., pp. 20-21.

96 Matt. 25: 40-45.

97 Keith Dowman, Introduction to Longchenpa, *Maya* Yoga, op. cit., pp. 18-9.

98 Ibid., p. 30.

99 El Morya, *Heart*, op. cit., p. 291.

100 El Morya, *Heart*, op. cit., p. 237.

101 James Irby, Introduction *to Labyrinths*, op. cit., p. xvii.

102 Shams-ud-din Muhammad Hafiz, *The Gift*, trans. Daniel Ladinsky (New York: Penguin Group, 1999), p. 84

103 Keith Dowman, Introduction to Longchenpa, *Maya* Yoga, op. cit., pp. 24-5.

104 Keith Dowman, Introduction to Longchenpa, *Maya* Yoga, op. cit., p. 41.

105 Saint Germain, *Pearls of Wisdom*, op. cit., Vol. 19 No. 27, July 4, 1976.

106 The Summit Lighthouse, Decree 7.26.

107 Ervin Laszlo, op. cit., p. 136.

108 Ervin Laszlo, op. cit., p. 157.

109 https://simple.wikipedia.org/wiki/Higgs_field

110 Ervin Laszlo, *Science and the Akashic Field*, op. cit., p. 64.

111 El Morya, *Heart*, op. cit., p. 217.

112 El Morya, *Heart*, op. cit., p. 170.

113 El Morya, *Heart*, op. cit., p. 19.

114 El Morya, *Heart*, op. cit., p. 46.

115 El Morya, *Heart*, op. cit., p. 195.

116 The Maha Chohan, *Pearls of Wisdom* (Gardiner, Mont.: Summit University Press, 1981), Vol. 24, No. 77.

117 El Morya, *Heart*, op. cit., p. 293.

118 El Morya, *Heart*, op. cit., pp. 309-10.

119 https://www.youtube.com/watch?v=j3qq1P9G3Uk Watching this lecture will be time very well spent.

120 El Morya, *Heart*, op. cit., pp. 268-9.

121 M. John Harrison, *Light*, op. cit., p. 80.

122 Ervin Laszlo, *Science and the Akashic Field*, op. cit., p. 28-9.

123 Ervin Laszlo, *Science and the Akashic Field*, op. cit., p. 142.

124 Taken from Time Ferris Newsletter "5-Bullet Friday" 10/26/18.

125 Ibid.

126 Longchenpa, *Maya Yoga*, op. cit., pp. 79-80.

127 Ibid.

128 Bhagavan Sri Ramana Maharshi, *Who Am I?* (Tamil Nadu, India: Sri Ramanasramam, 2010). pp. 8-9.

129 John Francis Xavier O'Connor, *A Study of Francis Thompson's Hound of Heaven* (John Lane Company, 1912), p.7.

130 The Aretha Franklin 60 Minutes Interview. https://www.youtube.com/watch?v=2dbf3HlNirE

131 John 5:30

132 John 14:10.

133 See https://en.wikipedia.org/wiki/Film_producer.

134 El Morya, *Hierarchy*, op. cit., p. 14.

135 http://www.wnd.com/2018/06/school-board-bans-fact-biological-sex-is-no-more/

136 El Morya, op. cit., p. 155.

137 Keith Dowman, Introduction to Longchenpa, *Spaciousness: Longchenpa's Precious Treasury of the Dharmadhatu*, trans. Keith Dowman (KeithDowman@gmail.com: DzogchenNow! Books, 2012, 2014), p. 19.

138 Ibid., p. 20.

139 Ibid., p. 22.

140 Ibid.

141 William Wordsworth, "Lines Composed a Few Miles Above TINTERN ABBEY On Revisiting the Bank of the Wye During a Tour."

142 Ibid.

143 Ibid.

144 Dowman, *Maya Yoga*, op. cit., p. 48.

145 El Morya, *Infinity - Book 1* (New York: Agni Yoga Society, 1930) #28.

146 El Morya, *Heart*, op. cit., p. 9.

147 https://en.wikipedia.org/wiki/Fierce_deities

148 https://en.wikipedia.org/wiki/Kundalini

149 https://en.wikipedia.org/wiki/Nadi_(yoga)

150 Jiddu Krishnamurti

INDEX

attuned xxxi, 97, 161, 180

attunement xvii, 53, 83, 108, 162, 163, 165, 212, 230

awareness xv, xx, xxi, xxii, xxxii, xxxiii, xxxv, xxxvi, xxxvii, xxxix, 3, 4, 8, 10, 11, 18, 23, 24, 31, 36, 44, 47, 48, 51, 57, 60, 61, 64, 65, 66, 70, 71, 75, 83, 86, 87, 88, 89, 95, 99, 100, 105, 107, 108, 113, 117, 119, 123, 124, 125, 127, 136, 138, 140, 142, 145, 148, 151, 153, 157, 163, 168, 173, 181, 183, 185, 186, 187, 190, 191, 194, 195, 197, 200, 204, 205, 212, 213, 214, 215, 229, 234

B

bad karma xxix, xxx, xxxii, xxxv, 21, 54, 76, 78, 83, 84, 86, 108, 111, 113, 123, 145, 146, 147, 148, 167, 176, 210, 222, 223

balance xvi, xxii, xxx, xxxiii, 5, 9, 81, 111, 112, 113, 147, 192, 204, 207, 231

bare wire Love 2, 3, 4, 5, 6, 11, 12, 13, 88

basic immaculate maya xxx, xxxiii, xxxiv, xxxv, 13, 50, 52, 53, 55, 57, 59, 61, 75, 76, 78, 81, 83, 87, 96, 106, 107, 108, 115, 123, 134, 136, 137, 139, 147, 157, 160, 172, 183, 190, 205

beauty 23, 79, 201, 224

beginningless xxxv, 24, 71, 91, 196, 219, 238, 241

Beings xvi, xviii, 3, 33, 49, 69, 104, 161, 162, 163, 166, 169, 217, 230

Binah 38, 40, 41, 56

boss xxxv, 25, 43

Brahman 71, 76, 82, 171

Brother Lawrence 36, 195

Buddha xv, xxviii, 32, 44, 46, 50, 65, 75, 107, 109, 134, 138, 170, 184, 217, 227, 228

Buddhism xxiii, 171, 220, 229

Buddhist xxxi, 43, 59, 71, 73, 96, 107, 115, 126, 136, 169

busybodies 2

busybody xxiv, 17, 72, 89, 99, 134, 163, 173, 218, 226

C

catalyst xix, 71, 72, 109, 177, 192, 198

catalyze 226

catalyzes 214

Causal Bodies 28, 30, 33, 40, 48, 214

Causal Body xxvii, xxviii, xxx, xxxiii, xxxiv, xxxv, 13, 27, 28, 29, 30, 31, 32, 33, 39, 40, 41, 45, 48, 49, 50, 52, 53, 55, 57, 59, 61, 76, 82, 86, 87, 96, 104, 105, 107, 109, 110, 113, 114, 115, 117, 122, 129, 131, 134, 135, 136, 137, 138, 139, 142, 145, 146, 147, 152, 158, 172, 174, 175, 183, 199, 200, 214, 216

center xxviii, 10, 34, 36, 37, 44, 46, 111, 116, 117, 165, 168, 170, 223, 232

centers 45, 69, 95, 99, 168, 212, 234

change xxiv, 2, 4, 11, 31, 46, 59, 63, 87, 130, 143, 151, 168, 172, 173, 177, 178, 187, 199, 221, 233

changeability 11

changes xxxiii, xxxiv, 8, 11, 31, 44, 113, 151, 187, 198

coherence 26, 126, 150, 158

collapse 123, 212

collapses 29, 106, 122, 123, 183

commanding Presence 72, 127, 136, 226, 237

complementary 27, 30, 31

confluence 105, 133

confluences 4

consensus 2, 3, 4, 5, 6, 7, 8, 9, 10, 12, 32, 91, 100, 121, 183, 184, 185, 187, 188, 193, 194, 195, 196

consonance xvi, xxii, 26, 34, 51, 54, 59, 95, 209, 213, 216, 230

Cosmic Being xv, xxx, 81, 93, 94, 101, 178, 215, 217, 228, 230

Cosmic Beings xxxvi, 9, 19, 23, 25, 33, 57, 60, 61, 69, 82, 108, 131, 145, 170, 218

cosmic mean 8, 89, 91, 120, 183

creative xvii, xxv, 23, 39, 47, 60, 115, 118, 172, 197, 200, 206, 244

creativity 18, 28, 60, 61, 62, 105, 109

cross of white fire 47, 68, 162

crystal cord 62, 63, 171

D

Dada art movement 90

decree 81, 86, 195

decreeing 35, 97, 98, 163, 173, 192, 216

decrees 86, 155, 216, 238

dimensional 24, 75, 96, 105, 112, 116, 129, 130, 178, 179

dimensions 51, 56, 96, 105, 112, 114, 130, 137, 162, 174

direct xvi, xxii, xxiii, xxxvi, 22, 45, 64, 70, 73, 87, 97, 98, 99, 132, 146, 147, 152, 163, 181, 211, 219

divine Love xxv, xxix, xxxii, xxxiii, 2, 3, 6, 19, 77, 83, 86, 87, 94, 97, 111, 120, 123, 142, 161, 180, 183, 211, 226

Divine Mother 84, 171

divine personality xxviii, 39, 55, 57, 59, 114, 135, 194

Divine Self ix, xxvii, 36, 55

divinity xviii, xxvii, xxx, 33, 41, 54, 119, 123, 129, 133, 181, 212, 216

dream xxxi, 122, 138, 151, 174, 180, 181, 182, 236, 237, 241

dreaming 37, 110, 174, 180, 182, 198

dukkha 86, 184

Dzogchen ix, xxii, 43, 72, 73, 74, 140, 160, 163, 169, 171, 194, 221, 222, 223, 225, 226, 227

E

Easter 23, 194, 241

Ein Sof 38, 41, 115

electron 106, 116, 156, 215

electrons 116, 122, 204

Elohim 24, 69, 71, 75, 214, 218, 228

emptiness 16, 72, 79, 89, 90, 126, 155, 185

empty 52, 78, 89, 90, 124, 143, 182, 183, 188, 199

endless xxxv, xxxvii, 9, 24, 25, 50, 56, 69, 71, 75, 91, 101, 132, 196, 219, 228, 238, 241

endlessly xxiv, xxxii, xxxvi, 78, 108, 191, 213, 217

energy xxv, xxix, xxx, xxxii, xxxiv, xxxvii, 19, 22, 23, 24, 31, 36, 38, 45, 53, 61, 64, 80, 82, 84, 86, 87, 88, 89, 90, 93, 95, 97, 98, 115, 116, 118, 123, 127, 128, 132, 139, 143, 144, 145, 146, 151, 152, 153, 154, 155, 156, 157, 158, 167, 181, 199, 203, 204, 211, 212, 229, 232, 233, 234

enlightened 71, 145, 151, 229, 231

enlightenment xxii, 55, 59, 70, 86, 174, 191, 197, 228

entanglement 30, 184, 187

N

O

CPSIA information can be obtained
at www.ICGtesting.com
Printed in the USA
BVHW071430110219
539954BV00004B/266/P